# NUBIAN
# ETHNOGRAPHIES

# Waveland Press, Inc.
## Prospect Heights, Illinois

# NUBIAN ETHNOGRAPHIES

Elizabeth Warnock Fernea and Robert A. Fernea

*with Aleya Rouchdy*

For information about this book, write or call:

Waveland Press, Inc.
P.O. Box 400
Prospect Heights, Illinois 60070
(708) 634-0081

Copyright © 1991 by Elizabeth Warnock Fernea and Robert A. Fernea

ISBN 0-88133-480-4

Printed in the United States of America

7  6  5  4  3

**Parts of this volume are from previously published works by the authors:**

Material appearing in Part I of this book has been reprinted in part from *A View of the Nile: The Story of an American Family in Egypt* by Elizabeth Warnock Fernea, originally published in 1970 by Doubleday & Co., Inc.

Material appearing in Part II of this book has been reprinted from *Nubians in Egypt: Peaceful People* by Robert Fernea (with accompanying photographic essay by Georg Gerster), originally published in 1973 by The University of Texas Press.

The concluding essay by Robert A. Fernea and Aleya Rouchdy (Part III) was originally presented as a joint paper at the International Nubian Studies Conference, University of Uppsala (Sweden), 1986. The proceedings of that conference were subsequently published in *Nubian Culture: Past and Present*, edited by Tomas Hägg, Stockholm: Almqvist & Wiksell International, 1987.

The Preface and Introduction have been written expressly for this edition.

**Credits:**

Cover photo and photo of woman painting house by Georg Gerster. Used with permission.

Photo of two women preparing food and photo of retired Nubian man by Tom Hartwell. Used with permission.

All other photos by Abdul Fattah Eid. Used with permission.

Maps by Diane Watts.

# Table of Contents

## Part III   EPILOGUE
*by Robert A. Fernea and Aleya Rouchdy*

# Preface

The Nubian Ethnographic Survey of which the research in this volume is part, was begun in 1960 as a salvage anthropology project. Its stated purpose was to record the culture and heritage of the 50,000 Egyptian Nubians before they were moved from their ancestral home along the Upper Nile. Their houses, fields and graveyards, along with hundreds of Pharaonic monuments (including the mammoth rock temple of Abu Simbel) were threatened by the rising waters backed up by the new High Dam at Aswan. As part of the High Dam project, the Nubians were to be compensated for the loss of their property, and resettled on agricultural land in Kom Ombo, north of the city of Aswan. The Egyptian government would provide houses and utilities as well as irrigated land and the Nubians would grow sugarcane, a cash crop useful to the nation, on their new allotments. By 1965, these events had all taken place. By 1990, the Nubians have been in their new homes for a generation and the villages of old Nubia have disappeared.

The Ford Foundation funded the Nubian Ethnographic Survey through the Social Research Center of the American University in Cairo. Laila Shukry al-Hamamsy, then the director of the Center, was crucial in implementing the project's aim — to provide a record of Nubian culture that would be valuable not only to the world of anthropology, but to the Nubians themselves. Robert Fernea was director of the project, which involved social scientists and researchers from America, Europe and Egypt, including some Egyptian Nubians. Three village studies took place in the three distinct linguistic areas of Egyptian Nubia. Charles Callender headed the team in the Kenuzi sector, assisted by Fadwa al-Guindi. Asaad Nadim and Nawal al-Messiri worked in the Arabic speaking region. South in the Mahasi area, Robert Fernea directed a team which included Karim al-Durzi, Bahiga Heikal, and Afaf al-Deeb. Abdul Hamid al-Zein later joined this group. A fourth village study was launched by John Kennedy, with Sohair Mehanna and Hussain Fahim, in Dar al-Salaam. This was a pseudonym for a village which had been settled by Kenuzi Nubians displaced after the raising of the first High Dam in 1912.

Thayer Scudder and Abdul Hamid al-Zein conducted a demographic survey of the entire area from Aswan to Wadi Halfa on the Sudanese border. Peter Geiser, with Mohammed Fikry and Aziza Rashad, interviewed Nubian families who had lived in Cairo and Alexandria as migrant laborers. Nadia Youssef also was involved in this sociological analysis. Additional work was later undertaken on Nubian architecture (Horst Jaritz, Hassan Fathy); Nubian funeral ceremonies (Najwa al-Shukairy); and Nubian languages (Aleya Rouchdy). The several books, theses and journal articles which have resulted from the project are listed in the bibliography.

An additional grant from the Ford Foundation made it possible for seven of the young Egyptian researchers from the project to continue their professional training in anthropology and sociology in the U.S. These included Abdul Hamid al-Zein, Sohair Mehanna, Fadwa al-Guindi, Hussain Fahim, Asaad Nadim, Nawal al-Messiri and Nadia Youssef. Of this group, three have returned to work in Egypt; three remained in the U.S.; and Abdul Hamid al-Zein, in the midst of a promising career in anthropology, died in 1979 while teaching at Temple University.

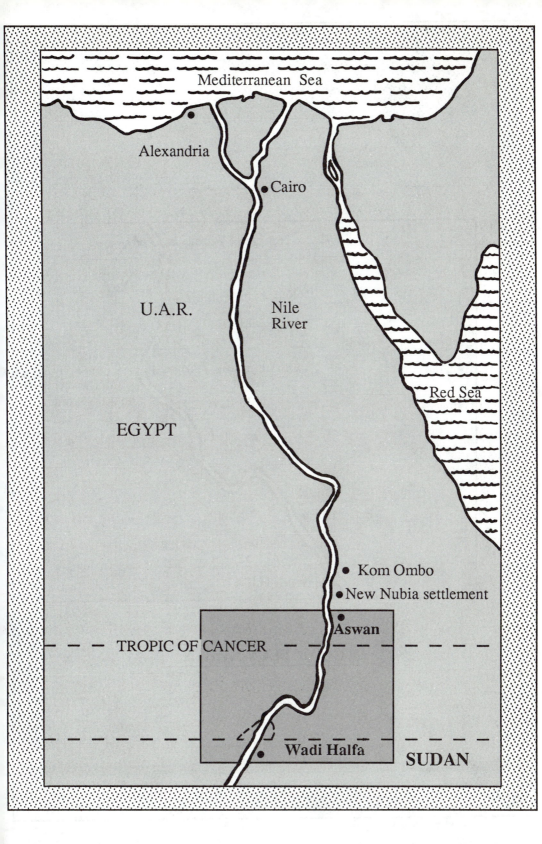

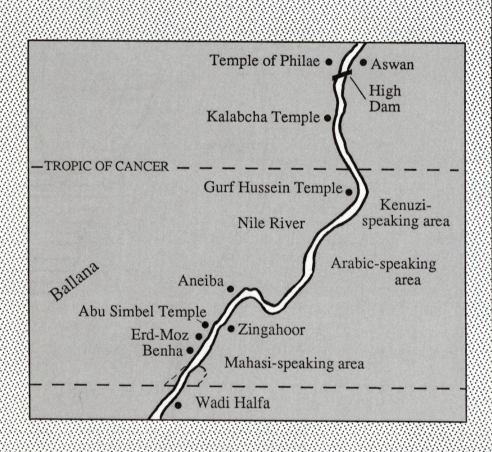

Temple of Philae • • Aswan

High Dam

Kalabcha Temple •

— TROPIC OF CANCER — — — — — — — —

Gurf Hussein Temple •

Kenuzi-speaking area

Nile River

Arabic-speaking area

Ballana

Aneiba •

Abu Simbel Temple •

Erd-Moz •

Zingahoor •

Benha •

Mahasi-speaking area

Wadi Halfa •

**EGYPTIAN NUBIA**

# Introduction

The book that follows is a chronicle of the period of Nubian history with which the Nubian Ethnographic Survey, a 1960s salvage anthropology project, was concerned. A follow-up essay describing Nubia today completes the book. The chronicle is told from several perspectives, Nubian and non-Nubian. These different perspectives allow the readers to see Nubians at different points in time, as well as through the eyes of different researchers. Through the different sections, the reader may also observe the changes in states of ethnographic writing that have taken place in the last thirty years, changes in both ethnographic method and subject matter.

Part I, by Elizabeth Fernea, is a personal account of the experience and process of fieldwork in Nubia, and of the author's interaction with Nubian society, particularly with the women and children. Written in the 1960s as the major section of *A View of the Nile*, it was published by Doubleday in 1970 as a non-fiction work, not an ethnography. At that time, ethnographic concerns were rather different than they are today. First, women's roles and children's lives were viewed as peripheral to the central concerns of a credible ethnographic account of any society or group. Women had not yet entered the field of anthropology in large numbers, and those who were becoming part of the profession studied what men perceived to be important: kinship, economics, politics, ritual.

The tone of Part I is related not only to the audience (the western lay reader) but to Elizabeth Fernea's own experiences in adjusting herself and her children to the isolation and scarce resources of the village. Her sense that Nubian women suffered from many of these problems is also conveyed. For Nubian women, the blessed land was not so blessed as for the migrant husbands who lived in Cairo and dreamed of home as an idealized refuge. The hazards of childbearing, high infant mortality rates, extreme temperatures, limited supplies of food, water and medical care, and the absence of husbands and fathers meant that Nubian women's lives were precarious, demanding and often lonely. Their perception of themselves as caretakers of households in the absence of men and as guardians

1

of family social and economic interests gave them strength, purpose and dignity. But everyday life was hard; many women spoke wistfully of the possibilities of an easier life in the cities.

Elizabeth Fernea was in Nubia not as an anthropologist but as a wife and mother, accompanying her anthropologist husband. She tried to gather material about women's and children's lives in order to understand their position within the larger society. For, in the master files of field notes that were kept for the entire project and organized according to the categories established by the respected Human Relations Area Files, no category then existed for "women" or "children." No clearer indication can be given of the priorities within the field at the time.

In addition, in those days, the ethnographer's presence was not recognized to be a factor affecting the description of a culture or the analysis of the data gathered. Therefore, any personal doubts or emotional reactions of the anthropologist were excised from the final text, for these were seen to be injecting subjectivity into what should be an objective account, and therefore undermining the legitimacy of the whole enterprise.

Today, however, new genres of anthropological writing are in process. Ethnographers are experimenting with different narrative strategies, attempting to represent their subjects and themselves in relation to those subjects. Elizabeth Fernea's account might be seen as an early expression of this new approach.

Part II of this volume is the text which accompanied a photographic essay in the now out-of-print book *Egyptian Nubians: Peaceful People* (University of Texas Press, 1973) by Robert Fernea with photographs by Georg Gerster. It is an ethnography providing an overview of Nubian society and culture, the result rather than the experience of fieldwork.

Even before the flooding by the High Dam in the early 1960s, Old Nubia had become a somewhat idealized homeland for most of its men, who were or had been urban labor immigrants. The Nubian migrants in Egyptian and foreign cities talked of their villages as places of peace and honesty, a "blessed land," they would say, free of the strife and conflict of urban life. It was a place where Nubian men were the princes of their domain, free from the orders of the housewives, hotel and apartment managers, and restaurant owners for whom many of them worked in Cairo or Alexandria. Nubia was an isolated, sheltered place, out of the purview of strangers, including government administrators. The beautiful villages along the Nile with spacious houses and groves of green palm trees *were* a place of peace and tranquility, even for the anthropologists engaged in their fieldwork.

By the time Robert Fernea began working on the text of his book, he had left Egypt, and Old Nubia had been under water for several years. His sense of writing about a world which had disappeared was very strong. Also, from the very beginning of the ethnographic survey one of the objectives had been to create for Egyptian Nubians a record of life in Old Nubia of which they could be proud. So, when Fernea was writing Part II, the audience he had in mind was not only Western readers but also future generations of Nubians. Hamza el-Din, the well-known Nubian musician, was then a visiting professor at the University of Texas at Austin and a colleague and close friend of the author. Fernea often wrote in Hamza's home while Hamza played the *oud* and sang. The music and conversation constituted an evocative context in which to formulate ideas and images of the ''blessed land,'' as Nubia was often called, at least by Nubian men. For Part II does reflect a male perspective as well as very positive feelings about life in Old Nubia. While the text in *Nubians in Egypt: Peaceful People* has never been published in Arabic, copies of the book are valued by Nubians today. Part II is then an account written not only about but also for the subjects of the narrative.

Part III was written by Robert Fernea and Aleya Rouchdy, a professor of Arabic and linguistics at Wayne State University, who is carrying out a long-term study of the Nubian language and its use. The joint paper was presented at the International Nubian Studies conference, held in 1986 at the University of Uppsala, and subsequently published in the proceedings of that conference. The essay builds upon several ethnographic studies by other scholars since the sixties to summarize events in Egyptian Nubian history since the resettlement in 1964-1965. Also, several times over the last twenty-five years Fernea and Rouchdy have independently visited the resettlement area of New Nubia north of Aswan. Rouchdy has found a steady decline in Nubian knowledge and use of their languages, which are also becoming more and more ''Arabized''; this suggests the languages will rapidly disappear. One might ask whether the Nubians, as a cultural and racial minority in Egypt, are also disappearing.

Future research may well address this issue. Are Egyptian Nubians developing a sense of self and other of their own or of other's choosing, which may make their minority status as a racial and ethnic group a matter of long term social consequence? How rapidly are they becoming absorbed into Egyptian society, something that has happened to other people from the south over the millennia of Egyptian history? These are the subjects for other studies; the book that follows addresses, in different ways, the Nubian past, not the future.

# PART I

# A View of the Nile

*Elizabeth Warnock Fernea*

# Chapter 1

# Our Thoughts
# Turn South

"You want to hear the story?"
   "Yes!"
"The real story, the true story?"
   "Yes! Yes, we do!"
"Well, this is the beginning, and this is how we did it!"
   (Cheers in the background, and drums)
"We built the High Dam!"

The popular voice of Abdul Halim Hafez singing "Sud el Ali, the Story of the High Dam," against a well-produced background of chorus and drums, was a hit record throughout Egypt that winter and spring of 1960. However, my mind was hardly on the High Dam. I was pregnant again, Laura Ann was teething, Fawzia's family had opened marriage negotiations with her first cousin's father (and where would I find another good nanny, I worried to myself). Bob had become fascinated with the idea of doing salvage anthropology in Nubia. That casual conversation in the garden of Chicago House at Luxor had been like a stone dropped into a deep pool; the circles widened every day.

But whether or not I wanted to think about the High Dam, it was with me everywhere I went. Taxi drivers turned their radios to full volume when Abdul Halim Hafez' voice signaled the beginning of "Sud el Ali." The choruses resounded from the coffee shops and record stores along Talaat Harb Street. "You want to hear the story, the true story?" came piping from the transistor radios propped up among the pyramids of pomegranates and the baskets of artichokes in the stalls of Bab el Loukh market. On 26th of July Street, the television sets displayed in Cicurel and Sednaoui department stores featured Abdul Halim Hafez in person, singing "The Story of the High Dam" on the Cairo television channel. Little queues of people gathered before this projection of the popular singer to watch, but also sometimes to clap in time.

At home, the Nubian *boabs* in our apartment building sported, under their white turbans, skullcaps decorated with the new High Dam design, a pattern in yellow and green and orange thread created by a Nubian housewife.

In the cinemas, the features varied: the new Egyptian film *Do'a el Karwaan*, based on a classic novel by Taha Hussein; an American hit, *The Guns of Navarone*; Russia's *The Cranes Are Flying*. But the short subject was always the same, a new documentary called, not surprisingly, *The Story of the High Dam!*

"Let's face it," Bob said to Nicholas. "The High Dam may change *our* lives, too, as well as the Egyptians."

"How?" I asked.

"Well, I mean, if I do get some money to do research and Nicholas does get a grant to lead an expedition . . ."

"I didn't realize. . . Nicholas was thinking of going to Nubia."

Nicholas laughed. "Who knows? One must think large thoughts these days. That's what the President is doing."

"And it seems to be working," put in Bob.

President Nasser was embarked on many projects to improve the individual's standard of living, to lift Egypt from nineteenth-century dependence on Europe to economic self-reliance. But the High Dam was the grandest of them all. He had taken Germany's offer to build an iron and steel plant, he had signed a contract with American engineers to develop new water sources in the oases, he concluded an agreement with the Fiat company to ship auto parts from Italy and assemble them in Egypt. Factories were being built and consumer goods appeared: drugs, cosmetics, plastic dishes, refrigerators, all with the proud label "Made in Egypt."

But none of these achievements had the popular appeal of the High Dam. More land—two million more acres of land—could be placed under cultivation when the dam was finished. That made sense to a people who knew from thousands of years of bitter experience just how many bushels of grain could be raised on a tiny strip of Nile-silted soil. Electricity, ten billion kilowatts of electricity, were promised. That made sense, too, to light the dim village houses, to power the television, the refrigerators, the radios that were to come with the new prosperity.

Think grand thoughts, Nicholas had said. Well. . .

"If you do go to Nubia, couldn't I come?" I asked.

"See," said Nicholas, "she's getting the bug, too."

"How could you?" asked Bob. "Bring the babies and live on a boat! Impossible!"

"Why couldn't we live in a village house?"

"B.J., I don't have the money to do *anything* yet. Nobody at Chicago House has even agreed I could bunk on their boat if I *did* have the money. Let's just wait and see."

I began to pay more attention to the daily news accounts of the High Dam's progress, to the government speeches about plans for the development of the city of Aswan. (Maybe I could live there with the children if Bob went to Nubia. It would be 750 miles closer than Cairo.)

Abbas was a Nubian. I asked him about the countryside, about the houses in the villages south of Aswan. Could I manage to live with two babies in one of those houses?

"They are nice houses," said Abbas doubtfully, "but they're made of mud and have no running water, and . . well, madame, I don't know."

I didn't know whether I could do it either, but I was willing to try. If the Nubian people were anything like Abbas, I was certain I would like them and enjoy living among them. I even began to listen more closely to "The Song," as we began to call it.

The curious thing about "The Song" was that it completely neglected to mention the Russian role.

"We built the dam, we built it with our hands, we built it with our money, yes, we built it, the High Dam!" sang Abdul Halim Hafez. I often wondered what the Russian Information Agency made of all this. Officially, the Egyptian cotton crop, main source of cash income, was mortgaged to the Russians for millennial years to pay for all those bright yellow bulldozers, for the Russian engineers and advisers, for the master plan of the largest earth-fill dam that had ever been attempted in the world.

But the Soviets got not so much as a footnote of popular appreciation in the songs and the stories that circulated throughout Egypt. It was true that the average Egyptian had almost no contact with the Russians, who arrived, planeload after planeload, and then seemed to disappear. They went directly onto the through train to Aswan, we were told, where they lived in a special housing project somewhat apart from the city of Aswan. If they stayed in Cairo for special duty at the closely guarded and walled Soviet Embassy, they still were not seen much in public, for they had their separate "leisure" compound.

We'd seen that compound. Its picket fence, which had allowed such interesting glimpses of the Russian children and their mamas, was now bricked in. Within its confines, we were told, were a social club, a dining hall, a school and a cinema. The Russians were required to spend most of their leisure there and were bused from home to embassy duties to compound in Soviet-hired vehicles. They did not even have servants, who could have gossiped about them. The ambassador had brought his staff with him from Moscow. The rest presumably needed none.

I saw Russian ladies in the markets in homemade cotton house dresses, their hair crimped and permanented, trying desperately to determine, through a dense language barrier, the prices of turnips, potatoes, cabbages, onions, beets.

"Parlez français? Ingleezie? Yonani?" The vendor would go through his five or six languages to no avail.

Occasionally I saw those ladies standing for long, silent moments in front of shop windows on Kasr el Nil and 26th of July Street, shop windows which Egyptians insisted were empty in comparison to the displays of previous years, but which apparently did not seem so to the consumer-goods-hungry Russians. And they sweated, how they sweated in the heat! Several years later, when Khrushchev made his official visit to Egypt, he was met at the Aswan airport by a solid mass of his fellow countrymen. One middle-aged Russian lady broke ranks when she saw him mopping his sweating brow, and bursting into tears, ran forward, crying, "The weather! The weather! Isn't it awful, Comrade Khrushchev?"

The privately circulated memoir of a Russian engineer who came to Egypt with the first contingent of technicians reported that he and his colleagues were "stunned" to be met at the Luxor railroad station by a crowd of enthusiastic Egyptians bearing placards lettered WELCOME BACK, OUR AMERICAN FRIENDS! At the Winter Palace Hotel, the multi-lingual bartender did not understand the Russians' carefully pronounced Arabic and was heard later remarking to one of the waiters, "What is the empire coming to when the British pashas drink vodka and cannot even speak proper English?"

The Russian Embassy was taking steps, it appeared, to bridge the cultural gap between the East and the Middle East. Dar el Shark Bookstore opened in the center of town, its windows decorated with photographs of Marx, Lenin and Engels. Translations of Russian books were offered at very low prices, and we enjoyed ourselves poking through the books and the inexpensive long-playing records, many still unavailable in the United States. The bookstore had soft carpets, cool whirring fans and reading tables where students might sit and browse. Yet it remained nearly empty, and oddly enough, there was scarcely a Russian in sight. All the clerks were Egyptian.

The Odeon Cinema, which advertised Russian films, was almost always empty. It was said that the ushers took down names or descriptions of all Egyptians seen entering the theatre, under orders from the secret police. The less dramatic reason given for low attendance at the Odeon was that the Russian films were not amusing.

*"Dem-el-thegeel awii!"* explained Omar, using the Arabic expression that sums up an attitude of life particularly alien to the Egyptian temperament; literally, it means heavy-blooded. If one has the opposite kind of blood, *dem-el-khafeef*, one is *sympatico*, gay, lighthearted, and can be counted upon to bear the vicissitudes of this life with a laugh, rather than a groan. It is, from an Egyptian, a high compliment.

"Certainly I am glad the Russians bring their heavy machines to build the dam," agreed Omar, when we pressed him, "but does that mean I have to sit and listen to their heavy-handed jokes?"

Perhaps it was only we Americans who were so super-curious about the Russians. Our Egyptian friends did not seem unduly interested, but then, they were not particularly interested in any foreigners as foreigners.

"I probably wouldn't see so much of you, if Bob and I hadn't both gone to the University of Chicago," said Omar, whose attitude was common. "Cairo has five million people," he would explain to me paternally. "The city has always been full of foreigners. Today it is full of foreigners from places I have never heard of. So? So."

The brief hiatus in international diplomatic and economic life, which came with the nationalization of the Suez Canal, was certainly over. Cairo, ancient crossroads of trade between East and West, was open for business as usual.

"Fascinating," Nick went around saying to anyone who would listen. "Look at the different combinations of people. History, history, all is history. A thousand years ago there were Syrian and Indian princes, even Chinese; five hundred years ago, Turks and Frenchmen. Now we are in a new phase. Africans. And the Chinese are coming back."

The Red Chinese were indeed coming back. Nicholas, who had spent his childhood in China with his foreign-service-officer father, visited with glee the newly opened Chinese restaurants, not one but two, and tried out his few words of remembered Chinese on the puzzled head waiter. (He had come from Peking to serve Arabs, not Americans, his expression seemed to say.)

We heard that the Red Chinese Embassy staff had increased from three to ten people. The next week rumors insisted that a staff of two hundred and twenty was handling stepped-up diplomatic relations. The week after that we were given to understand that more than three hundred Chinese specialists were infiltrating the Arab Socialist Union and sitting on mats in village courtyards, explaining Mao Tse-tung to the fellaheen.

"No, no, no!" protested an American Embassy political secretary. "Everyone knows the Egyptian Communist party is illegal, and no Red Chinese employees are even allowed to leave Cairo! Think of what would happen if they got to Aswan unannounced. Sino-Soviet friction here? That is hardly what President Nasser has in mind."

We saw President Nasser for the first time when he returned from his visit to the United Nations in New York. Busloads of fellaheen, shouting, "*Ya* Gamal! *Ya* Gamal!" had been arriving all day in the city, brought in from the country, it was said, and given lunch at government expense to swell the crowds. But such measures did not seem to be really needed, at least in Liberation Square, where the sidewalks were jammed with people, the windows and the roofs facing on the maidan were crowded with onlookers, and even the lampposts were topped with small boys, waving happily from their precarious perches. We stood on the balconies of the American University and listened to the wailing of the sirens, heralding the approach of the *polis el negda*, official motorcycle escort of the president.

"*Ya* Gamal! *Ya* Gamal!" chanted some of the onlookers. A loud spatter of steady applause erupted as the President drove past, standing up in the open car, hatless, a tall man in a dark pinstripe suit, smiling and waving to the people, whose pride he had restored and whose stains of poverty he had promised to erase.

But how could he do it? The problems were so gargantuan, the balance between a small amount of land and an enormous population so uneven.

Yet those were the years when it seemed possible. The High Dam was under way at last, and the UNESCO campaign to save Abu Simbel Temple from the dam's backwaters was focusing international attention on Egypt and its problems. The most cynical of our Egyptian friends admitted to a cautious optimism, and Nasser's enthusiasm was communicating itself to his people and to the foreigners who had come to Egypt.

The oasis of the American University was widening to include Japanese businessmen and African exchange students studying Arabic, young Egyptian clerks learning English in the extension evening classes. The parties we went to were marvelous cosmopolitan conglomerate gatherings of cultures and races, of political ideas and multilingual jokes. Even the *ganeena* had its share of thrills; the children and nannies would run to the fence to watch the motorcades roar by along the Corniche bringing President Sukarno of Indonesia, Ben Bella of Algeria, Prime Minister Nehru of India, or Marshal Tito of Yugoslavia in state to the President's house.

Gay and hopeful, confusing and amusing, they were, as Omar said, "Real *dem-el-khafeef* [light-blooded] days." And always, now at the back of my mind, lay that magic image — Nubia!

"Come with us, Susan," I would say, without thinking.

"Come where?"

"To Nubia, of course."

"Why not?" Susan would answer.

"I thought your esteemed husband was only planning a tiny piece of research," Nick would put in.

"You're the one who encouraged me to think big, Nick," Bob would say. "I'm putting together a proposal to show Professor Wilson when he comes.

"Oh?"

"Yes," Bob answered eagerly.

He, too, was thinking about Nubia all the time. The more he had inquired about those "few, small" Nubian villages, the more interested he had become.

One hundred thousand people were to be moved from their homes and resettled. Very little was known about them. Some work had been done on the Nubian language, and the Egyptian archeologist Ahmed Fakhry had gathered informal notes about Nubian customs and superstitions. But anthropological studies? Ecological studies? Nothing.

Bob assembled as many facts as he could, made some rough cost estimates, and went to see Dr. Laila, director of the Social Research Center at the American University and an anthropologist herself. If he could get bed and board on the Oriental Institute boat, would the Social Research Center be willing to sponsor a small bit of salvage anthropology on the Nubian people?

"Yes," said Dr. Laila. "Most definitely, yes. When will you know? I have to submit budgets, too.

"Professor John Wilson can give us a reasonably definite answer," said Bob. "He's coming from Chicago for the UNESCO commission meeting on the Save Abu Simbel campaign. Can you come to dinner then?"

Dr. Laila could.

The suffocating warmth of an early summer night in Cairo is mitigated and finally dispelled by the natural air conditioning of Mediterranean winds, fresh and sea-laden, which arrive regularly from the north each evening about dusk. But, of course, on this particular evening, with Professor John Wilson and twenty other guests coming for dinner, no breeze had yet come. Bob suggested closing the shutters again — the shutters we fastened tight in the morning to keep out the heat and opened in the evening to take advantage of the winds. We closed the shutters and turned on the fans. Then we opened the shutters again and tried putting the fans in the windows. Neither ploy helped. It was as hot and close outside as it was inside, the air pressing on one with an irritating close breath of its own.

"Maybe we'll have a *khamseen* tonight just to make everything lovely," Bob said cheerily. "Do you think so, Abbas?" It was *khamseen* season all right, when the hot, dry winds came from the desert, bringing sandstorms with them.

"No," said Abbas. "*Khamseens* don't start at dusk."

Laura Ann, crowing in her bath, seemed the only comfortable one in the house, though Abbas, in a fresh white *gullabiya* and turban, looked unruffled, as did Mohammed, his cousin, brought in to help for the occasion. Fawzia didn't look too harassed either, I thought. It was only Bob and me, fussing.

"Why tonight?" I muttered to myself as I walked around the apartment, checking ash trays, nut dishes, straightening cushions. The hot rooms were filled with the insistent scent of a great bouquet of creamy white tuberoses standing up stiffly in a brass urn in the dining room. Nothing moved in the apartment, not the spiked leaves of the tuberoses, nor the filmy bedroom curtains, not even the paper lantern in the hall.

"What time is it?"

"Seven," answered Abbas.

"We have an hour. Maybe the breeze will get here by then."

"If it doesn't the party will be ruined!" pronounced Bob in his own special voice of doom. He had already showered and dressed and was pacing up and down the length of the apartment. "No one will want to stay in this hot box for a fraction of a second longer than they absolutely have to for politeness' sake. How awful it is!" He marked off a few more paces.

Laura Ann was brought out, cool and happy in a batiste nightgown, kissed and jounced and taken to bed.

"Oh *where* is that wind?" cried Bob. He was on the balcony now, staring up and down, searching the air for sound, looking for the wind, but only the rude honking of taxis on the Corniche and the beat of the cha-cha-cha, carried across the still river from the night club on the opposite bank, answered him. That and the hushed conversation of all our neighbors, who were also out on their balconies looking, like Bob, for the wind.

"It will come," said Abbas shortly. He and his cousin Mohammed moved the dining table to a more central location for the buffet, the table draped in our best tablecloth for UNESCO. Abbas knew all about UNESCO and he had heard bits of Bob's plans to "do something" on the Nubians. After all, Abbas himself was a Nubian, from the Sudan. He had known the great temple of Kerma as a child, which was more than any of us could say, as Nick pointed out. Abbas had even heard of John Wilson.

"Maybe you should take those flowers out," suggested Bob.

"The tuberoses? But why? They have a lovely scent."

"Maybe too lovely. Why suffocate on hot, scented air rather than on just plain . . ." Bob mopped his forehead. "Really, B.J., I . . ."

The doorbell rang. Abbas opened the door to admit Professor Wilson and Omar.

The party had begun. The wind had not come, and even a plentiful supply of gin-and-tonics was no proper substitute.

"When shall I serve dinner?" Abbas asked me. "Everything's ready."

I glanced about at our guests, who by now filled the rooms and seemed to make them even hotter than before. There was nothing I wanted less at that moment than food, and I was sure they felt the same. And yet the lamb wouldn't wait forever, nor would the rice and Abbas' good casserole of squash and lentils and tomatoes and onions. The salad would wilt, the rolls dry up and the wine grow warm in the heat! I could have wept when I thought of the hours of preparation Abbas and I had put into that meal. A slight hush had descended on the crowd. They are trying to think of a polite way of leaving, I thought bitterly.

Abbas held up his hand.

It was a very slight movement, a faint whisper from the dusty leaves of the casuarina trees in the *ganeena*, taken up and passed like a message through the drooping foliage of the cottonwoods.

We waited.

Another whisper, another flutter.

"It is the breeze," announced Abbas with certainty.

Everyone rushed onto the balcony to watch the leaves move, the branches sway. We gulped the delightful air. In a quarter of an hour the temperature had dropped ten degrees and the breeze continued to blow. The guests sailed back into the dining room and consumed all the food and drained the wine, poured by Abbas (though with compressed lips—a good Moslem, he never touched alcohol himself). Laughter and conversation filled the apartment.

Dr. Laila, in a white and silver dress which set off her vivid coloring, sat with John Wilson and Bob in the living room, talking animatedly and gesturing. The two men talked, too, and gestured, on the couch under the windows where gusts of that cool sea air wafted through, ruffling in an attractive way Dr. Laila's dark shining coiffure, moving the tuberoses in the hall and actually blowing up the comers of the tablecloth!

"We're not the only people partying," Susan pointed out.

The roof of the Czechoslovakian Embassy across the *ganeena*, so tightly closed and guarded by day, was ablaze with light. The beat of a folk dance boomed into the night, and the Czechs polka-ed and laughed and slapped their knees, little knowing that the wind brought each slap and guffaw across to us in blasts of sound. Next door the colored lights strung about the Indonesian Embassy garden glinted on the silver of the ladies' saris, on golden epaulets and campaign medals and ceremonial swords. The ambassador was having his military evening, decorous and quiet except for military marches performed in unfamiliar Southeast Asian rhythms.

Laila and Bob and Professor Wilson talked on.

During dessert, the almond soufflé that was Abbas' specialty (he had been given the secret instructions by the landlady's cook in exchange for his bread recipe), I could not keep myself from that animated trio under the window any longer. What were they deciding about our future?

Professor Wilson smiled. "I think I've persuaded Bob and Laila," he said, "that their plans should be made on a grander scale."

"The idea," said Laila in a rush, "is that the Ford Foundation should be asked to support a long-term project to record Nubian culture."

"Salvage anthropology, but also cooperation with the ministry that's resettling the Nubians," explained Bob, "and training graduate students."

"What you should stress, I think," said Professor Wilson, "is the international cooperation in the social sciences angle, just as the archaeologists are collaborating to save Abu Simbel. The Nubians, after all, are an ancient and proud people, one must remember that. They're mentioned in Pharaonic sources, they are painted on the walls of tombs."

"Do you think the Ford Foundation would be really interested?" I asked.

"It seems a natural to me," answered John Wilson, "with all the attention Nubia and Aswan are getting these days. Nobody has yet given much scholarly thought to the people. Why not you and Laila?"

"If Ford isn't interested, there are other foundations," said Bob.

"B.J. can bring the family down and set up housekeeping like she did in Iraq," went on Professor Wilson.

"I can?" I looked at Bob.

"Let's try anyway, Laila," said Bob. "We've nothing to lose."

"Exactly!" agreed Laila. "And potentially who knows what we might gain?"

Professor Wilson shook hands. We parted.

Would all these possibilities have arisen if the evening breeze from the Mediterranean had not chosen to blow up the Nile that early summer evening? Sometimes I have seriously doubted it.

# Chapter 2

# Nubian Adventures Begin

N ubian fever gripped us all that autumn. Bob and Dr. Laila submitted a formal proposal to the Ford Foundation for a Nubian ethnological survey. It would be, as envisioned, a three-year program covering a great many aspects of this soon-to-be-lost culture. Nicholas had decided, after talking with ministry officials and with other archaeologists, that the American Research Center in Egypt, his sponsor, could very well apply for one of the permits being issued by the Ministry of Antiquities to excavate Nubia.

"If the Poles, the Dutch, the Russians and the Austrians can do it, why can't we?"

"Why not?" asked Bob. "Nicholas, I have a great idea, a kind of interdisciplinary plan."

"Now what?"

"If you excavate near one of the villages where we will do long-term community studies, perhaps we could even compare data later on."

"Ho-ho, my good friend!" responded Nicholas. "Capital! The compleat history of the area from prehistory to 1960!"

We toasted, in Stella beer, that particular inspiration.

"You should see those villages," Omar exulted.

Omar dominated every gathering of Nubia-philes because, although we all talked about Nubia, he was the only one of us who had been there. The Ministry of Antiquities had sent him with a group of archaeologists to survey major temples to be recorded and photographed for posterity. Then, should the UNESCO campaign fail, history would still have some record of the drowned monuments.

"At first I could not believe that simple people had built such sophisticated dwellings—and of mud!" continued Omar.

"Tut, tut, Omar! Your prejudices are showing," chuckled Nick.

Omar did not laugh. He was tall and dark and elegant and joked most of the time, but at this moment he did not laugh. "You must see the villages for yourself," he said. "I'm glad, Bob, that you're going to study these people. I had no idea there was a culture like this within the boundaries of my own country.

"Can you find me a job in Nubia so I can come?" asked Susan.

"Me, too," chimed in Aziza.

"Aziza! You in a village!" Omar did laugh now. "You'd be no good at all. You'd only slow them down; where, my dear, would you have your hair done?"

Aziza rapped her brother on the shoulder. "I could take an anthropology course," she suggested gaily. "It might be fun!"

"Well," said Bob, "plenty of time to decide. We won't be going for a while. Even if we hear about the grant by Christmas, there is much to be done before we actually go down."

Yes, I thought, planning on many levels to be done. Our second child was due before Christmas and if all went well, Bob planned to leave for Nubia in January and get settled in a village by late spring; he was determined to do a community study himself rather than stay in Cairo and administer the proposed project, as everyone expected him to.

Next fall, with Laura Ann two and the new baby nearly a year old, I would take the children and join him in the village.

"All we can do now is wait," said Bob.

But our new baby, it seemed, did not feel like waiting. He had indicated rather firmly his intention to arrive before his time.

"Hurry, can't you tell the driver to hurry, I don't know what's going on, it's not at all like Laura Ann," I wailed to Bob as we whizzed along the Corniche at midnight on our way to the hospital.

Dark, it was much too dark. The coffee shops had snuffed out their colored lights, the slender minarets of the Zamalek mosque library, without their garlands of electric blossoms, had become only shadows, mere frightening ghosts of minarets in the shadows. The Nile was still, only a dark, scarcely rippling path between the two banks.

"Oh, no!"

"What?" said Bob in concern.

"Oh, look, on the curb."

Were those vagabond boys planning to descend on the lone vendor up the street? He started to move, evidently thinking so too, pushing his lighted glass shop-on-a-cart ahead of him home, and with each bump in the street, my stomach jerked, the pains flashed, and the peddler's white enamel bowls of rice pudding and jello, the brown clay pots of yogurt rattled and banged against the walls of the van, walls painted in lurid colors and topped with cuttin curlicues and towers.

"Bob!" I cried.

"What?"

"Nothing. Really, it's nothing."

Had it been only a year since the doorkeeper ushered us into the Coptic Hospital for the first time? Where would we be this time next year?

Our second child came into the world in silence, and in the several lengthened ticking seconds before the silence became a muffled gurgling and finally erupted into a full-fledged human cry, my mind wandered again, panic-stricken, over those darkened whizzing scenes which we had passed in our midnight race to the hospital. The dark, smooth, rippling path of the Nile, the frightened peddler bumping his cart, the dark, nameless boys in the gutter after him, armed with broken sticks.

"Congratulations, Mrs. Fernea!" cried Dr. Zaki. "It's a boy. We're lucky. The cord was tight around the baby's neck. If your labor had been longer, he might have strangled."

But from the piercing wail now emerging nonstop from my newborn son, strangling did not seem an imminent danger, and my midnight fantasies receded. I thanked God for the strength and timbre of that cry.

Little did I know that the wail would go on and on. Many times in the following months I had to remind myself how grateful I was that the baby's lungs were clear and well formed. The only visitor that David Karim's bellow did not send scurrying out was Abbas, come with a loaf of bread and a sponge cake to dispel the monotony of hospital food.

"Oh," he said cheerfully, blinking at the volume tiny David seemed capable of producing ad infinitum, "this boy is a strong one, may God protect him!"

We brought our son and heir home to a veritable phalanx of neighborhood greeters. Bob, for the first time in years, seemed embarrassed.

"Did they all expect a *baksheesh*, Abbas?" he asked afterward.

Abbas shrugged. "Well, if you'd given them one, they wouldn't have said no," he answered. His face softened. "But everyone likes babies," he added. "They are gifts from God. Everybody wants to see a new boy."

After three weeks of nonstop crying, we visited Dr. Hanna.

"Just relax," he said calmly. "The child had a bad time coming into the world. Didn't you just about lose him twice? He simply has an unusually severe case of colic."

"But. . ." said Bob wearily, passing a hand over his eyes. He had his son to worry about now as well as Nubia. "Dr. Hanna, isn't there something you can give him to stop the crying?"

Dr. Hanna smiled. "You might try a weak infusion of caraway seed, with a bit of sugar. Or tilleul which is only lime flowers."

I stared. "Fawzia suggested that, but I didn't pay any attention. I thought it was some old wives' remedy."

"Usually my American patients expect a more scientific answer," said Dr. Hanna smoothly, "and if I were to say that a simple infusion, such as is used by the very poor, would help, they might think that I, a doctor in an under-developed country (isn't that the phrase?), was ignorant of recent advances in international medicine. Tilleul and caraway tea are not things I learned to prescribe in American medical schools, but American mothers, as I'm sure you have realized by now, madame, have different problems than Egyptian mothers."

He smiled and we shook hands.

In the following weeks of Davy's life, I was very grateful for tilleul and caraway tea. It had been so simple with Laura Ann, who nursed and ate well, slept, smiled, grew round and pink with scarcely any effort. I had felt pleased (a bit too pleased) with myself when I wheeled her along, past mothers with unpleasant cross children and whining unattractive babies.

"Really," I had said aloud more times than I care to remember, "all one needs to do is relax. Simply a matter of a calm environment."

Along had come Davy to end my smug theories. The tilleul didn't work miracles but it helped, and Davy was gaining weight. "Food and mother's milk and tilleul," twinkled Dr. Hanna and I nodded humbly.

The new year passed. Bob was depressed and worried. It was difficult to say whether Davy's problems made Bob more edgy over not hearing anything definite about the Nubian project, or whether they merely substituted an immediate, somewhat remediable problem for one that had no ready solution.

He fretted. Dr. Laila fretted. The Ford Foundation office in New York seemed a long way from Cairo.

"What we're up against," said Bob, as we sat in Dr. Laila's garden with the local Ford Foundation representative, "is time!"

"The first group of Nubians, you see," explained Laila, "has to be moved to new houses before the Nile is diverted into the side channel."

"And how long is that?"

"Two, two and a half years at most," said Bob. "If we're going to do this thing, we must do it quickly."

"What do you suggest?" asked the Ford representative.

Bob looked blank for a moment. "Well, er, rather than waste valuable time just sitting and waiting, maybe I could do a quick preliminary survey of Nubia for six weeks or two months."

"Alone?"

"No, I could take Karim with me. None of us actually knows what the situation is, you know," went on Bob, warming to his subject. "Will we be able to rent houses in the villages? Or will we need tents? How many people for each community study? Which communities, for that matter? Will we need motorboats? Donkeys? Water filters?"

"But how can you do such a survey, Bob?" interrupted the Ford representative. "You've told me yourself the Sudan Railways steamboat is the only public transportation in the area and it only stops in three or four places. This would hardly provide you with the information you say you need."

"Well—" said Bob, and he sat up suddenly and the words tumbled out of him, "we could hire a felucca in Aswan."

He smiled and I realized he was absolutely delighted at the thought.

"A sailboat could pull in any place along the river, and we could stay wherever we wanted as long as we needed to. Why not? It couldn't be that expensive to hire a tourist sailboat. At the end of the trip we can take the Sudan Railways express boat back from Wadi Halfa or Ballana."

"Where will you *sleep* and eat, for that matter?" asked Laila.

"On the boat," said Bob quickly. "On the boat. We'll get a sack of rice and a primus stove and sleeping bags . . ."

"Shades of Alan Villiers!" cried Nick in glee. "Two hundred miles in a felucca! You're not serious, Bob!"

"Of course I'm serious," answered Bob.

I realized the idea had just come to him in the past several minutes, but already it was taking shape in his mind, and he could visualize himself at the prow of a felucca (wearing a *gullabiya*, perhaps, and a pith helmet), sailing up the Nile with his primus stove, his typewriter and his Swiss army knife.

I had to laugh. I couldn't help it. Then I realized ruefully why I was laughing.

"She laughs," said Bob to Nick. "Ha! She laughs, but she is just jealous."

"Excellent idea!" cried Laila. She was laughing, too, and I fancied she wouldn't mind going along on the felucca, either. "Wait until Karim hears about this."

Susan reported that when told of his role in the forthcoming Nile expedition, Karim, one of the bright younger research assistants in the Center, turned pale. Any comment he might have made was drowned in the excited clamor of the office staff.

I wondered about Karim, a nervous and intense young man. He was intelligent and well educated, but had never lived outside a city, and the cultural milieu within which he grew up did not include summer camps. Those were for poor orphan boys whose families could not afford vacations on the beaches of Alexandria. Thus Karim had no nostalgia for the great outdoors. But he said nothing. He bought supplies and began to fill, systematically, a metal first-aid kit the size of a suitcase.

Bob scoffed. "For heaven's sake, Karim, we'll never use all those medicines up in fifteen years!"

"I am thinking in broader terms, D-Dr. Fernea," stuttered Karim. "This is for the big project, eventually, for all three camps.

"Oh, good," answered Bob, "but there won't be room for it on the felucca. Take out everything except aspirin, entrovioform, sulfa powder, a few basics."

Karim peered doubtfully after Bob's receding back. I bent over and helped remove the vials and jars and bottles.

"But we must have the anti-snakebite serum," insisted Karim, "and the anti-scorpion medicine. I got it with a special permit from the Ministry of Health."

"Well, if you think so," I said doubtfully.

"Yes, and the penicillin and the splints and the malaria medicine . . ." He looked at me and said quickly, "I'll carry it all with my luggage, and Dr. Fernea won't have to bother about it."

On a cold, dank February evening, Bob and Karim departed for Nubia, Bob with his mind full of ideas and plans and his briefcase full of papers. Karim had arrived early and stowed the first-aid suitcase under the seat of the Cairo-Aswan sleeper, I noted.

"Beni Suef, Assiut, Luxor, Aswan!" called the conductor.

"Karim's mother asked me just now if I would ask you to be kind to her son," I whispered to Bob.

"He can only eat, apparently, the special food she cooks for him, and she's worried," added Susan.

Bob stared. He looked at Karim, jumping about nervously in the huge crowd of friends and relatives who had come down to see him off.

"Kind?" he said, amazed. "Why on earth would I be *un*kind?"

The train began to move. Bob and Karim climbed aboard.

"God go with you!" cried the crowd of well-wishers.

"Wear your scarf all the time, dear!" begged Karim's mother.

"Don't drink the water!" called someone.

The crowd laughed loudly. Steam rose around us. Karim's mother dabbed at her eyes as the train chugged out of the station. The Nubian adventure had begun.

"Nubia," wrote architect Hassan Fathi, "was like a world so new, so fresh in invention and artistry that we were enchanted . . . we could not believe it to be true. Most of us" (artists sent by the Ministry of Culture to record impressions of Nubia for posterity) "had never visited this part of our own country, and the clearness of the architectural purpose, the procession of glistening white houses on the banks of these ancient shores, was like a dream from another age."

We awaited letters in like vein from Bob and Karim. But traveling, as Hassan Fathi had, on a well-staffed luxury boat was rather different from Bob and Karim's plans to hire a garden-variety felucca and drop anchor at every village along the way.

"Well," wrote Bob finally and brusquely, "we're setting off at last. Four days in Aswan to line up a felucca and crew. No one seems to want to make such an unorthodox trip, the local Nubian sailors are unwilling to give up transporting tourists around the cataracts. Infuriating waste of time. We go through the locks at Aswan tomorrow before sunrise, and then on to Nubia!"

Karim wrote, "Can you believe, dear friends in the Center, that we are actually on the river almost all the time, Dr. Fernea and me? The boat is very small, I must say. We bobbed up and down in the locks like a cork! It makes one rather nervous. I sleep on the boards on top of the boat, like the sailors in old-fashioned English novels. My transistor radio has run out of batteries. I feel very far from Cairo and my friends, from the coffee shops and the tea garden of Groppi."

"*Le pauvre!*" enunciated a pretty research assistant, as this letter was read aloud to the breathless office staff.

"Now Bob's new letter," prompted Susan, who was working part time in the Center.

"The river is trickier than one would think," Bob had typed. "For instance, yesterday we came very close to grinding a hole in the bottom of the boat, on a submerged tree. There are hundreds of them, especially along the shores, trees that were covered by the flood after the 1933 raising of the dam. I suggested we steer a course closer to the main stream of the river, but the boatmen absolutely refuse, say it's dangerous and so on. I suppose they know what they're doing, that's what I hired them for, after all, but I'm beginning to wonder."

The girls stifled tiny yawns.

"Is that all?" asked the pretty researcher.

"Well, oh yes, here's a nice part. 'The villages are quite something, very clean, some houses have porches with pillars, like southern mansions. Yesterday we found a whitewashed staircase coming right down to the water line; we moored the boat and walked straight up to tea. We've seen sculpture in mud brick, very good some of it, decorating the houses, and also colorful paintings on the walls and doors. By the way, how are the children?' "

The girls oohed and aahed. I felt a pang which I tried unsuccessfully to suppress. Whitewashed pillars and sculpture along the quiet Nile. A long procession of days in the warm winter sun and nights sleeping under the stars. I wouldn't have thought of leaving the children, and yet. . .

Abbas was in good form these days, as manager and protector of the household. From years of living and traveling on the river, he knew it well, and each evening after we had gone over the daily accounts, he found occasion to tell me some story about the Nile, the first cataract at Aswan, the second at the Sudanese border, and the third and final cataract of the river near his own home of Kerma in New Dongola. His eyes shone as he talked and I wondered again what we were all doing up here in Cairo when we could be trail-breaking along the second greatest river in the world. Then I shook myself and wrote a long letter to Bob, full of the children's newest words and accomplishments.

The next thing that happened was a telegram.

"Don't worry!" the transcriber of the cable had typed, suitably punctuating the phrase to alert me at once. Don't worry about what? "We are o. k. will cable when more news love Bob."

Had the boat sunk? Had they been attacked by scorpions or chomped upon by crocodiles?

"Don't worry," repeated Abbas. "Probably they went aground. The Aswan boatmen don't know the southern channels."

Abbas' tone was brisk and his advice seemed sensible. Not to worry. But how could I help it when I had no idea where Bob was or what had happened to him?

Four days passed without word. "They may have to wait three or four days, a week maybe if they are aground," cautioned Abbas.

"Why?"

"Till a bigger boat comes along to pull them off," he answered.

"But the steamboat goes past every three days!"

"Yes," said Abbas, "but the steamboat doesn't stop for every felucca that goes aground. They might be in an empty place or in a cove, out of sight."

Empty! Now in my dreams, footage of the river and the stars combined with a frame of Bob and Karim, stretched on the sand in the classic lost-in-the-desert pose. I knew this was perfect nonsense, but still. . . . Did they have water canteens with them, I wondered, and sat up in bed in the middle of the night. Why hadn't they written or sent another cable? A week had gone by, eight days.

"Dear friends in the Center," Karim's letter brought me down to the office posthaste in a taxi to hear it read aloud. "I know you will not believe it, but I think I have gained several pounds on Dr. Fernea's cooking. It is horrible, but rice and bully beef are filling. I do not even take my sleeping pills and aspirin before bed as I am so tired I fall asleep at dark and there is no radio to keep me awake.''

The girls babbled all at once.

"Karim fat?''

"*Incroyable!*''

"Karim without his pills?''

"Can Dr. Fernea cook?''

"Oh,'' sighed the pretty research assistant, "he was so thin and elegant, Karim. I shall have to plan a small *regime* for him when he returns.'' And she giggled.

This letter did not make sense in relation to the "Don't worry'' cable. I pored over the postmark after the girls had gone back to work and finally realized the letter had been mailed before the cable was sent, so was not actually news at all.

Then where were they?

"Two weeks,'' I said to Susan, who was staying with me while Bob was gone. "Two weeks is a long time not to hear a word. He could have sent a cable.''

"Maybe there's no place to send a cable from.''

"Don't worry, madame,'' repeated Abbas.

Next morning the letter did finally arrive. I skimmed over the beginning, he did seem to be all right, and yet. . .

"Yesterday,'' wrote Bob (the letter was dated more than two weeks before), "we were skidding along the edge of the river again as usual when we ran over a submerged palm, just as I had predicted days before, and tore a hole in the bottom of our boat. Water poured in, great confusion. It wasn't very serious, as it turned out, and we easily made it to shore but as far as our sailors were concerned, that was that. They put us and our belongings ashore, turned the boat upside down and announced that as soon as it was repaired they were heading back to Aswan! We could go to hell and so could our 'agreement'! We're currently bargaining with a vendor of salted fish and other salables to abandon his trade for a time and take us on for a month as passengers. Here's hoping we're successful, as I don't fancy spending the next month in this particular village, though there are interesting things about it.

"When we first arrived we were taken to one elderly man who addressed us in good English with a strong southern accent. While Karim and I sat there with our mouths open, he told us his tale; he'd worked as a steward on a merchant ship out of Suez, had jumped ship in New Orleans and lived there for twelve years. He even married a New Orleans woman and they ran a restaurant together. One day, it appeared he got homesick for Nubia and for his Nubian wife and family, and got an Egyptian ship to take him on again. Sounds like an unlikely story, doesn't it, but he certainly knew New Orleans inside and out. Seems the Nubians are going to offer us plenty of surprises of this kind. I mean, one might not be too amazed in Cairo, but imagine finding a man who knew all about the restaurants in New Orleans living happily in a little village on the Nile halfway through the Sahara desert!''

Susan and I looked at each other appreciatively.

"Is there more?'' she asked.

I nodded.

"I don't fancy going on in this other boat either, smells of rotten fish from stem to stern, but we're stuck, and we will be lucky if we can get them to take us on. The post boat is coming soon so I want to mail this letter. Will let you know what happens next time I get a chance."

Next morning, not only was Abbas grinning from ear to ear for having diagnosed the situation correctly from the beginning, but two more explanatory letters arrived, together.

I took the children for a walk along the Corniche, trying to feel virtuous and motherly. It was not a success. "All I need now," I told myself, "is a truly lyrical letter about Abu Simbel."

Eventually that letter arrived, too.

"The yellow acacia tree is in flower, it provides a nice foreground for the temple."

Could that really be Bob writing?

"We spent the night sleeping on shore in front of the four mighty colossi of Ramses. At dawn, just as the books say, the rays of the sun do strike the inner sanctuary of the temple. The light was a bit off the altar though, since we are past whatever day the sunrise is supposed to strike full center.

"Actually, sleeping on the sandy shore sounds romantic, but it was most uncomfortable because of the insects, which reminds me, don't forget to send us some more insect repellent, c/o Dr. Riad at Sebua, we will pick it up at the post office."

Yes, that was Bob writing. But there was more.

"Karim and I took the day off to look at the temple, the big one dedicated to Ramses, and the smaller one, his queen's. One feels one knows a bit what the earlier explorers of the Nile must have felt like. Here we are, all alone, the river, the empty sand, everything so quiet, and this great monumental temple just standing here. The place is most memorable. You must see it."

Yes, I thought, I'd like to very much.

In the office, the girls were once more agog over Karim's prose in praise of Abu Simbel.

"They all want to go to Nubia," said Dr. Laila. "And when I think that two years ago, we couldn't have paid enough to one of those girls or to the boys either, to go to a village, any village and work. . . ."

She paused. "Egypt is really changing," she said. "The only problem is, well, you know."

Yes, I knew. Money. There still had been no definite word from Ford.

The bright, clear days of February passed. Ramadan began, and special preparations were under way in the kitchen each day for the *iftar*, or breaking of the fast. Abbas jounced Laura Ann and now Davy, who had passed his howling days and except for a stubborn cold seemed finally to be enjoying life for the first time.

Bob wrote about the temple of Derr, the pottery-makers of Sebua, of the village near Abu Simbel where he hoped to base one of the community studies, of Faras on the Sudanese border where archaeologists were uncovering medieval Christian churches with Byzantine frescoes. "Karim and I seem to be thriving in this air. I can understand why the Pharaohs used to come to Upper Egypt for their health. WHAT GIVES WITH FORD?"

What indeed? I did not know. Neither did Laila or the Ford office in Cairo.

Could Ford say no? Of course they could. And then what would happen to the Nubian idea? A little piece of research, perhaps, one man on the University of Chicago expedition boat, as Bob had originally envisaged it. It would be all right. Not so grandiose, but useful and interesting. Things had gotten beyond that stage, however, and we all entertained bigger ideas. Setting up field camps. Spinning up and down the river in motorboats. Seminars with the Ministry of Social Affairs, which was handling the Nubian resettlement. A chance to be of some real service perhaps. UNESCO cooperation.

I met Laila at a large cocktail party for an NBC correspondent in Cairo on his way back from filming the Upper Nile.

"Everybody in New York wants to see Abu Simbel these days," he explained. "So we have to give the public what it wants. Vince Halliday. How do you do?" He was ruddy faced and his thickening chin above the fashionable shirt hinted at middle age, his boyish shock of graying hair brushed the top of heavy horn-rimmed spectacles.

"You've just come from Abu Simbel?" I asked eagerly.

"Yes," said Vince. "New York won't believe what Roger and I went through to get this footage . . . just to hire the boat, I mean.

Laila and I looked at each other.

"Fantastic place, though," went on Vince. "Worth it all. And we ran into a couple of guys traveling by sailboat. Like to do that myself if I were twenty years younger."

"Really?" I began. There couldn't be that many people traveling coursing up the Nile in a sailboat, could there? "Who were they?"

"Nubians told us the tall thin blond with the stringy beard was a Swede, and the other, a chubby dark fellow with a big bush of a beard, an Ethiopian.

"Were they?"

Laila giggled. Vince looked at her. "Well, no," he said. "We got them to give us a live interview, which we sold to the 'Today' show. Quite an interesting bit. Bush Beard was a Palestinian and Thin Beard was, honest-to-pete, ladies, an American. I discovered I'd been working in Chicago when he was there, and they ended up staying to lunch. Can you believe it? In the middle of the desert?"

Next morning Laila telephoned.

"I've just sent a cable to Thin Beard," she said.

"Asking him to give up the lie he's been leading all these years and send in his Swedish passport for validation?"

"B.J.!" cried Laila, exasperated. "Listen to me! This is the cable. 'Ford has given us the grant!' Did you hear that?"

"Yes."

"Well, say something. Isn't it wonderful? *El Hamdillaa!* Thanks be to God!"

The Nubian Ethnological Survey was about to become an actuality.

"We'll be here three more years," I told Abbas.

He grinned. "Nubia is a fine place," he said.

Three more years. Three more years of our lives to be lived abroad, in Egypt, three more years of our children's lives. We had not thought this far in advance when we'd come from America less than two years ago. But now it seemed a fine thing. What would my mother say, and Bob's mother? Their grandchildren raised in foreign climes? Why? Well, why not?

"It seems that Thin Beard has triumphed at last," I told Susan at suppertime.

"*El Hamdillaa!*" she pronounced. "You'll take the children and go down in the fall, then, as planned."

"Yes, if Davy gets over this stubborn cold."

"A cold! For heaven's sake, B.J., don't turn into a fussing mother just when we're about to embark on our Nubian adventure," said Susan lightly, and added, "I'm sure he'll be fine in a few days."

"You're probably right."

We sat on the balcony, watching the lights wink along the Nile, and thinking of Bob and Karim, sitting beside this same beautiful river, but closer, far closer to its source.

# Chapter 3

# Up the Nile to Abu Simbel

The ancient Egyptians believed the Nile to be the center of the world and that the source of this great river lay in a narrow rocky gorge near Aswan. Within the gorge, the myths say, the mysterious Spirit of the Nile, the god Hapy, unleased the miraculous waters which flooded the land with rich loam and "divine sweat" and allowed men to survive in the desert.

As usual, the myths bore some resemblance to reality. For the first cataract of the Nile is at Aswan, the last natural obstruction in the river's three thousand miles of wanderings from its source in the mountains and lakes of central Africa. And the Nile, as it rushes through the cataract, does seem to be beginning, to be gathering momentum and strength for the remainder of its journey to the Mediterranean Sea.

From the canopied veranda of the Old Cataract Hotel in Aswan, high on the sandstone cliffs above the riverbanks, one can see occasional quiet pools, reflecting the golds and reds and darknesses of the wide, clear sky. More often the river boils and froths, surging around islands of palm trees and whitewashed houses and Pharaonic temple ruins, around granite boulders polished and worn into curious shapes by centuries of the passage of these foaming waters.

The Nile winds, as it has always wound, above and below the cataract, but a railroad has never been finished beyond Aswan. The only overland traffic which pushed south into Nubia was that of the caravans, the camels and donkeys of the Bishareen nomads who circumnavigated the rocks along the riverbanks and traveled inland along the desert of the valley floor. Today even this traffic is thinning, as the Aswan Dam rises and its backwaters are slowly covering Nubia with a vast lake. Most southbound passengers are now flying south or taking a circuitous ocean route through the Red Sea and the Gulf of Aden.

27

But before the days of the High Dam, passengers could go on by water, as Bob and Karim had done earlier in their hired felucca. The river was the main highway through Egyptian Nubia, a three-hundred mile stretch of country between Aswan and Wadi Halfa, in the Sudan. Feluccas sailed up and down the Nile with loads of dates and grain, with sheep and goats, salted fish, straw mats, produce to be traded in Aswan or Halfa for cloth, tea, tobacco, pots and pans and gold. Smaller feluccas ferried the Nubian people across the river to grind grain at the mill, to see the government doctor, to visit friends, to celebrate feasts. For more affluent travelers, the Sudan Railways operated a twice-weekly steamer, an unpretentious but cheerful riverboat, with an adequate sun deck, a dining room and small but well-kept cabins. At Wadi Halfa the voyager could, if he wished, connect with the train to Khartoum and Juba, on the edge of Uganda and the Congo, near the source of the Nile.

It was this Sudan Railways steamer we boarded one January morning, after a bumpy night on the Cairo-Aswan sleeper. We stood on the dock at the little port of Shellal in the crowd of gesticulating Nubians, shouting porters, a handful of tourists and a few harassed-looking Egyptian customs officials in wrinkled white uniforms. Bob and Susan and I, with Laura Ann and David, were bound for Nubia at last.

"A pleasant trip for all of us," Bob had predicted. "Abu Simbel's the last stop before Halfa, we'll wait at the temple and someone from the village can come pick us up. Two days and a night with nothing to do! What more could one ask? Riverboat travel is very relaxing."

Well, we can all use some of that, I thought, feeling suddenly tired although it was not yet noon. Bob, too, had a harried look. Only Susan appeared her normal calm self, holding Laura Ann by the hand and pointing out the exciting parts of the steamboat we were about to board.

"See, Laura Ann, that little white platform is the bridge, and the man with the gold shoulder tassels calling through the megaphone is the captain. Those are the lifesavers if we fall in the river."

"Fall in river?" Laura Ann pulled forward to the edge of the dock where the shining water dropped to unknown depths. Susan pulled her gently back.

"And there," cried Susan, "look at the big wheels in back turning, they'll push us up the river!"

The science of paddle steamers seemed beyond the ken of two-and-a-half-year-old Laura Ann, but Aunt Susan's enthusiastic tone was bound to rivet her attention. She stared in fascination at the big wheels at the rear of the boat which were, indeed, beginning to turn in the depths of the Nile.

It had been many months since Ford had given the money for the Nubian project, and Bob had been back and forth between village and city ever since. Davy's stubborn cold had developed into what the doctor called allergic asthma; he had sprouted various fungus infections and was losing weight; Dr. Hanna had begun treating him with cortisone. I was pregnant. For a time it had been give-and-take whether I would get to Nubia with the children at all. Finally, Dr. Hanna admitted that Nubia's dry climate might help Davy, since he was not improving in Cairo. Dr. Zaki had agreed that if there had been no trouble by the beginning of my fifth month, I could go to Nubia (provided I did nothing foolish, he said firmly; I had laughed to myself at that). Yet here I was, already tired, not the proper beginning at all for such a long-anticipated and momentous journey.

"Oh!" I cried. "Oh, no!"

A huge wooden box teetering dangerously on the bent porter's back missed Laura Ann's head by a quarter of an inch. I turned away so she would not hear my involuntary cry, and found myself staring at a young tourist couple. Slender, smooth-skinned, they smiled and held hands, obviously honeymooners.

How gladly, for one moment, I would have traded in my ponderous self for the lighthearted slimness of the girl, would have exchanged my diaper bag and our other odd-shaped pieces of luggage (water filters, kerosene lanterns, cans of powdered milk, motorboat parts, sleeping bags) for the chic compactness of their single suitcase, their cameras on narrow straps.

"Where are the vaccination certificates, B.J.?" shouted Bob above the noise.

Oh, dear, where are they, I wondered. I passed Davy to Susan while I rummaged, in the midst of the crush, in my catchall purse.

Shellal, although still in Egypt proper, was the official border crossing point into the Sudan.

I'd expected the extensive baggage searches in progress; Bob had explained that much petty smuggling went on between the two countries. But I'd forgotten that health checks were made here, too. *Where* were those certificates, ah, at last.

We were scheduled to sail at eleven. It was now past noon and the customs officials were still combing through the bags and bundles piled on the dock. They were looking for something or someone, Bob whispered; he'd never been held up this long.

Our valises, I noticed, did not have the neatness of those carefully sewn cloth bundles which the white-robed and turbaned Nubian fathers carried on their shoulders, leaving a hand free to hold a child. The little girls, wearing red-fringed head shawls over bright flannelette dresses, a warm red to set off their dark brown skin, stared with round eyes at Laura Ann's big baby doll, clutched to the bosom of her blue sweater. The boys were not so distinctive; they wore the casual *gullabiya* found throughout Egypt; only the design and color of their hand-made skullcaps showed they were Nubian.

Like me, many of the Nubian women carried a baby, but more resourceful than I, they also managed their luggage at the same time, big baskets of beige, purple and orange, which they balanced as easily as hats on their black-veiled heads.

"Maaaa! Maaa!"

The protesting bleat of hobbled goats and sheep tore through the din. People were beginning to board. Crates of clucking poultry were being passed into the hold, and sacks of sugar and tea marked with the sign of the government cooperative stores. Mailbags came last, precious mail-bags containing money from fathers working in the cities to their families in rural Nubia.

Bells clanged, motors roared, the paddle wheels turned the river to froth. The customs search had apparently been fruitless, for the signal had been given to depart, and the gangplank was hoisted up. We were on our way to the little village of Erd-Moz, where Bob had begun his community study.

"How many people will be able to say, my dears," Bob joked to Susan and me, "that they lived when young beside the drowned temple of Abu Simbel?"

Laura Ann's blonde head did not quite touch the top of the ship's rail, where she stood with her father, watching the shoreline while we steamed slowly upriver. The granite boulders, which had seemed so picturesque in the changing light of Aswan, were bleak here, strewn high upon each bank and tumbling down crazily and seemingly haphazardly to the lapping river.

"I thought Nubia would be just sand," I ventured.

"Nonsense," said Bob crisply. "Why?"

"Well, it's a desert, isn't it?"

"Yes, but a mountainous desert, and it's all around you now. Over there to the west is the Sahara and to the east the mountains and valleys go on until you reach the Red Sea. There is no habitable land anywhere except this bit along the water's edge."

And that doesn't look like much, I thought to myself. In Cairo the strip of cultivated land was wide and lush; one was not as aware of the hovering presence of the desert. Here in northern Nubia the riverside vegetation had been covered by the waters of the first Aswan Dam, erected in 1933; all that remained was this waste of rock and coarse sand.

Earlier, we had passed a few villages where, Bob had said, the population consisted almost entirely of women and children; the men had gone to work in the cities.

"I can see why," said Susan. "How could *anything* grow here?"

There was obviously no source of livelihood left on the barren shores. The houses stood up among the rocks, small and bravely whitewashed but these, too, we had passed, for the landscape became more empty and silent with each mile we traveled south toward the Sudan.

Davy, in Susan's arms, strained upward toward a white bird with long, lazily drooping legs and wide wings. The bird swooped and rose, swooped and rose with the gentle undulations of the churning steamer.

"Davy'd like to fly, too, I think," said Susan.

Davy was still not walking. "He's weakened from the months of coughing, remember," Dr. Hanna had said. "When he is strong enough to walk, he will walk'"

"Is that a stork?" I asked.

"Could be," said Bob.

"Yes, a stork," volunteered a small bearded gentleman standing near us at the rail. "Gurf Hussein," he added, and pointed to a mound of broken stones in the distance. "Perhaps you would care to see?" and he offered us his binoculars.

He smiled in a friendly, one-passenger-to-another way. "What you see is the remains of the colonnaded court which stood before the rock temple."

I could not find anything too remarkable in the cluster of broken stones but the little man was awaiting a reply.

"So many antiquities in Nubia!" I remarked rather stupidly. "I had no idea of that. I suppose it's because Abu Simbel gets all the publicity."

David sat on the deck at my feet. He held onto the iron netting which fenced the rail, pulled himself upright for a moment, sank down wearily. Bob picked him up. Laura Ann and Susan began a game of hide-and-seek between the canvas deck chairs.

"Ah, dear madame," the little man spoke with a distinct French accent, "Nubia is a veritable treasure house of the past."

With a sweeping gesture he encompassed the tumbling white wake of the boat, the vast empty stretches of rock-strewn desert land on either side of us, the disappearing broken remains of the Gurf Hussein Temple. "Pharaonic, Greek, Roman, Byzantine, Islamic, the entire panorama of history before the Middle Ages has left its traces here."

"Really?"

"Yes, but all these records will soon be under water, lost to humanity forever!" he declaimed. "Because of one dam."

Bob handed Davy to me. "The whole country is full of antiquities," he pointed out. "Nubia is not unique."

"We do not know," admitted the little man, stroking his beard. "I, with some others, believe that if Nubia were to be explored thoroughly, our whole idea of the history of Egypt would change."

"The dam, though," put in Bob, "is very important if the Egyptian economy is to survive."

"Perhaps," the little man allowed.

We took turns looking through his proffered binoculars at the distant mountain, the changing landscape. Occasionally, clusters of palms and light fringes of grass appeared softening the harshness of the rocks. Was it because we were leaving that section of Nubia which had been flooded by the first dam? I turned to ask Bob, but he was listening to the Frenchman who, with gestures and little quick nods of his bearded profile, was delivering a brief lecture.

"The Nubian kings rose to power," I heard him say. "They had waited a long time." Battles, slaves, caravans of ivory and ebony and spices, gold mines opened, resumption of trade with Africa. "Greek soldiers actually wrote their names in the temple of Abu Simbel," he said, his voice rising. "That is how we know the campaign came so far south. You will see the stone."

"I have seen it," said Bob.

The little Frenchman paused, but not for long.

"And then we come to Juvenal."

"Juvenal, the Roman satirist?" I was jolted from my reverie. I had not pictured Juvenal, somehow, in this wild, remote land.

The Frenchman chuckled. "I can see, madame, that you indeed are not aware of the extent of Nubia's place in ancient history. Yes, Juvenal" — wagging a finger at me — "was banished to the most remote frontier of the Roman Empire, that is, to Syene, near Aswan, as punishment for his biting attacks on the Roman court. That is interesting, no?"

Laura Ann rushed toward us, and I was afraid she would bump into the French-man with her hard little head. Whoops! She did.

He looked offended.

"Here, on this side, Laura Ann, run to Aunt Susan."

But our shipboard acquaintance, though shaken, had not been deflected from his course. "Romans, the Nubian Christian kingdoms and bishoprics . . ."

I watched Laura Ann out of the corner of my eye as she crept up on Susan from behind, barely able to contain her excitement.

"Byzantium!" declared the Frenchman, raising his hand as if to bless us.

I shifted Davy from one shoulder to the other. "Long after the fall of Constan-tinople, Byzantium flourished here in Nubia, madame."

Laura Ann ran, shrieking, toward us again. Short yellow hair flying, brown eyes sparkling, she was a sturdy, pretty child.

She smiled at the Frenchman.

He beamed. "You are taking your children, madame, to see the ancient temple of Abu Simbel?"

"Well, not exactly," I answered, looking about for Bob who had drifted away down the rail. Antiquities had never been his number-one nor even number-two interest in life.

"Excellent," replied Monsieur, as though I had not spoken, "for when this young lady is grown, she will be able to tell her children she saw the temple before the Nile covered it."

"I thought they were hoping to save it."

A wave of his small, compact hand. A scarab ring set in gold flashed in the sun. "Fantasy. Sheer fantasy," he answered. "This hydraulic lifting process, you mean? Hmph! One millimeter of a mistake, and the entire temple will lie in ruins. It is impossible!"

"That's not what John Wilson says."

Our French shipmate looked closely at me. "Your husband is an archeologist? I don't believe I have had the pleasure . . ."

We exchanged handshakes and names. Gaudet. Archeologue. Fernea. Anthropologist.

Bob came back.

"I'm making an ethnological survey, yes, in a village with my wife and children. . . oh, the village houses are quite adequate for us. . . . We are planning a study of each of the three different linguistic areas of Nubia. . . . Actually, we know almost nothing of Nubian culture. . . yes, of course there is a culture. . . . No, I prefer to call the southern dialect Mahasi, not Fedicha. . ."

Again I was only half listening, watching my son in the arms of Susan, Susan who had volunteered to spend her winter vacation helping me in the village. Dr. Zaki had said I could not go without help, and taking Fawzia was not the solution, Bob had decided. The Nubian women did not work for others and would have patronized poor Fawzia; this would have created tensions before we had even begun our work, Bob felt.

Now Susan had made Davy smile. And he smiled so seldom these days. He . . . what if he . . .

"Are we not scheduled to reach Abu Simbel tomorrow afternoon?" M. Gaudet was asking.

"If the weather stays calm," Bob answered. His mouth was tight with worry. I knew why. Would the boat from Erd-Moz be at the temple to meet us? Was the village house Bob had rented going to be adequate? What had Karim accomplished while Bob had come to Cairo to bring us all down? What would he, Bob, do should something go wrong suddenly in my pregnancy? Would Davy be all right?

I glanced away, but the little Frenchman stepped forward and touched Bob's arm.

"M'sieu," he said gently, "do not look like that. To see the mighty rock temples for the first time at sunset, in their natural setting, approaching slowly up the river, as the ancients must have done, on their way to the great religious celebrations-ah, this is a rare opportunity which you are providing for your family and Mademoiselle Susan, an opportunity. . ."

The gong sounded.

"An opportunity," went on M. Gaudet, undeterred, "that they will not forget!"

He snapped his binoculars into their worn leather case, patted Laura Ann on her shining head, and we went into lunch.

The calm weather held. By the next afternoon we had left behind the empty, rocky landscape of lower Nubia and had reached a different land. In the south the countryside had been less affected by the first dam's flooding. Grain grew green in square plots on the western bank, below the wooden arms of water wheels thrusting diagonally across the wide sky.

"Are those flowers I see painted on the walls of the houses?" asked Susan in amazement.

"Yes," answered Bob. "They are. The women decorate their houses. Some villages have only white designs, in other villages they use every color of the rainbow."

"And I," added M. Gaudet, joining in, "have even seen pillars on the verandas which the people must have copied from the temples. The ancients have had their influence," he said, stroking his beard thoughtfully, "incredible really, pillars made of mud brick in the old mold, and finely carved."

Near the clusters of low houses stood palm trees, their height and luxuriance a testimony to the long history of these southern villages. The afternoon sun poured light on the dark green palms, on the river and on the mountains of the eastern shore, mountains higher than any we had seen, lying like dark islands in yellow lakes of sand.

"*Voilà!*" M. Gaudet pointed toward the shadowed western bank where a great elbow of rock narrowed the upstream path of the Nile. "That, *mes amis*, is the backbone of the temple of Abu Simbel." He spoke the phrase like an incantation.

Upon the bridge of the riverboat a bell clanged shrilly. The tourists, cameras ready, were assembling at the rail.

"Slow—ly it comes now!" breathed M. Gaudet at my side.

"Mama!" Laura Ann, sensing the general air of excitement, jumped up and down beside me.

Davy, too, reached forward, in Susan's arms, again toward a bird skimming the shining path of water leading to the mountain ahead.

A bell shrilled again and the engines were cut. The ship seemed to pause momentarily in midstream before drifting slowly forward toward the mountain which was being transformed before our eyes. Giant sculptured heads, shoulders, knees emerged from the natural surface of the stone.

"Ramses II, Pharaoh, Beloved of Amun-Ra," chanted M. Gaudet, "King of Upper and Lower Egypt, Lord of the Two Lands, the Living Horus. It was he who immortalized himself thus four thousand years ago. Can it be imagined or encompassed by the mind, that?"

Susan and I were silent before the spectacle of the changing mountain, mighty stone figures taking shape as we approached, giant hands folded peaceably in stone laps, stone feet on the edge of the moving water.

"Great! Isn't it great?" The voice of the young honeymoon husband came to us down the rail.

"He, too, even senses it," M. Gaudet pointed out happily. "Would you like to view through the binoculars? Perhaps M'sieu Fernea . . ."

But Bob had moved away, to the far end of the rail where he peered intently toward shore, shading his eyes with both hands against the afternoon sun.

"He's looking for the Nubians who are coming from the village to meet us," I explained. "Knowing my husband, he'll worry until we've actually reached the village."

I tried to laugh. It was not a success. What if the Nubians don't come, I asked myself. There was no rest house, no hotel at Abu Simbel, no telephone to the village. Where would we spend the night after the steamboat had gone on? In the temple?

"As many times as I have seen it, the temple, as many times," M. Gaudet said, "I am always moved by the natural splendor of the setting."

"The great builder, Ramses was called. The great egoist might be a better sobriquet, don't you think?" M. Gaudet was chattering on, more to himself than to us. "Imagine building not one, but four colossal statues of oneself, each more than sixty feet high!"

Susan chuckled politely. I watched Bob. He did not seem to have picked out any familiar figures yet.

"Queen Nefertari's temple, as you see, faces inward, toward that of her king and lord," M. Gaudet said. "A charming invention on the part of Ramses' architect."

"They're here, there's Mohammed," cried Bob, coming down the deck at a trot, his face momentarily cleared in relief. "See, there," and he pointed to four men on the sand, near the dock where the Department of Antiquities boat was moored, and next to it, a small felucca.

"We're going on in that felucca?" asked Susan. "I thought there was to be a motorboat."

"No," said Bob. "They couldn't run the boat without the part we picked up in Aswan. Never mind, it's all right. There's a wind blowing. We should easily reach Erd-Moz before dark.

"So, Monsieur Gaudet," said Bob, "it has been a pleasure."

M. Gaudet shook hands solemnly. "Since you are a non-archeologue," he said, "I would like your assessment of Abu Simbel."

"Impressive," said Bob, "but only a monument, when all is said and done."

"*Mon Dieu!*" ejaculated Monsieur Gaudet. "What is the world coming to when one of the great achievements of ancient civilization can be dismissed with the word that it is 'only a monument!' "

Bob stared. "What are we coming to, indeed," he returned, "when millions of dollars are spent to raise a monument of stone, and scarcely a fraction of that is spent on the thousands of people who must go the way of the monument!"

M. Gaudet stroked his beard a moment. "It is a point of view, I grant you," he allowed with a smile. "A point of view. *Au revoir.*" He patted Laura Ann on the head.

"*Au revoir.*"

We crossed the gangplank onto the sand, and in the shade of the yellow-blossomed acacia tree between the king's temple and the queen's temple, we were introduced to the four Nubian gentlemen: Abdul Majid, the village schoolteacher; Saleh, a retired, middle-aged man from whom Bob was renting a house; Abdou, Saleh's one-legged brother; and Mohammed, young, handsome, and, Bob said lightly, in his obvious pleasure at seeing them all again, "Mohammed is the best tambura player and the most famous duck hunter in the whole Abu Simbel area."

The colossal sandstone figures of Ramses Pharaoh glared white in the brilliant sun, almost as white as the towering turbans and blowing *gullabiyas* of our dignified Nubian escorts, who were gaily greeting the children.

"*Ya*, Daoud!"

"Lor-Ann!"

Mohammed picked up Laura Ann first; she squealed with delight. Then he threw David up in the air and tossed him to his father while I held my breath.

In the background I could hear the resident guide beginning his piece. "The edifice, ladies and gentlemen, is 181 feet long, carved directly into the living rock. There are eight main chambers, some as high as . . ."

Bob caught me looking wistfully after the tourists filing into the temple.

"Come on, B.J.," he said. "We'll come back and look at Abu Simbel later, when we can have it all to ourselves."

Sails billowed out on the felucca from Erd-Moz. It looked very small beside the colossal temple cut out of the towering mountain. Children and bags were passed hand to hand, and I climbed, after Susan, unsteadily into the swaying boat. Waves rocked us from side to side. Davy buried his face in my shoulder. Susan held onto squirming Laura Ann, Bob gripped the rudder, and Mohammed steadied the yard. The two small boys who had helped push off stared at us in a rather friendly, curious way, but the Nubian men sat impassively in the stern, their hands placed carefully and formally upon their knees, like the statues of Ramses II, Beloved of Amun-Ra.

We crossed the choppy water to the center of the Nile, Mohammed and Bob tacking skillfully until our sails caught the evening breeze blowing from Egypt south to the Sudan.

"We should make it to Erd-Moz in record time with this wind," shouted Bob.

He was actually smiling.

The sky, clear and wide and uncluttered as far as I could see around and before us, was pale and luminous. The river—Pop! A strategic button on my woolen maternity jumper broke from its moorings and clattered to the sloshing bottom of the felucca.

The Nubian men opened their eyes, Bob tried not to notice, and Laura Ann, escaping from Susan's grasp, retrieved the button.

"See, Mama!" She was very proud of herself, and I tried to smile, sitting there, annoyed, holding that button foolishly in my hand, examining with great care the beveled edge, the four holes with the bit of wet thread hanging from them.

Here we were, in a romantic lateen-sailed felucca on the Upper Nile, leaving behind the world-famous temple of Abu Simbel, and the only emotion I seemed able to summon was irritation at the fates for loosening the thread on a single, small button! What was the matter with me? I took a deep breath, guided Laura Ann across the watery boat bottom to Susan, and shifted Davy forward on my lap, using him as a shield while I covered that gap across my middle with a large safety pin.

"Stop *wiggling!*" I whispered.

"Ah—oooooooooo!" My human shield let out a blood-curdling yell.

He had shifted at the wrong moment. I knew it had hurt because I had gotten the pin full in the finger.

"Davy!" Susan took him, and I rummaged, cursing, in the purse for a hand-kerchief, a scarf, anything to wrap around my bleeding finger. But when I caught sight of Bob, I had a mad impulse to laugh. For there he sat, looking steadily out at the palm trees, the remote dark mountains, the water reflecting that glorious luminous sky, trying, it appeared, to establish a mood of patient tolerance that would get him through the last of this journey. Why, that stiffly dignified back seemed to ask, had he *ever* urged me to come down to Nubia, a pregnant mama so clumsy she allowed her son to sit down on the point of a safety pin in the middle of the Nile? Why, indeed? I was beginning to wonder myself. At least nothing *else* can happen, that stiff back seemed also to convey, and I agreed.

We were wrong. The brisk wind died and we were becalmed. Becalmed is not quite what we were; the boat was becalmed, but the children were restless and noisy. They were hungry; it was hours now since lunch, and our stores of biscuits long since finished. I sensed both Davy and Laura Ann were working up to a good cross cry, and I did not really blame them, while we waited and waited for the flapping sails to be furled, the oars to be fitted in the oarlocks, the rowing to begin.

The sun was sinking, the sky was reddening slowly. I rummaged in my purse, but alas, not even a dusty date could be found in its depths. Susan rescued us all by producing lumps of sugar from her pocketbook and popping them in the children's mouths as we slowly forged ahead on the still river.

"Hobby of mine," she announced briskly, with a professional smile. "Collecting sugar, I mean."

The marvelous quiet produced by those paper twists of sugar (packets marked Sudan Railways, Nile Hilton, Semiramis Hotel) was broken only by the creak of the locks, the steady splash and drip of water from the oars and Bob's conversation with Saleh.

"Has the house been cleaned?"

"Yes."

"Is the bed ready, that I ordered for the baby, and the chairs?"

"Yes, Karim has arranged everything."

Six or seven sugar lumps later, we tied up at a little stone wall built into the riverbank where Karim waved and some children waited for us, shouting and calling, "Ahlan! Ahlan! Ahlan wusahlan!"

"Where's the house?" I looked toward a grove of palm trees into which our bundles and bags seemed to be disappearing, each in the hand of a different half-grown Nubian boy.

"We have a little walk," said Bob heartily. "Up to the dune ridge."

"UP?" I remembered Dr. Zaki's last warning, "Promise me you won't try to climb any hills," and my blissfully ignorant reply, "Oh, there aren't any hills in Nubia, only sand."

Bob must have been thinking the same thing, for he added quickly, "You don't have to do it in one sprint. Go up slowly, zigzag."

Laura Ann, delighted to be out of the confines of the boat, skipped along the narrow mud footpath, jumping over the tiny feeder canals with Susan's help, the canals cut from the riverbank which watered the grove of date palms, the small orchard of fruit trees and the grain growing in every inch of free soil between. Davy jogged happily ahead in Karim's arms.

Several Nubian girls passed me, balancing on their heads shiny kerosene cans filled to the brim with river water. One of them was pregnant. They were not going up, zigzag like me, they were heading straight up, up the dune to the row of long, low mud-brick houses on the topmost ridge above. I knew that I did not have the strength to do that, even without a heavy can of water on my head, and I felt again that surge of unreasoning weariness that had come over me on the dock at Aswan. Was I going to have to climb up and down this hill every day?

Maybe Dr. Zaki was right, and I shouldn't have tried to come. What if I turned out to be more trouble than I was worth? That would hardly speed the progress of Bob's work. For the first time, I felt apprehensive and also very sorry for myself. Stop it, I told myself, watching the straight-backed Nubian girls mounting easily the hill before me. Stop it and start walking. You wanted to come. You know it will be worth it.

"You all right, B.J.?" Susan called.

"Yes, just want to look at the view."

Women had assembled at the top of the dune. They sat in front of their houses, or stood, eyes shaded against the sunset glare, to watch my slow ascent. Bob had been in the village off and on for nearly five months; he had told me the men as well as the women were eager to look over his family. I needed a moment, not only to catch my breath, but to compose myself before the introductions began, to the Nubian ladies I would live among during the coming months.

The table-topped mountains on the eastern shore were clearly outlined against the bronze sky. The sand had darkened. But the river was still alight, and it turned southward in a shining arc around the mountain where the architect of Ramses II had declared to the workmen that here, just here, in that fold of hills, the temple of Abu Simbel would be carved out of the solid rock. It was a magnificent scene, the grandeur of the natural landscape complemented by the inspiration and workmanship of the architect and the sculptor, and while I absorbed its beauty and harmony, I tried to quiet the turbulence in my mind, the pounding of my tired heart.

"Come *on!*" called Bob.

The seated women rose as I reached the last ridge of dunes. They came forward in their long, black, full-sleeved garments, trains dragging over the sand behind them like court dresses. They smiled, flashing teeth in dark faces, and shook hands, some of the older women wrapping their hands in their veils before clasping mine. They nodded at Susan, pinched Davy's cheeks, stared at Laura Ann, as curiously as she stared at them, and gazed with undisguised interest at my safety-pin-covered bulging stomach, my black tights and loafers, my uncovered brown hair.

"*Mascagna!*" cried several of the women together.

"It's a Nubian welcome," said Bob, who was watching carefully, I noticed, the impression his family was making.

With several Nubian men, he stood to one side, not exactly mixing with the women but not exactly excluded from their presence, either. This was apparently going to be a different situation than in Iraq, where the village men and women were socially segregated.

"The women speak Arabic less than their husbands, but you can reply in Arabic. Most of them will understand," he prompted.

I did, and that was the language in which we conversed for the rest of my stay in Erd-Moz.

"Come and see your house!" offered a young woman. She was very pretty and she carried on her hip a son almost the same size as Davy.

"*Your* house!" echoed another woman sarcastically, an older woman with buck teeth in a thin, middle-aged face. "Listen to her!" she mocked the younger. "Come and see the part of *our* house which we are renting to you," she announced ungraciously to me.

"I will take them in," said Saleh.

He led us across the colonnaded veranda to a heavy door where a design in brass nails surrounded the carved wooden lock. Three flowered china plates had been unexpectedly set into the lintel above the door.

"Is that Meissen?" asked Susan. "And why is it above the door?"

"It's symbolic," answered Karim, who seemed glad to be our tour guide in Nubia, more at ease here than he was in the Center at the American University in Cairo. "The plates above the door mean the man of the house is alive, Susan. If Saleh were to die tomorrow, his women would break the plates."

The house was large and well laid out, a series of open spaces surrounded with rooms, some entirely enclosed, some partially shaded by half roofs. The floors were of sand, the roof beams were of palm wood, and a paved walkway circled the central court, which was wide and open to the sky.

"We have camp cots in our room," said Bob. "Surprisingly comfortable. Susan and Laura Ann have the two wooden bedsteads in this room. And how do you like the crib I had made for Davy? Interesting process. They split the palm wood into different widths, and sort of weave it together in various patterns."

So little light seeped into the windowless children's bedroom (cooler in summer that way, fewer drafts in winter, Bob explained) that I could scarcely see the crib, but it appeared adequate.

"A nice house, don't you think so?" Bob ventured.

It *was* a nice house. Everything seemed neat, orderly and well-planned, though obviously not planned for us, but for some other mode of living with which we were not at all familiar. Different things took place in these houses, different schedules had been organized. A clay water jar suspended in a wooden frame had a tight wooden lid to keep out the flies, a drip pan beneath it to catch the evaporating moisture. Several squat storage jars the size of bushel baskets, of clay and painted in different colors, lined a shaded wall. A container of water with a spigot and basin stood on a small table beside the porcelain water filter, which I recognized as part of the expedition gear. These objects, with our beds, comprised the sum total of the house's furniture.

The last rays of sun shining through the woven, rush half roofs created pleasing patterns of shadow on the floor of the court, but there was little other decoration to be seen. Three kerosene lanterns hung on nails, a tin cup hung above the water jar.

"Wait till you see the *diwani*, though," said Karim. "The bride's room really. The bride and groom sleep together for the first time in the little bedroom there, then they come into the *diwani* in the morning to receive guests and presents and entertainment, and to eat their special wedding breakfast."

At the entrance to the *diwani* we stood in silence for a moment.

"But it's quite beautiful!" exclaimed Susan in surprise.

"Why are you so surprised?" returned Karim. "The Nubians have very good taste."

I looked at him. For an Egyptian city boy to make such a remark about his peasant countrymen was rather startling, but Karim was obviously sincere.

What limited resources were available to the Nubian housewife with a flair for interior decoration had been used here in ingenious ways that would never have occured to me. The family's collection of reed plates, locally woven of palm fiber dyed in various hues, had been hung at eye level in a neat row, rather like an ornate wallpaper border on the walls, walls whose smooth matt gray mud surface provided an ideal background for the display of design and color.

"But aren't those the plates they clean the grain from the chaff with?" I asked. Bob had mentioned noticing these plates, which I had seen used similarly in Iraq.

Karim smiled. "Oh, they have plain ones for work," he said. "These are just to be looked at for pleasure."

The palm fiber strips, in orange and purple or wine and natural pale-straw colors, had been used to weave a whole series of variations in design on the plates: whorls and diagonals, circles and squares, and below the plates, on the mud-paved floor, reed mats of the same colors had been laid. From the beams in the ceiling were suspended, like a series of chandeliers, scores of painted bowls and china plates, easch nested in a swing of plaited leather. The mock chandeliers were decorated with streamers of the same plaited leather, ornamented with clusters of white shells. Wind stirred the shells to a mild clacking, reminding me of the oriental wind chimes which my aunt had hung in her Chicago garden.

"Where do we bathe?" inquired Susan.

"Oh, you can bring a couple of buckets of water into the *diwani* and lock the door. Nice ambiance in that room for baths, eh, Karim?"

Karim and Bob smiled at each other obliquely but Susan, used to a shower a day, did not appear amused. She did not comment, however.

The total effect of my rented Nubian house (except for the riot of color in the *diwani*) was austere, even bare, but pleasing. In another mood, say that of the slim tourist bride on the steamboat, I would have been enthusiastic about the simplicity and functionalism of the basic design. But foremost in my mind now was not design, but the need to establish my own routine in this alien place. Boiling water to mix with powdered milk, mashing baby food, washing diapers, where were these tasks to be accomplished? The shells clacked softly once more above me, the sound was soothing; surely something could be arranged. Put a table there, and. . .

"Where do you sit down?"

Bob smiled. "On mats, of course, on the floor just as you saw in the *diwani*. There are some rolled up in the bedrooms. You can bring them out when you like. The women sweep them off and roll them up to keep them clean."

"You eat and type and so on, on the *mats*?" I contemplated getting my ponderous self up and down from the sandy floor forty times a day; my natural childbirth exercises seemed built into this situation; I decided I would worry about them no longer.

Bob smiled once more, to himself. "I was putting you on, B.J. We do have a table and chairs in the *mendara*, the guest room. It has its own separate entrance from outside, so the house is more or less private for you and Susan and the children. Karim sleeps in the *mendara* and only comes here to wash his face and go to the toilet."

I looked around for some evidence of such a facility, but found none.

"The Nubians are very clever about everything," said Bob.

He took me to the innermost court, where a long open stairway led up to a closed door on the brink of the roof.

"*Voilà*, as our friend M. Gaudet would say," Bob said. "Right up at the top of the stairs. Open to the air, but shut off from the rest of the house. Chilly at night, but very sanitary."

A cold wind swept through the almost empty rooms. I shivered. M. Gaudet. Had it really been only this afternoon that he had entertained us with his gentle, courtly lectures about ancient Egypt? It seemed in another age, another world.

Darkness was almost upon us; it lay in pools of shadow in the central courtyard, where Davy and Laura Ann played, happy to find at the end of the long trip the surprise of a built-in sandbox.

"Come into the *mendara*. Susan and I have set the table." Karim stood at the door with the lamps, the Coleman hissing white, the kerosene lanterns flickering yellow.

Saleh brought in a tureen of vegetables and meat. The steam rose upward from the aluminum camp table to the dark beams of the ceiling, and we ate the thick soup gratefully, eagerly.

It had been years since I had eaten by lamplight. The children felt the strangeness, too; they clung tightly.

"Where's house, Mama?" asked Laura Ann, thinking, I was sure, of our warm, electrically lighted apartment in Cairo, which seemed thousands of miles from this little oasis where we ate soup by lantern light and Karim fiddled with the tape recorder, finally triumphantly producing a faint recording of a Bach double piano concerto.

"Our house is still there in Cairo, but we're going to stay here for a while, with Baba," I explained.

She slurped a little soup. Her eyes drooped.

"Where's my bed, Mama?" she asked, and her lip quivered.

Bob went out suddenly and came back with suitcases. Susan and I put on the children's sleepers, went through the motions of washing hands and faces in half a basin of cold water, and carried them, wrapped in blankets to the bedroom, Davy snuffling and sneezing, Laura Ann almost asleep.

> "I gave my love a cherry
> without a stone."

I went through the lullaby ritual and covered the children with all their blankets against the cold which grew with the darkness.

Bob was waiting in the court with a lantern. "I'll stay here," I said.

"You don't need to, B.J. Saleh's women sleep just the other side of the wall and can hear every breath the children draw. We can, too, for that matter, since there's little intervening noise. Come have some tea. It will warm you up."

We stood on the veranda for a moment. The night sky lay above the river and the mountains like a vast splendid coverlet, the stars so thick I could scarcely distinguish one from another in the blaze of light.

"I'm awfully glad you're here, but it won't be easy, you know," said Bob in a worried undertone, the timbre of his voice at odd variance with the serenity of the sky and the river, the stillness of the sleeping village, dark except for faint flickers of lantern light from a house down the hill, silent except for a peeping of Bach from Karim's tape recorder, a bawling of a calf for its mother.

"I knew that before I came."

Susan coughed from behind the closed shutters of the *mendara*.

"There's a doctor not far up the river. You must tell me if you feel bad, have strange pains or anything."

"I will."

"The boat stops at Abu Simbel twice a week, and you should plan on leaving anytime you want to, any time the going seems too much. I want you to share Nubia with me; it is a beautiful place, but I don't want you down here if it will damage your health or Davy's."

"Yes," I said, and we went in and sat in the *mendara*, listening to the Bach on Karim's tape until sleep reached us.

# Chapter 4

# The Village of Erd-Moz

The houses in Erd-Moz commanded their fine view of the river and the mountains, not by chance, but by design. Erd-Moz was a planned village in the ideal sense of the word, planned by the occupants, each house designed and constructed by its owner, with the help of local mud-brick masons and wood carvers.

Half a century ago Erd-Moz had been a compact cluster of smaller houses closer to the shore of the Nile, in the midst of palm groves and strips of the cultivated land. The villagers traveled up to the hills only to look for fuel, to graze their goats and sheep on the tender camel's-thorn, to bury their dead under piles of the flinty stones which littered the mountains behind the dunes.

"My great-grandmother did not have to go so far for water," I was told by Khadija, the young and beautiful niece of our landlord Saleh "Our people were frightened of these hills then."

Moving the village to high ground had taken place long before Khadija was born, in 1900, after the first Aswan Dam flooded land in northern Nubia. The southern area near Abu Simbel had been scarcely touched by the waters, but Khadija's ancestors had been prudent men.

"If we have to move now, we may have to move again," they reasoned. "Who knows what the British will do to the river next?"

Thus the village was laid out on the highest ridge of dunes, and in 1933 when the first dam was heightened for the third time, the people of Erd-Moz received cash compensation for their flooded land. With this money added to their average annual income (which was probably not more than $250), they built larger and more elaborate houses. The women plastered the walkways smooth with mud, painted walls, doors and shutters with designs in bright colors; they decorated

43

the lintels of their doorways with china plates set into the plaster, those dainty plates that would be smashed if the man of the house were to die.

Compared to the French-Oriental villas of Cairo, Nubian houses like the one in which we were living were simple dwellings. But compared to the huts in the Delta where lived fellaheen of similar income and status, or even to the average two-bedroom California ranch house, these Nileside homes were mansions—spacious and neat, well arranged for comfort in both summer heat and winter cold. A large central courtyard, surrounded by bedrooms, a *diwani*, or bride's room, *mendara*, or guest room, a storage room, a summer kitchen and a winter kitchen, a separate toilet room, an outside fenced shelter for the animals: These were basic features of almost every house in Erd-Moz. Inner courts, covered walkways and patios, wide porches with benches upon which one could sit and admire the view—these were added, depending on the needs of the family, the size of its income.

We lived in half of a semidetached dwelling, which Saleh had designed to keep his two wives content in separate domains and at the smallest possible expense (most men had settled their wives in separate homes, often even in separate villages, which raised the cost considerably). I remembered buck-toothed Dahiba's ungracious welcome. Since she was the displaced wife, it was hardly surprising that she was the least friendly of the occupants of Saleh's house: Hanim Ali and Dahiba, his wives; Khadija and Naima, his nieces; and Abdul Nasr, Khadija's infant son. Hanim Ali and Dahiba were childless, but they lavished affection on Abdul Nasr, whose father worked in Khartoum. Khadija and Naima's own father was also reportedly in the Sudan. A disgraced younger brother of Saleh's, he had disappeared after being accused of some crime.

"We heard your son coughing all night long," Khadija reported two or three mornings after our arrival. "Did he get that awful cold on the express boat?"

"He was sick before we came."

I sat on a straw mat beside the sunny courtyard wall. Khadija offered me tea while Davy's lunch cooked and drinking water boiled (we had no stove in our house). David and Khadija's son, Abdul Nasr, had been born the same week, we discovered.

"Was yours a difficult labor?" she asked.

"Not too bad, but the pregnancy was terrible."

"So was mine; my labor was awful too, it was my first child," confided Khadija. "Fourteen hours."

Abdul Nasr, a wiry baby with bright eyes, wore a short cotton *gullabiya* and a sweater; he tottered barefoot about the court on sturdy legs. But Davy, full of vitamins and antibiotics and cortisone, shielded from drafts by pants, sweater, shirt, socks and shoes, could not even crawl after Abdul Nasr. He tried, but in a moment, wheezing and out of breath, he settled for sitting instead.

"My boy hardly ever gets colds," said Khadija, "but when he does, I give him date honey. Would you like some? We make it from our own dates."

"Thank you, Khadija, I'll try it."

Naima had finished washing all the breakfast dishes, including ours, and had laid them out to dry on a bare wooden bedstead set in the sun; she was now sweeping the bedrooms. Dahiba was squatting some distance away, rinsing clothes in a large flat pan of water. Hanim Ali, on the mat with us, was packing Saleh's water pipe with honey, tobacco and *kamanja*, the local species of hemp or marijuana, tamping the fragrant mixture down into the narrow-necked glass bottle, its sides painted with flowers.

"The pinch of *kamanja* with the honey gives a pleasant smoke," said Hanim Ali, smiling under hennaed hair, which she had arranged in two coquettish wings on her forehead below her black head scarf. As was proper for a woman past the age of childbearing she wore no gold necklaces and bracelets, but on her brown fingers, twisted with work and age, were a number of curious rings, dull silver, brass, set with rough-cut stones of turquoise, carnelian, onyx. I asked about them, but she pretended she had not heard me. Many weeks later Khadija told me they were sacred rings, magic rings, and Hanim Ali never discussed them, for fear of dispelling their occult powers.

Khadija sewed while chatting with me and keeping an eye on her son's perambulations around the court, here for a bit of bread from Naima, there for a kiss from Dahiba, back to sit with Davy and play with a duck pull toy. She was making a dress for herself, a flower-printed cotton to wear under the sheer black *gargara*, or overdress, that was standard southern Nubian garb.

"They say the sleeves will be shorter this year," remarked Khadija. "The fullness will be taken up by more tucking here," and she demonstrated on a sleeve of her own *gargara*, a garment which seemed to me highly impractical for life in Erd-Moz, a wide, full dress with a train that gathered dust and bits of straw when one walked in the sand, and sleeves so wide they had to be folded back when one cooked over an open fire.

"It is lovely, the *gargara*," went on Khadija, "but hard to keep clean."

The garment, if impractical, was exceedingly feminine.

I had already noticed men turning to watch the way a woman walked down the village street, a shining kerosene can of water balanced on her graceful head, the *gargara* trailing behind her like a black peignoir upon the golden sand.

The train, we were told, erased the women's footprints as they walked and thus kept secret their indiscretions.

"Your vegetables are going to burn," said Dahiba pointedly from her laundry position near the stove.

I pulled myself up off the mat, took the pot off the stove and sat down again with the pureer. Every meal which Davy ate had to be prepared immediately beforehand, since our kerosene refrigerator, imported and shipped to Nubia at so much trouble and expense, worked only erratically. I was not very efficient with the pureer, and I could tell by the side glances from Saleh's women that they thought so, too. I'm sure I presented a wan, incomprehensible picture to them. After all, what was the matter with me except pregnancy? And did I not have Saleh to cook most of my meals, Naima to bring water from the river, a woman to wash clothes for me?

Fortunately, the ladies seemed inclined to take a charitable view.

"You're tired, I think," said Hanim Ali. She propped her hand covered with those odd rings under her chin and gave me a look.

"Yes," I answered, "the trip, the pregnancy." I did not add, squatting, sitting, bending, walking in sand, trying to impose our own routines, our ways of living upon this new and strange environment. Baths, electricity, running hot water, a pharmacy around the corner, a doctor at the other end of the telephone, how long had I taken these things for granted? I knew rationally that they were not vital; the children would survive without a daily bath, we had plenty of medicine, there was a doctor about an hour away by boat (if the motors were working), boiling the drinking water purified it, obviously, and a little diarrhea was not a disaster. It did not seem to me that during our years in Iraq, either Bob or I had been so fussy about the details of our daily lives, but then, the children's presence changed things. The rational point of view faded before the awful "If."

"Pray to God," Hanim Ali was saying to me, glancing at Davy involuntarily as she spoke. She inserted Saleh's pipe into the painted glass bottle full of honey and tobacco, turning it and straightening it with a good wifely gesture, then placing the pipe at the edge of the reed mat where Saleh would sit and smoke after lunch. "Pray to God," she repeated. "God knows best."

She rose, lightly and easily though she must have been fifty, while I stumbled up from my squatting position, feeling a clumsy fool; the women watched without comment.

"Pray to God you carry a stronger child within you," concluded Hanim Ali and went into the kitchen to start a fire for the daily bread baking.

At lunch, Bob told me to visit elsewhere.

"Saleh's family is not typical," he said, "and our relationship with them is complicated."

"Why?"

"We are renting part of their house. The women perform services for us, bringing water and so on. You know the women don't like that, they aren't supposed to work for other people, they don't want other people to know."

"What about the woman who washes our clothes?"

"Saleh says her husband is the descendant of a slave, and that family has never had much pride. But, anyhow, it's better to make friends outside. Dahiba is already annoyed to be jolted out of her house, you can see that. Go to Abdulla's house. His mother is the midwife."

"The midwife?" My voice came out higher than intended, and Bob's face tightened.

"A professional visit you have in mind yet?" said Susan lightly.

Bob laughed, and I silently thanked Susan. She had decided, I realized, and rightly, that her role in Erd-Moz was not only to help me with the children but to ease, with wit, the atmosphere of worry and fear within which Bob and I were operating. Defusing a potentially explosive conversation was one way, and she was very good at it.

"Not exactly," he answered, with an amused glance at me. "That is, it might be interesting, but I doubt that B.J. would agree. Anyhow . . . oh, I don't care. Go to the schoolteacher's, Abdul Majid's, or to Mohammed's. He's our best friend here, and he'll be very hurt if you don't appear soon at his house so his wife can say you've come. I don't know much about his womenfolk, though I feel quite close to Mohammed, curious.''

"You didn't know much about the women in Iraq either," I pointed out, "at least from their men."

"It's a bit different here, I think," mused Bob, "but I don't really know. That's why I want you to visit and see."

"The women are more independent than *I* expected," put in Karim, "maybe because the men are often away and then they have to take charge of the farming, even. They certainly seem to control the purse strings."

"Susan, you choose. Where shall we go this afternoon?"

"Well," confessed Susan, "when Laura Ann and I were looking at the sheep this morning, a woman invited us to tea. Her name is Sherifa and she lives down the hill a bit."

"The schoolteacher," prompted Karim. "Abdul Majid."

Six ladies had assembled in Abdul Majid's spotless and well-furnished guest room (sofa, table covered with an embroidered cloth, chairs, cushion, photos and calendars lining the mud-brick walls). They had come to get a look at us, and they sat comfortably, cross-legged on a mat, all in proper black *gargaras* over printed cotton, their long, sheer head scarves wound about their heads and shoulders, trailing yards behind. It was Susan and Laura Ann and me, David in arms and sniveling and wheezing, who sat stiffly upright on the sofa with Sherifa's sister, Sitta. Sherifa, after greeting us at the door, had departed, presumably to make the tea and to satisfy the needs of her three toddlers, which were more immediate than ours.

Six pairs of adult eyes and those of several uncounted children, in arms or on laps, stared at us; the eyes were bright with interest and the throats and ears and wrists and ankles were bright with the gleam of gold and silver. Gold earrings at the tops and bottoms of the ears, long necklaces of round gold pieces, of agate and silver beads, silver or bright plastic bracelets, a few heavy silver ankle bracelets. Against the somber black gowns, the shapes and colors of the varied jewelry looked, as the fashion magazines say, exactly right.

The women's brown feet were bare, for were they not sitting on a mat inside a clean house? Beside the door stood a row of plastic shoes, like shower shoes, in glorious shades of orange, turquoise, pink and green. I smiled in a patronizing way at the plastic shoes that first day, but I lived to regret that smile. Plastic shoes were excellent for walking in the sand (and so easy to empty out); they wore like iron and all they needed was a dip in water to look as bright and clean as the day they'd been bought. I would have liked a pair myself.

"You have come to Nubia for your son's health?" inquired a middle-aged lady. Scarification marks, like the traceries of a fine pencil, ran high up her brown cheekbones.

Startled by the question, I mumbled something about the dry climate.

"Far better than Cairo, certainly," said another. She held a tiny baby, swaddled in flannelette. "There you breathe dirt from the factories and dirt from so many people. Here the air is clean. . . . I am so glad I came back to deliver my baby *at home*."

"When I think of Cairo—"

"That awful city—"

"It's not awful, they have cinemas, electricity—"

"Electricity!" sniffed the woman with the scarification marks. "What is that? They charge for it, don't they? And you pay for every date, every grain of sand. You have to buy sand little by little, like fruit. Here *some* things are free."

The speed of the conversation made it hard to follow. The women spoke in Arabic and in their own dialect alternately, translating back and forth for each other, and it was soon apparent that unless we entered in, the conversation would go on without us.

"You've been to Cairo?" Susan broke in.

The young woman with the baby laughed. "Have I been to Cairo?" she asked the group mockingly. "Yes," she said to Susan, "five times I have been and five times my husband has tried to persuade me to stay and live there. But I said no. Those apartments in Bab el Loukh! Phew!" She held her nose. "You can scrub and scrub those toilets, they never get clean. Where do you and your cousin live in Cairo?"

"Garden City."

The middle-aged lady with the scarification marks, the widow Fatooma, nodded her head. "Well, that's a pleasant enough quarter. I lived there when I was a child. My father was a *boab*. Is the *ganeena* as clean as it used to be?"

At this juncture, Sherifa rustled in with the tea tray, and Sitta served us, from rose-sprigged bone china cups, the best tea I had tasted for months.

"Where did you get the tea?" Susan asked. "It's excellent."

"It's English tea from the Sudan."

"Sudan? But how do you get it through the Egyptian customs?"

The women laughed and nudged each other, white teeth flashing in the dark faces, gold and silver clinking and gleaming against the black *gargaras*.

"We have ways," said Sitta, one of those bandbox women who always look as if their clothes had been freshly pressed five minutes before, "ways and means."

"She means smugglers," I said to Susan in English. "There's quite a bit of border trade in consumer goods, Bob says."

At the sound of the English, a slight hush fell, and I could tell from the dark eyes that they realized we had understood.

"Ali should be here next week to take orders," said the widow.

"We'll let you know when he comes."

"He also has good needles and German paring knives and very light, warm English blankets."

Laura Ann was playing in the court with Sherifa's children, but Davy still sat on my lap, reaching for this, reaching for that, whining a little, wheezing a little. The poor child was constantly uncomfortable, hence never content.

"Why don't you let your children drink tea?" our hostess Sherifa asked. "Tea would be good for your son's cough."

How did they know I didn't give the children tea?

"Give him some now, it will calm him."

Sitta, without waiting for my answer, half filled a cup with tea, stirred in milk, sugar, blew on the mixture to cool it and offered it to Davy, who, with her gentle, efficient help, slurped it up eagerly, down to the last drop.

The ladies were delighted.

"You see?" said Sherifa. "He likes it."

"What did we tell you?"

"It will help him, you'll see."

I looked around the friendly group, for they were friendly, informal, kind ladies, all of them.

"What else should I do to help him?" I asked.

They all broke into speech at once.

"Give him cumin seed tea."

"Mastica will stop the cough."

"Rub his chest with oil and put newspaper on his back and chest when he sleeps."

"Keep his head wrapped up at night."

"Dress him all in flannelette or all wool, but not half and half, like he is now."

I looked startled at the wool sweater, the corduroy overalls. Maybe they thought the corduroy was flannelette?

"Otherwise he will chill," they finished.

But in this rush of suggestions, Sitta had remained watchful and silent.

"I am surprised that you ask us," she said. "After all, you can take him to doctors in Cairo and get him good medicine."

"I have, but it hasn't helped."

And feeling suddenly that I was not up to a question-and-answer session on Davy's condition and prospects, I stood up, making excuses about the small tasks that had to be done before darkness came.

Sitta and Sherifa saw us to the door, Sherifa apologizing for the untidy courtyard, her children rushing about with Laura Ann, chickens scratching in the sand, lines of laundry drying, fuel half stacked into several piles, tea dishes to be washed.

"There is no one here but me," she said. "Sitta lives near the temple of Abu Simbel. She is here to help me today because you came."

"Your husband works at the temple?" Susan asked Sitta.

"No, he is in London."

"LONDON?" repeated Susan in astonishment.

"Yes," said Sitta, and drew herself up, a bit proudly, in those pristine ironed-looking clothes. "He is a chauffeur for the Egyptian Embassy in England. I went with him to Tunis and Damascus, but London was too far. Besides, I wanted the children to go to school here in Nubia, with their own people."

"Didn't you like Damascus and Tunis?" I asked.

Sitta sighed. "Oh yes, Damascus is beautiful, and I made many friends in Tunis. But—well," she turned to me, "don't you ever miss your family and your country of America?"

"Yes, I do."

"That is how I felt. London might be nice, but here I have my own house, my own date trees; my husband will come in summer. He sent us some English books for the children. Perhaps you and your cousin could come to my house one day and read the English to us? The children will study English in school when we go to Kom Ombo."

"Thank you, Sitta. I would love to," I answered.

The distance between London and the tiny village beside the temple of Abu Simbel seemed immeasurably great by almost any standard, distance, culture, technology, language, yet Sitta found it quite natural that her husband should be there now but would return in the summer, bringing, no doubt, a tin of good Darjeeling tea and British woolens from Marks and Spencer for all the family. She was secure in her knowledge of her place in the world, secure like my friends in a small Iraqi village had been. But she had traveled, as they had not, and she had met and observed many kinds of people, as they had not.

Yet, exposure to other ways does not always change one's view of the world. Often it serves to strengthen one's views. Sitta was a perfect example of something Bob had noted about the Nubians in the few months he had lived among them. They, like Sitta, had been observant in new surroundings and had adopted some things they liked, but had maintained their own values.

Susan interrupted my dune-climbing reverie home. "What did Sherifa press into your hand?"

"Tea," I replied. "I protested, but she said it was English tea for Davy."

"Very nice of her. They were all very nice, I thought. Sitta was quite remarkable, don't you agree?"

"I agree."

"What else did Sherifa say? You talked for quite a time at the door. I could hardly keep Laura Ann from rolling down the hill in the sand. That child is strong!"

"Sherifa's pregnant again, and has bad backaches the way I do."

"Really? Poor thing."

"She didn't seem to feel that way," I answered. "She lost a baby last spring, but she has three sons and perhaps another on the way. She said she was luckier than I."

'Well, perhaps the English tea will help us all feel better," Susan said gently.

Each morning, the women swept the rooms and the walkways of their houses and once a week, at least, they changed the sand in the central courts. The old sand was carried out and thrown over the hill, and with the debris from the houses, and the dried goat and sheep droppings everywhere, it was surprising that the outside sand retained such a bronzed, clean look, a golden sand, still only a shade or two lighter than the rectangular flat-roofed houses set upon it.

"Oh, we have lots of sand, sand everywhere, it cleans itself as it goes down," explained Fatima airily.

She was that kind of person, breezy, good-natured, anticipating little but taking from life what it offered to her, eagerly and with thanks. I had expected someone quite different, though what I had expected I could not have said. True, she was the wife of Abdulla, a man of some status in the village, for he was not only the barber, the circumciser and the official registrar of births and deaths, he was universally respected as a lay religious dignitary. He offered the call to prayer during Ramadan and he was regularly asked to lead the Friday morning services in the village mosque. Further, Bob had told me, he was much in demand as a mediator in family quarrels. Perhaps I had thought Fatima would be a lady who rests on her dignity. She was not.

"*Mascagna!*" she called out to us cheerfully the first time we went to tea. "*Mascagna!*" greeting us in Nubian and waving at us from down that sandy street that cleaned itself.

"*Mascagna!*" we echoed, a bit self-consciously.

"*Na!*" repeated Laura Ann, jumping about on her sturdy legs.

"Rrrrrrr!" Fatima nuzzled Laura Ann in the cheek with her fist, and Laura Ann smiled with pleasure. It was not often people in Erd-Moz paid that much attention to her. "Ah! Your children will learn to speak our language. You learn, too! Good! Come and have tea!"

Sailing gracefully down the street, Fatima made me ashamed of my plodding. Today I did not even have Davy as an excuse, for Susan was carrying him, but Fatima held a small sickly baby in one arm and had a toddler hanging on her long black skirts, pulling on her trailing black head scarf which she was constantly readjusting and patting back to place. He tripped over her train and bawled in anguish after her. Fatima would set him on his feet again, placate him with a kiss, then turn and greet the women standing at their doors to watch us pass.

"Well!" shouted Fatima gaily. "Can't you speak to our guests? They don't care whether you talk Arabic or English, they're going to learn our good Nubian language, *aren't* you, Beeja?" with a quick glance at me.

I nodded, but Fatima had already turned back to another neighbor.

"Come on!" she called. "Cheerful greetings, please! It's a beautiful day!"

Every day we had been in Erd-Moz had seemed a beautiful day, but Khadija warned me darkly that I had seen nothing yet. Bad sandstorms in spring, unbearable heat in the summer more than made up for these mild sunny days of winter, she said.

However, Fatima was a different sort of person. Khadija, for all her dusky beauty, was not happy; she was known in the village as one who looked on the dark side.

"It's her husband, she's lucky he's away in the Sudan," the women said. "He drinks, and when he drinks, he beats her. She hopes he will not come back."

"Fatima on the other hand," our informant had said, "has a good, steady, loving man. She enjoys what there is to enjoy in life."

She did seem to, Fatima.

"*Yallah!* Gamal!" she called to a small boy, perhaps five or six, with a goat in tow. He had white teeth and a neatly shaved head and obediently joined our parade, the fuzzy brown goat trailing behind.

"*Mascagna!*" The women raised their hands to us and chuckled behind their head scarves.

Down the sandy street that cleaned itself we marched, the strong clear sunlight warming us all, Laura Ann with her yellow hair wisping out of its pony tail, Fatima with her necklace of massive gold coins, Gamal with his white shining teeth, Davy with his white face, too white against Susan's Shetland sweater.

"*Mascagna!*" The greeting followed us to a green door where Fatima shifted her baby around, slapped the goat out of the way and worked her long-pegged key into the carved wooden lock.

"*Ya*, Gamal!" The boy sprang to hold the door open for us, and when Laura Ann skipped through, he touched her hair gently, as one touches a strange bird or an unusually colored butterfly.

Fatima caught my eye above the heads of the children, one so dark, one so light, and she smiled. In the pointed face, her deep-set eyes flashed black; her front teeth protruded slightly in an appealing way; even in repose, Fatima looked on the verge of a giggle.

"Let Lor-Ann play with my boy Gamal in the court," she suggested. "We'll go in to Aisha."

After the bright glare, I blinked in the dark and smoky room. A tiny fire burned fitfully in the traditional hearth, a three-legged clay griddle fashioned by the Nubian housewives themselves, and so cleverly designed it concentrated the heat of the smallest fire.

Around the hearth mats were laid, and from a pillow close to the fire an old woman raised her head and stared at us with sightless eyes.

"Must be Aisha," whispered Susan. "The midwife, Abdulla's mother."

Aisha cocked her head. She had heard that whisper. "*Mascagna! Ahlan!* Welcome to our house!" she called out in a deep, imperious voice.

She was in black, without jewelry; from a scarf of bright orange satin tied tightly around her head, two thin braids of gray hair fell onto her sloping shoulders. Raising her arms in their full black sleeves, she commanded us, with grand sibylline gestures, to be seated.

Aisha smiled with nearly toothless gums. She bore no facial tattoo marks, only the usual scarification lines, which seemed, in her aged face, simply wrinkles, a special set of wrinkles cutting across the grain of her brown skin.

"Ah!" she expelled her breath. "So this is the Amerikiya, wife of the doctor, come at last! Aha! And her cousin Susan, too."

She smiled and stroked my arm, smiled and peered at the floor as though she could see the forest-green wool of my sweater projected upon a screen in her innermost eye.

"Fatima!" She spoke to her daughter-in-law in Nubian, quickly, commandingly. Fatima did not seem to be offended by her tone.

"Aisha wants me to tell her everything you have on, you and your cousin, every single thing and its color," she translated.

Halfway through Fatima's catalogue of our clothes, Davy began to whimper, and Aisha stopped her daughter-in-law and said to me, "I am sorry for your trouble with this boy. I have heard about him. Tell me his symptoms more carefully. Perhaps I can help. I used to be able to cure with herbs and cupping or burning, if it were bad. But children are difficult."

"Why?" asked Susan.

"Because sometimes it is God's will that they are not strong enough to live. Then there is nothing we can do."

I saw the expression on Susan's face—pure, clear distaste for the old woman. I gulped and impelled myself to say, "Look, Aisha, he is not so weak, it is only that he wheezes and coughs. He has the asthma."

Aisha raised a hand. "Don't tell me. I may not see, but I can hear well enough to know that. He is a year?"

"More. Thirteen and a half months."

"He walks?"

"No."

"He has been circumcised?"

"Yes."

Aisha ruminated, clearing her throat loudly and looking at the floor. I watched Fatima's movements about the room, putting the blue enamel teakettle on the hearth to boil, feeding the fire with tiny sticks, taking pots from hollowed niches in the walls, cups from neatly arranged shelves, shelves edged with strips of newspaper, hand-cut into lace, an attractive border against the gray mud wall. Beneath one shelf, a woven reed plate hung, and two dish swings, the Nubian method of keeping food out of the reach of mice. In the *diwanis* or brides' rooms of the houses the dish swings were merely decorative, but in Fatima's kitchen, beside the hearth, they were put to use.

"Give me your boy for a moment."

Pretending not to notice Susan's unwillingness to let go of Davy, I pushed him forward. Aisha groped for him, found his hand, ran her strong brown fingers up his arm, across his chest and back. He drew back, wheezing softly.

"Yes, yes," muttered Aisha and let him go.

She looked down at the mat again. "Cupping, no, not cupping, that would not help," she said to herself.

The door burst open. "Careful, children, careful!" called a younger version of Fatima, balancing in her hands a large platter of dates and popcorn, the traditional Nubian offering to visitors, and trying to push ahead of her into the room Laura Ann, Gamal and several other children.

"My oldest daughter, Wahiba," Fatima introduced the girl, who resembled her mother but lacked the deep eyes and the slightly jutting teeth that gave Fatima her individuality.

Susan said, "Fatima, I can't believe you're old enough to have a daughter this age."

"Really?" Fatima grinned broadly. "You think I look young? Well, thank God, I have a strong constitution or I'd never have lived through it all—eight children, five living and three dead."

Aisha's head jerked up at a giggle from Laura Ann.

"That is your other child," she said to me. "I want to see her. Come here, girl!"

Laura Ann, recognizing the tone of authority, came, Gamal with her. "It's my grandma," he was saying, "she can't see you so she wants to touch you."

Aisha began feeling Laura Ann carefully all over, legs, arms, stomach, Laura Ann standing quietly enough until those sensitive hands of Aisha reached her head.

"Now! Now!" chided Aisha. "You're a girl, aren't you? A nice girl, and you must learn to be still."

To my surprise, Laura Ann did stand still, staring at the long wrinkled face beneath the orange scarf, the deep caverns of the eye sockets where the dead eyes were buried.

"Strange, it is so smooth, her head, what color is her hair?"

"White, Grandmamma," responded Gamal with a smile, kneeling beside Laura Ann to support her during this thorough investigation of her personality. Daughter Wahiba looked on silently, Fatima's sickly baby cradled in her lap.

"Your daughter has been circumcised, of course."

I ignored the question. I knew the Nubian custom of circumcising girls as well as boys, "for reasons of health," but I did not want to engage in an ideological battle on the subject with old Aisha. She, herself, as a midwife, performed such operations. Only the clitorectomy was done here now, said the women, not the more radical operation known as Pharaonic circumcision, which had been forbidden by the government as well as the Islamic religious authorities. The men had told Bob circumcision was good for emotional as well as physical health; it calmed a woman's sexual desires and made it easier for her to remain faithful if her husband had to go away and work in Cairo, for example. The women themselves believed circumcision made them healthier, but more important, made them more feminine, more truly a woman. I disagreed, but there seemed little point in arguing about it.

"Aisha," said Fatima, "let the child go now."

"All right, all right," the old woman answered pettishly. "Go then," and with a last pat on Laura Ann's head. "You don't need me, thank the good God for that. Here," and reaching forward to the platter of dates and popcorn which Khadija had placed before me, she burrowed into it with sure fingers and came up with a large date. "Here, take this."

Laura Ann took it and laughed, leaned down and picked out another date for Gamal.

He looked at his mother. "Take it, the guest gives it to you," she said. "Now go!"

"Let the other children have some," said Susan.

"No," said Fatima. "They must learn what it is to respect guests and to wait their turn. You have to begin early with children or they stay animals all their lives."

And although three small children sat on the other side of the fire, in full sight of that fulsome platter of dates and popcorn, not one moved, not one asked for food.

Fatima served us tea from a painted wooden tray and poured a cup for Aisha.

"Here, Um Abdulla!"

"No! No!" Aisha waved a hand impatiently. "Not till the guests have drunk. I'm not that old!"

But I could see the corner of her mouth twitching. She needed that tea and was sorely tempted to help herself.

"Come, Um Abdulla," I said, "you'd honor us, since you are older than we, and wiser, by drinking with us."

Aisha, making mock protest, took the cup which Fatima placed carefully in her hands, and sipped the hot tea loudly and appreciatively. It did taste good, that tea, I felt it all the way to my bones, tired and cramping from the hour of sitting cross-legged on the mat.

"Fix *me* some tea, Wahiba," Fatima said, and to me, "I need the milk. I give this baby the breast all the time, but she is never satisfied."

"How old is the baby?" I asked. With sticklike arms and legs, an overlarge head, she looked at best perhaps two months.

"Oh, nine months, ten months," said Fatima lightly. "She was born after the last big feast, I can't remember exactly how old she is.

"God's will be done!" pronounced Aisha in a ringing voice.

"God's will be done!" assented Fatima, trying to cradle the pitiful lolling head in the crook of her arm so the baby could hold onto the nipple more easily.

"But about the boy," Aisha began, thwacking my knee with a long strong finger. "We will think together and we will pray."

"Yes, Aisha, thank you." I stretched my legs in preparation for departure but crafty Aisha was before me.

"Uh-uh-uh, don't go yet," she ordered, that thwacking finger on my knee again. "I want to talk to you about your pregnancy."

She cleared her throat professionally and I sat back automatically, like a patient responding to the voice of a familiar doctor. Aisha had that effect on everyone, I was to find.

"The child moved when?"

"Four months, about."

"Good, You carry the child high or low?"

"High."

"How does she look, Fatima, her eyes, her skin?"

"Terrible," laughed Fatima, truthfully.

"Mmm, that complicates things," mused Aisha. "Carrying the baby high, probably a girl, looks terrible, probably a boy."

"We must go," I said and rose from the mat, breaking the spell Aisha was beginning to cast.

"No, no!" cried the old woman. "You have come a long way to get to Erd-Moz, and we are only beginning to know each other."

"Yes, Aisha, but soon it will be dark and the children will be asking for their supper, and my husband is waiting for me. Another day I'll sit with you for a long time. Because I want to know you also. I hear you are the best midwife in the whole Abu Simbel area."

Aisha reached up and pulled me down again with those iron hands.

"Ha, ha!" She gave a cracked, pleased laugh. "She's heard of me, has she? Well, I *am* a good midwife. See my hands?"

She held the long, seamed brown hands close to my face. "They are strong, you see, but they are also gentle, from years and years they know the way the baby comes and they bring it easily, at exactly the right moment! Why go back to Cairo to have your baby when I'm here?"

"I'm sure you are very good, Aisha," I said politely, "but—"

Aisha scoffed. "I know what you're thinking. You think I can't see, eh? Who needs to see? I'm a better midwife without sight than most of the new ones who have both eyes and no skill. Skill is what it takes, and strength and kindness. Believe me, my girl, I don't leave my patients alone with their pain the way those modern men doctors in Cairo do."

I stood up and moved out of range of Aisha's hand. We *had* to go. We were shaking hands with Wahiba, with Fatima, but Aisha was not to be ignored.

"You listen to me, you Amerikiya!" she cried, reaching out with those hands, raising her sightless eyes under the orange scarf. "I'll wash my hands in hot water, I'll make a good strong knot in the cord, so—" she snapped the long fingers to punctuate her offer. "My son Abdulla can do the circumcision, if it's a boy. I'll do it if it's a girl, and all for nothing. Doesn't that sound good? What else do you want?"

"Yes, yes, thank you, thank you, we'll talk about it," I temporized.

Fatima's eyes were bright with mischief. I could see she had enjoyed the exchange between Aisha and me.

"She's strong, isn't she, my mother-in-law? Well, women have to be strong or they don't live long in *this* world. Gamal!" she hollered after her son, running with Laura Ann, dodging in and out of the long shadows cast by the houses on the darkening sand of the street.

"Let him come home with us. I'll send him back," I promised.

"All right, but don't let him stay and bother you," insisted Fatima. "Good night! Good night! God go with you!"

She was gone in a trail of black dress and veil, a whiff of sandalwood perfume in the acrid dust our footsteps raised in the street.

"That old woman!" said Susan crisply. "Cupping, burning," she shifted Davy to the other shoulder. "She'll wash her hands in hot water, will she?"

The sun was poised, a flattened orange disk, on the very rim of the mountains. Twenty more minutes before total darkness fell, I calculated, and the women in their long black dresses hurrying home with loads of fuel and cans of water, the children driving goats and sheep toward shelter, seemed to share my view.

"B.J.?" It was Susan.

"I can always say my husband won't allow it," I answered.

"Well, why didn't you?" Susan was quite indignant. "Circumcising, too. My God!"

"Laura Ann! Laura Ann!" Karim called.

Time for the nightly ritual of play before supper that warmhearted Karim had introduced into the family routine. In her joy, Laura Ann ran to him and to her father, her new friend Gamal forgotten.

The women of Erd-Moz were proving to be far more independent and far more knowledgeable in the ways of the world outside their tiny village than any of us had expected. Bob had discovered that most Nubian adult men had spent some time working in the cities of Egypt, and therefore he was not too surprised to find the men showing a great deal of sophistication in dealing with him. What was surprising was that the women, theoretically more secluded and isolated, should also demonstrate a certain worldliness, a certain awareness of other values.

Sitta, whose husband worked in London and who had herself lived in Damascus and Tunis, was not unique, we found. Every woman in Erd-Moz had been at least to Aswan more than once; most had lived for extended periods of time in Cairo, Alexandria or Khartoum. Many women echoed ideas about health and child care which I thought they must have heard from Western-trained doctors or from their own husbands.

Bob had told me about the forward-looking ideas of Mohammed, the handsome tambura player who was becoming his best friend in the village. Mohammed moved easily in many kinds of worlds—among his own relatives and friends, with Egyptian archeologists at the temple whom he took duck hunting, with transient European tourists whom he often invited to stay in his house.

I suppose, after the example of Sitta and others, that I rather expected Mohammed's women to follow his lead. His wife, Nezla, and his mother, Shemessa, were very proud of their beautiful double cradle, made to order after a European model, for Mohammed's youngest children, twin baby boys. It was true that when we went to tea at Mohammed's house, tins of lard and folded clothes reposed in the cradle, and the twins were cuddled in the arms of their grandmother Shemessa. But I had not really given the situation much thought, except to note that the twins were whisked out of sight as soon as I arrived and inquiries about their health were met with an abruptness bordering on rudeness. Why?

Nezla was timid and sweet, with a frail beauty gradually being eroded by hard work and childbearing. Shemessa, her mother-in-law, was a tall, commanding person, who ordered Nezla about in an especially unmerciful way, even in a setting where brides can expect little quarter from their husband's mothers. Neither woman appealed to me particularly, yet suddenly and involuntarily I found myself in the middle in a struggle between old and new which was being waged, quietly but fiercely, in the house of modernist Mohammed.

It began one day at lunch.

"Mohammed has asked me if you'll show his women how to take better care of the twins," announced Bob.

"What? You can't be serious."

"Well, Mohammed is."

"Bob," I said, "Shemessa has raised five children, Nezla has three others besides the twins."

"Mohammed really wants you to help."

I frowned. "No," I replied. I could not think of anything worse than becoming identified with the men of Erd-Moz in some kind of struggle against their women, women whom I liked and admired (though it was true I did not much like Shemessa).

"No," I repeated.

"But those twins are constantly sick, eye infections, ear infections, cough, dysentery," observed Bob. "Why not help Mohammed out and give the women a few suggestions."

"If Mohammed is as progressive as you say, why does he need me? He can take the babies to the doctor in Benha."

"He has," said Karim, "but the women forget to put the medicine in or they give too much or too little."

"Let the doctor explain to the women," I argued.

"They wouldn't listen to the doctor, they tune him out. He's a man and not their relative. Mohammed thinks they might listen to you, since you're a woman and have children too. You should be flattered!"

"Ha!" I laughed hollowly. "Nezla and Shemessa listen to me? They're suspicious of foreign medicine to begin with and they can see it doesn't help."

"What do you mean? They haven't given the medicine a fair chance."

Susan intervened. "That's not what B.J. has in mind. Everywhere we go the women look at Davy and say, 'Don't you give him expensive medicine, how come he's still sick?' "

"They begin muttering in dialect," I said, "and they mean, why should we bother? We hardly present a shining example of what Western miracle medicine can do!"

The subject was dropped. I visited Mohammed's house again, but I felt more uncomfortable than before; it was hard to explain why. Then the twins, with dysentery, began passing blood and mucus. "Would I please come?" Mohammed asked.

"You'd rather not meddle in local customs but let the twins die instead," said Bob to provoke me.

This I could not take. "I'll try, I'll try," I said, "but Nezla and Shemessa don't want me messing with the twins; just ask Susan."

"B.J.'s right in a way," said Susan. "It's not the same as at Abdul Majid's or even Saleh's."

"Hmph," retorted Bob. "Feelings. Impressions. Give me some concrete evidence."

I reminded Bob and Karim of all the Nubian beliefs about twins; they were really cats; one twin could not live without the other; they flew out at night; beliefs which Bob thought had developed to explain multiple births and the inevitable death of one or both babies, since it was unlikely, in a subsistence economy, that more than one baby could survive. The Evil Eye figured in all this, too, and I could see it in Nezla's and Shemessa's treatment of the twins. Though they were boys, they wore girls' dresses and frilled sunbonnets, their necks were hung with charms to ward off the Evil Eye.

Bob heard me out and said, "What does all that have to do with you?"

"They think I'm bad luck, too."

"Oh, B.J., don't exaggerate."

"I'm not exaggerating, you should see the way they *look* at me."

"They seem to be *watching* B.J. all the time," put in Susan.

"What imagination!" expostulated Bob.

I said nothing, but I felt Shemessa's nearly open hostility and I also felt, from the bottom of my heart, the same uneasiness and distraction in Nezla, the same sense of inadequacy about those sickly twins that I felt about Davy. I knew enough, I hoped, not to be driven to tie beads around Davy's neck or put hot nails on his forehead to drive out the evil spirits, but I was worried all the time. Nezla knew less about the causes of illness than I; she was worried, too, and an unknown quantity like me only added to her burden. But I agreed to go down the next morning and administer the medicine Mohammed would bring from Benha that afternoon.

I set off alone after breakfast, down the wide street of sand, not relishing the prospect of my mission at all.

"*Mascagna!*" called the women on their way to the mountains to gather fuel.

"*Mascagna!*" called the old widow Fatooma, sitting alone before her door, weaving a small reed plate. "You're going to Mohammed's, hey, to see the sick babies?"

"Yes," I answered.

"Leave them be," she advised. "They're twins!" And she jabbed her long needle between the rows and brought out the free end of palm fiber. "Twins!"

"Yes, I know!"

At the open gate of the primary school, the doorkeeper sat, rolling himself a long, thin, brown cigarette. He nodded to me as I passed. "Off to see Shemessa, eh?" he remarked.

Did everyone know my destination this morning? I could hear the drone of the morning lessons, boys and girls together, reciting.

"What is the capital of America?"

"Washington!"

"What is the capital of Egypt?"

"Aswan!"

"Idiot! No, it is not Aswan. What is the capital of Egypt, children?"

"Cairo."

"Right. Now repeat after me . . . the capital of Egypt is Cairo."

Cairo. I had a full moment of homesickness, not for America, but for Cairo, crowded streets, cinemas, coffee shops, the entire restless urban bustle of my adopted home. I knocked and knocked on Mohammed's door. Finally it gave a crack, and the narrowed eyes of Shemessa met mine.

"*Ahlan wusahlan!*" she said in a falsely bright voice and threw open the door.

"How are the twins?"

"Fine, thank you, just fine."

I was in the court now and Shemessa, winding and unwinding her head scarf, was pacing back and forth and darting glances at me from narrowed eyes while she called, in that falsely bright voice, "Look, Nezla! It is Beeja, come to drink tea with us."

"No, thank you, Shemessa, no tea. I have only come to help you give the babies their medicine. Mohammed, your son, asked me."

Shemessa stopped in her nervous pacing.

"Medicine? What medicine? The twins are fine, just fine. A bit tired this morning is all"'

"I'm glad," I answered.

What to do now? I could not tell Shemessa that I knew she was lying, for Mohammed had stopped last night at our house and shown me the bottle of antibiotic he had brought back.

"Well," I said cheerfully, "then you don't need me. I must be getting back to my children.

"Oh, no," cried Shemessa, "you must have tea first. You will shame our household."

She blocked the door. "That we would let a guest come in through our door and not offer them something?" Her voice shook. "My son Mohammed will not forgive you."

I stood irresolute, realizing only too well that it was Nezla and Shemessa that Mohammed would not forgive, and in that moment Nezla emerged from the kitchen, a twin baby whining on each arm and her face twisted with worry.

Do your duty, I thought to myself, and get out. "I only stopped to inquire after the twins and help you put in the medicine, Nezla," I said.

"I can't *find* the medicine!" wailed Nezla, "and Mohammed made me promise to have you give it to them, and he will be so angry."

"Shhhhhh!" hissed Shemessa and swept the twins out of Nezla's arms, disappearing into one of the bedrooms.

"How are they?"

"Not good," said Nezla, and bit her lip, for in her distress she had done a bad thing. She had admitted to me that the babies were ill. One never admitted in this society that *anyone* was ever ill. He might be a little tired, very tired, might not eat, might be able to take a little tea only, but he was never, never ill.

Suffra, Mohammed's sister, banged open the door, her year-and-a-half-old son on her hip. "How are the twins? Have you come to give them their medicine," she asked me, "like Mohammed said?"

I nodded.

"Well, get it, Nezla," said Suffra. "It's in the *mendara*, I saw my mother, Shemessa, hide it there this morning, after Mohammed had gone."

We sat in the court while the medicine was produced and measured out, Shemessa blustering, "Why do they need this, they are all right, a little tea, it will help, that's all they can take."

Nezla looked from me to Suffra to her mother-in-law, no doubt feeling, as I did, the disapproval in the older woman. Poor Nezla. She seemed torn between her distrust of what I represented and her own beliefs, yet she obviously wanted to do something for her babies. They were so thin and small, their faces so pinched under the frilled bonnets.

"Don't forget the ears are infected, too," reminded Suffra, in a matter-of-fact way. "Mohammed made you promise."

The bonnets were untied, Shemessa hardly able to contain herself, and I bent close over those running, suppurating ears, hardly able to contain *myself*, but for different reasons. The twins were so weak they did not even cry out when the ear drops, warmed briefly as per instructions, went in. They simply closed their eyes, and I saw that the thin eyelashes were matted together with pus.

"Oh, that!" said Nezla. "All the children have eye infections, that is easy to cure; I put the medicine in myself."

"My children have them, too," I said, and in a strained voice I added, "let's put some medicine in now."

This was difficult, but finally, accomplished, Suffra again officiating, holding the babies eyes open until the drops and the ointment went in, Nezla and Shemessa looking at each other wordlessly above us. It was like a pressure, a drift of air, so intense was that silent struggle, and Suffra must have felt it, too, for she said something in dialect and Nezla got up and left the court.

"Put some in my boy Elias' eyes too," Suffra said unexpectedly when we were finished and the pathetic babies had been bundled off by Shemessa, presumably to be put right after my ministrations.

"Now you must have tea, I have already made it," Nezla said, looking exhausted.

We sat together in the sunny court, quietly, while the water jar in its wooden frame gently dripped into its pan and the pigeons in their cotes high on the courtyard wall sounded their low throaty calls.

The atmosphere gradually softened, portents and presences fading, with the departure of their object of concentration.

"Ah, Beeja," said Suffra, half jokingly, "what will we do for him?" picking up her Elias, wiping his runny nose, hugging him and setting him on his unsteady legs to walk again. "He's too old to be satisfied with my milk but too young to eat meat. Here we don't have any food between the milk and the meat that children can grow strong on."

Shemessa had come back just in time for this last complaint. She drew herself up. "Nonsense! We have mashed potatoes, rice, you can soak some bread in milk for him. Babies that are meant to live, live. It is God's will."

"Why is it only God's will in the country?" Suffra asked scornfully. "In Cairo the babies don't die for lack of food. They have beans and bananas and eggs. By God, I will be glad to leave this place and move to Kom Ombo."

"Suffra!" remonstrated her mother. "Don't speak like that of our blessed land. We have enough. We should be content!"

"Enough for old people, yes," agreed Suffra.

I remembered she had recently lost a baby, so perhaps Shemessa was being lenient with her; it was not acceptable to contradict one's elders.

"The city is not perfect either, my girl," and with a glance at me, Shemessa lapsed into dialect.

I knew what they were saying, look at Beeja's baby, expensive medicines, doctors, warm woolen clothes and still. . . the morning had come full circle. It was time to go.

Shemessa rose, almost friendly again after having satisfied herself once more that what will be, will be, despite the efforts of modern upstarts to change anything.

"You should not leave your son alone," she cautioned me. "He needs your protection all the time."

When I smiled and thanked her for her advice, however, she pushed her face close to mine, all the muscles working and the eyes narrowed to slits, and whispered hoarsely, "Who knows where the Evil Eye hides, hey?"

I shivered in the sunshine, and the peaceful courtyard seemed once more to be filled with portents of unknown, unexplained evil. The shudder was involuntary, but Nezla had seen it, for she said quickly, "When one is pregnant, it is hard to keep the other children always with you."

I looked at her. Something in the face. . .

"You're pregnant, Nezla?"

"Yes, I think so. Two or three months."

The sun was hot, the street was empty. Bob and Karim and Susan were in the *mendara* with the children.

"Well?" said Bob meaningfully.

I told the story of the morning, leaving out my own reactions to Shemessa for I felt embarrassed and could not explain them even to myself. But when I thought of Nezla at the end, that sad, tired face, I felt angry. All the tumultuous emotions of the morning crystallized in anger, and I found myself shouting, "Nezla is pregnant again."

"Really?" echoed Bob. "Well, you don't have to yell at us. I'm surprised. Mohammed hasn't said anything.

"Probably doesn't consider it worth mentioning," I burst out. "Mohammed and his modern, progressive ideas!"

Since Bob and Karim said nothing, I raced ahead. "I am sure," I said, feeling like the seer of the mountains after my skirmish with mother-in-laws, folk medicine and the Evil Eye, "that when Nezla delivers this child, the twins will die. The poor woman can hardly produce milk enough for one baby, let alone three!"

"Don't get so excited," said Bob mildly. "You can't do anything about it, so why don't you write down what happened or rest or something while Karim and I finish our morning notes."

What *could* I do? Nothing. I did not feel like writing about it, so I reached for Davy and went outside with Susan and Laura Ann to sit in the sun until lunchtime.

The afternoon had been set aside for our official visit to the *omda*, chief of Nubia's Ballana district. "A pleasant outing," Bob promised, "but be sure to put on your best clothes and clean up the kids. The *omda* is a distinguished man!"

I laughed hollowly to myself. Two weeks of bucket baths, hand-washed clothes, straight hair, sunburned face, swollen ankles and front, it seemed unlikely that I would make even a mildly favorable impression on the *omda*!

But the visit to the *omda*'s did turn out to be a pleasant change. We buzzed upriver in the *Susan*, one of the three motorboats Bob had ordered for the project's field camps. Motors had come from Europe, but the boats had been built in Cairo, and Bob had originally thought of them as communicating links between the camps, emergency transport in case of illness. He and Karim did use the *Susan* to do surveys and interviews in villages around Abu Simbel, to go to Benha for supplies, to the temple for mail brought by the post or express boat. He had planned to use them more than he really did, for the problems of shipping gasoline south of Aswan were great and one or the other motor was always out of order.

Today, though, the *Susan* was purring along on both motors. I breathed the clear soft air; a flock of birds rose winging south to Africa, calling across the river to each other, the river which seemed so wide and vast from our position in the tiny boat. I watched Laura Ann trailing her hand in the water, clutched from the rear by ever watchful Susan, and I held Davy tighter and cast off the mood of depression that the morning had produced. Bob and Karim too forgot, for a moment, their concerns with land tenure and irrigation and cow ownership, and actually laughed at a new joke about the government cooperatives, which had found its way to us, even in this remote place.

I found I responded almost gaily to the *omda*'s formal welcome and even his silent perusal of sniffly Davy and his single comment, "and this is your *only* son?" did not disturb me as much as usual.

We sat on the *omda*'s freshly scrubbed white porch overlooking the river and the ruins of the Islamic fort of Jebel Ada and had a curiously urbane conversation with Suliman Ali Mahmoud Haj, *omda* of Ballana province, descended on his mother's side from the Kashifs, Turkish overlords in Nubia until Mohammed Ali's reign, and descended on his father's side from the Nubian family of Rashwan, a family who had lived in Ballana, it was said, as long as anyone could remember. The *omdas* had once ruled the districts of Nubia, under a broad grant of power from the central government. Since 1952, the government had taken a more direct interest in Nubian affairs, but the *omdas* still remained figures of some importance.

"Do you prefer plane or boat travel, madame?" asked the *omda*. He lounged, a slight elderly figure, in one of his cretonne-covered porch chairs. He had offered us English cigarettes, which he smoked in a long ivory holder. Ivory to match the rest of him; except for the pale coffee-colored leather of his face and hands, he was white, spotless *gullabiya* and turban, white beard and mustache, even immaculate white shoes.

I said that I preferred boats, especially on warm winter days like this, when the breeze was not too strong.

The *omda* agreed. Feluccas, he found, were by far the best mode of travel when the object was pleasure. "But I am glad they have invented airplanes," he said, "so that unpleasant trips may be over quickly."

"You have a beautiful view," offered Susan.

"Yes, I like it," responded the *omda*, and after a magnificent tea had been served, with biscuits and pound cake and raisin cookies, he instructed his servant to bring dates.

"These are our best dates," he admitted when we oohed and aahed about their sweetness, their flavor. "We pack them in fat to keep them soft. Let the boy have more," and with that, he excused himself, he had other urgent business.

"He's a shrewd old bird, that *omda*," mused Bob, as we putt-putted back down the river toward Erd-Moz. "He's still a force to be reckoned with, despite the fact that he's not supposed to have any power at all."

"How can he be a force?" asked Susan. "The Egyptian government is in close control of everything now, I thought."

Karim, at the wheel, his wrinkled white sun hat pulled down over his curly black hair to the rim of his sunglasses, smiled. He would never laugh at our innocence, but he quite often smiled that smile.

"Americans sometimes do not understand," he said gently, "about power. There are lots of ways of keeping it, once you have it."

We were nearing the palm groves that marked the boundary between Dekhla and Erd-Moz. Davy and Laura Ann were unusually quiet, lulled by the purr of the motor and the piles of the *omda*'s best dates which they had consumed.

"He's most impressive," I said.

"Impressive, but perhaps a bit out-of-date," said Bob.

I remembered the sitting room of the guest house where I had gone to change Davy midway through tea. Chintz sofas and chairs, a table beneath a window through which was framed, and not by chance, I thought, the broken towers of the old Jebel Ada fort. Was it the silver inkwell and pen tray, the wooden shutters over glassless windows, the pound cake for tea that gave the *omda*'s riverside house an air of the colonial past, of a time finished and completed elsewhere but still persisting here?

Bob cleared his throat. "I don't want to bring up the business with Mohammed's babies again," he said, "but aside from that, how do things seem to be going with the women?"

"Well enough. Everyone is kind and friendly."

"No problems of rapport, no awkward pauses and so on?"

Susan laughed. "Awkward pauses?" she hooted. "Come along some day and watch us try to keep the children's little hands out of the food."

She went on to recount our disaster of yesterday afternoon when Laura Ann, after admiringly watching a small girl strutting about the court with an empty plate on her head, was suddenly moved to action. I saw her small hands fold around the huge plate of popcorn and dates laid out for us; Susan and I both moved, but too late. Laura Ann raised the plate on high and popcorn and dates rained onto the fine sand of the court, a shocking thing to happen in a society where food is considered sacred, and even dirty or spoiled bits of food are blessed before being given to the animals.

"Never mind," our hostess had muttered automatically but made no move to help as Susan and I picked out of the sand, one by one, the grains of popcorn and the flat dried dates. When the plate was refilled, one of the women took it away, and general conversation was resumed.

We tied up at the dock, Bob took Davy from Susan and hoisted him to his shoulder for the climb to the top of the dunes. Laura Ann clutched Karim's hand happily and I dropped behind, taking the safe, slow way upward, greeting the women with their evening water cans. Fatima's son Gamal, his brother by the hand, was skipping stones into the muddy water of the shallow canal. In some shelter nearby a cow bellowed to be milked. One week more and Susan would return to Cairo. Beryl would come to help me with the children, but I scarcely knew Beryl. Mona would come from the American University as a research assistant, to work with the women, and I didn't know her at all. One day at a time.

"Bob has promised to take me to the temple tomorrow," called Susan from above, where Bob sat with the men admiring the sunset. From the west, the fading golden light slanted across the veranda, giving the mud-brick pillars a look of monumental stone. Bob's face was lost in shadow, but the turbans of Mohammed and Saleh and the china plates above the door gleamed white against the gray mud wall.

"How could I ever explain to my relatives in New York that I lived beside Abu Simbel for three weeks and never got inside it? You and Karim are my witnesses. He has promised!"

Karim waved his white sun hat. "Okay, Susan," he answered.

The women resting before the houses, Khadija, I thought, and Hanim Ali, were laughing at our long-distance interchange. Susan turned and laughed too and sank down on the sand with them.

Abdul Nasr crawled into her lap beside Davy.

# Chapter 5

# Nubian Housekeeping

W hen I was a child, I was fascinated by those pale images of the roadside reflected in the window of our moving automobile. One image unrolled at eye level, like an over exposed filmstrip—fields of corn, red barns, blue silos, children waving and running past white farmhouses on the gentle slopes of rolling hills. But the reflection of the opposite side of the road seemed to have been threaded wrongly into the projector. The landscape whipped past at an unpredictable angle, lop-sided farmhouses, crazy half hills, oddly suspended children disappearing diagonally into an unknown sky. I would find myself glancing quickly, furtively, across the highway to check on the second half of the landscape, to make certain that this odd imprint which I watched was an illusion.

In Nubia my fears for Laura Ann and Davy were like that distorted reflection, an unreal image I tried not to face directly, while the field work moved along reasonably easily, like the eye-level landscape of my childhood travels. Beryl, who had come with Susan's departure, was not only helping me with the children; like Susan, she entered spontaneously into our work. The new research assistant, Mona, had also been quickly absorbed into the life of Erd-Moz, rather to everyone's pleased surprise, including her own. Mona's comfortable upper middle-class Cairo home, staffed by many servants, could hardly have prepared her for the difficult life in the village, one would have thought, but Mona reminded us that she had spent her summers on the family farm estate in the Delta.

"I feel at home in the country," she said.

"And the Nubians are a very appealing people," added Beryl.

Both girls were intelligent, but it was their warm hearts, I thought, which contributed more to their obvious enjoyment and appreciation of life in Nubia.

66

At first together and then often separately, as we developed our individual friendships, we visited the women of Erd-Moz and they visited us. We sat together in the courtyards or on the tawny, sun-drenched dunes before the houses, listening, talking, trying to understand the people among whom we were living, to record the techniques and skills that the women had developed to deal successfully with home life on the Upper Nile. This was a life far from the lives we had led and known, a life which made different demands upon wives and mothers and daughters than any we had experienced before.

Mona, challenged one day by laughing and teasing friends, had attempted to imitate that deft movement of both arms for which Hanim Ali was famous. With only a flat reed plate as a sifter, Hanim Ali could separate, we were told, a bushel of wheat from its chaff without losing a single valuable edible grain. Mona tried valiantly, but stifled giggles from the audience soon erupted into loud laughter, and Fatima, her eyes streaming with tears of mirth, finally took the plate away.

"You don't want to waste all my grain, do you?" said Fatima, and at Mona's stricken guilty look (several scores of grains of wheat had disappeared into the sand during the experiment) she patted her on the shoulder. "Never mind, Mona," she said, "it takes years of practice, and even though I've been doing it since I was a little girl, I'm still not as good as Hanim Ali."

"You can do other things we can't do," reminded Wahiba.

"Like what?" pressed Beryl.

"Well, er. . ." Wahiba looked around her, "read, things like that," she gestured widely in the hot cloudless air.

Reading, I thought, could be learned by Hanim All more easily than I could ever learn that rhythmic sifting movement. A bushel of wheat without losing a grain? Incredible.

Sherifa was drying mint when we went to tea, sorting the leaves and laying them in the sun upon the woven leather "spring" of the classic *angareeb*, the Nubian bedstead with feet carved like the feet of Pharaonic furniture. One of these bedframes stood in almost every bare courtyard, used to keep the freshly washed dishes as well as the drying vegetables off the ground.

"My children have coughs all winter long," Sherifa said. "Mint tea settles their stomachs and soothes their throats and Abdul Majid likes it, too."

The mint was tied into bundles with shreds of palm fiber before being hung with the strings of okra and green beans from the rafters of the warm summer kitchen.

Mona walked to the mountains with Wahiba and Fatima to graze the goats and gather dead branches and shrubs for fuel. Beryl, taking Laura Ann by the hand, walked to the river with Naima, Khadija's young sister, to watch the nomad camel caravan pass. I listened to Hanim Ali's tale of woe as she lay in her bedroom, ill with stomach trouble, dosing herself with a purging brew and clenching her fists, covered with those magic rings, to keep herself from crying out with pain.

The women had long ago learned to take advantage of every single resource available to them in their limited environment. Empty kerosene cans, for example, were not thrown away; they were used as water cans, or, hung high on the walls of the courtyards and with door holes cut in the sides, they became pigeon lofts.

In the mud-brick walls of the kitchens, niches had been carefully hollowed out to serve as special built-in cupboards, a small niche (high up and away from children) for the matches, a long flat deep hollow for fuel, shorter ones for the primus stove, the cooking pots. A place for everything and everything in its place was the neat Nubian housewife's motto.

It was in the care of their floors, however, that they seemed to me to exercise the most ingenuity. Cleaning and changing the sand in the courtyards every week was not enough; the walkways and doorways had not only to be swept, they had to be renewed regularly. Each year, before the two principal feasts in the Moslem religious calendar, the women gathered together and pooled their energies in a final orgy of spring cleaning and house refurbishing. Not a quilting bee nor a roof raising, but a complete floor replastering took place in each household.

Khadija came in the day our house was to be done, carrying great flat pans which she had filled with a mud and water mixture.

"Who's coming to plaster?" asked Beryl.

"Almost everybody, except Nezla, who isn't feeling well—the twins again," she threw out offhandedly, "but Suffra will take her place. After all, the floors are a big job. Everybody must help. Whoever doesn't come here, well, we won't go to *her* replastering."

Using their hands, the women spread the mud and water plaster over the walks and doorways, smoothing it and edging it carefully with a knife. The new coat of mud baked in the sun to a hard smooth gloss by the end of the afternoon. A final swipe with the broom and presto, chango, shiny new mud floors, thresholds and doorjambs, a surface which would have degenerated quickly under the impact of leather shoes, but lasted a long time with the barefoot tread of our friends (who carefully left their shoes outside when they entered a house).

One day Karim and Bob reported that a strange leafless tree had been carried with some ceremony into Mohammed's house. What, they wanted to know, would they be using that oddly shaped tree for, if not for fuel? We waited an hour and then "visited" to find Nezla and Shemessa and Suffra mixing a kind of spaghetti to be used in a special sweet for the feast coming at the end of Ramadan. The dough went into a meat grinder and came out in strings. And the tree? It had been carefully chosen by Shemessa herself as a special drying rack, since for this task the bedstead would simply not do, she said. The spread between the branches and twigs allowed each string of spaghetti to be draped separately and dried individually in the sun.

Mona shared *iftar* with Fatima, the breaking of the fast during Ramadan, and was treated to *gargabida*, paper-thin slices of crisp bread soaked in lime water and served as the first light refreshing taste of food and drink after the long day of fasting.

After the joyous *iftar* meals, Beryl practiced traditional dance steps with Wahiba and Naima and the other unmarried girls. In the cold winter moonlight, which cast their vague girlish shadows on the darkened walls of the houses, they danced to a drumbeat punctuating their own singing.

"Now that I've seen you," they chanted,
"O my love,
  How can I live without you
  O my love!"

It was Beryl perhaps who came closest to actually taking part in the life around us. She was younger than Mona, without the traditional attitudes of Egyptians toward their less fortunate fellow countrymen; she was younger than I and unmarried, more open to new impressions, not bound up in the wife-mother sets as I had become. She danced and sang and learned the steps, and years later, in Cambridge, she sang my children those old Nubian songs.

But wherever I went, whatever I did, my fears for David and Laura Ann were with me, irrational fears, that at night before sleep or in unexpected moments during the day would unwind before me and flash like that other nightmarish landscape reflection of my childhood, diagonally into the unknown sky. In my dreams the figure of my own mother, the white farmhouses of Wisconsin childhood summers appeared confusedly in company with blind Aisha, with Shemessa hissing about the Evil Eye.

Davy's asthma, contrary to our hopes, had not improved, but on the other hand, it had not worsened. His fungus infections seemed to be slowly drying up, but he was plagued by new irritations and illnesses; ear infections, eye infections, dysentery (like the twins, the dreams whispered). Laura Ann had several eye infections and developed a hacking cough. We dosed them both with antibiotics from the first-aid suitcase which Karim had prepared so meticulously in Cairo more than a year ago. The infections, the cough, the dysentery got better, only to recur.

"That's the way children are, Beeja," Fatima said. "One day they're sick, one day they're well," and she gestured to her sniffling three-year-old. "What else do you expect?"

I was silent. Should I ask Fatima about the other problem that had risen to haunt me, Laura Ann's relationship to the village children? Abruptly I burst out, "What about Laura Ann?"

"Our children don't mean any harm," said Fatima.

Perhaps they didn't. Probably they didn't. But Laura Ann, our once happy daughter, was miserable. We had thought that since Laura Ann had, practically since birth, played in the *ganeena* with children of all sizes and colors, her attitude toward the Nubian children would be a perfectly natural and friendly one. We were right. What we had not reckoned with was the attitude of the Nubian children toward Laura Ann.

"Mama! Mama! Play!" Laura Ann had insisted excitedly those first mornings in our new home, entranced at the thought of all that sand, all those children, all those donkeys and goats and geese and chickens. Dressed and breakfasted, she would race out and head for the nearest cluster of Nubian children, drawing pictures in the sand with pointed sticks, playing jacks with small stones or practicing the ancient jumping game depicted on the walls of Pharaonic tombs. One hand high, two hands high, three, four and six hands high the little boys would jump.

As Laura Ann approached, however, the children would stop their play, still their chatter and their gay, high-pitched laughter. I would watch through the cracks in the shutters, praying that today things might go differently.

"Play?" Laura Ann would go up to a child. "Play?" she would repeat, trying it in English and Arabic, in a piercing little voice I could hear all the way to the house. The Nubian child would back away, good-humoredly enough, but still back away, and in a moment, blonde-haired and white-skinned Laura Ann would find herself the center of a tight ring of dark children, with flashing eyes, skullcaps and *gullabiyas*, tight little pigtails under their red shawls.

"Play?" she would say once more, for at first she had thought this was a new kind of game. But it was not "Farmer in the Dell" or "Drop the Handkerchief." After a brief silent pause the teasing would begin. One child would rush forward and pull on Laura Ann's red sweater. She would turn, to find someone yanking her hair from behind. Another child would lean forward and pinch her leg. By this time, a number of dark mothers would have emerged from doorways to admonish their children and the circle would break.

The Nubian children would laugh and run away, and Laura Ann, left alone, would burst into tears and run for home. After about ten days of this treatment, the poor child refused to leave the house without Susan or Beryl or me.

When I saw her on the porch, rocking back and forth with her dolly, her little face tight with unhappiness, I would ask myself, what am I doing? Why am I allowing her to go through this? Is it really necessary for me to stay here? To whom do I owe my first responsibility? Bob? But what about the children? Don't I owe something to them, too?

Fatima pointed out that her son Gamal was very fond of Laura Ann. "You see how nicely they play together here," she said.

True. Alone, Gamal was very kind and gentle with Laura Ann and she would follow him devotedly, carrying a stick when he carried one, sipping water from the water jar when he did. But in a crowd, Gamal would not stand alone against all of his friends and relatives.

"They just want to make sure she's real," Khadija laughed. "Watch how Abdul Nasr, even, touches her hair and feels it, he's never seen hair like that before."

I thought she had probably come closer to the truth than anyone, but it was difficult to explain this refinement to two-and-a-half-year-old Laura Ann.

Every few days Bob and I would discuss the current problems with the children, and I would decide to leave; I had done my duty, it seemed, by demonstrating that my husband was a respectable family man who could be trusted to supervise properly these unmarried research assistants. Bob would make reservations on the express boat. But before the boat arrived, Davy would improve or worsen, Laura Ann would be uncomfortable with another eye infection or would seem momentarily happier, and the long, arduous trip to Cairo would be postponed again.

So the winter days passed, warm and sunny, with windy nights and freezing mornings. Before sunup I would hear Davy wailing and, struggling up from sleep, I would throw my clothes on in the icy cold, rush across the court and get Davy quickly before he woke Laura Ann and Beryl. Bundled in sleeper and blankets, he would stop crying when we came out of the dark bedroom into the predawn light of the court.

Even in my cold, blurred sleepy state, I could see why the child quieted and looked. From the porch the dark mountains on the opposite shore seemed gilded with an edge of radiant gold; the sun was rising. Khadija, a heavy shawl over her head, would emerge and nod before heading down the hill to feed the cows bawling with hunger in the cold.

A dog woke and barked.

The sky was red, the palms a dusky green beside the dark river. Saleh would come out, his head shrouded in white; in his hand the primus stove blazing and ready for me to cook Davy's early breakfast in the *mendara*.

"Good morning!" he would say between chattering teeth.

Davy, pointing upward into the lightening sky, would answer, "Bird" (wheeze), "bird!"

Saleh would laugh in the cold and nod at Davy, yes, there were always birds flying over the village toward the river, the flapping of their wings unnaturally loud in the early morning quiet.

The sky lost its redness while I knocked at the door of the *mendara* where Karim was asleep on a cot; Saleh would leave the primus stove hissing beside me.

"Karim!" I'd call again, banging on the shutter to get in; he would answer sleepily he'd be dressed in a moment.

The sky was now clear and limpid, the enormous round red sun showed above the mountains and slowly, as it rose in the sky, seemed to diminish in size, while the palms, the river, the mountains and the sand dunes beside me took color from its light.

Cocks crowed. More dogs barked.

The primus stove hissed yellow, blue, red and back to blue.

Just at the moment when I felt on the point of desperation, jumping up and down to keep warm, Davy struggling to get out of his nest of blankets, the primus stove threatening to die in the morning wind, always at that point, it seemed, Karim would unbolt the door with a loud thonk.

"Good morning!" he would say briskly, rubbing his eyes and adjusting his glasses. "Excuse me, please." Huddled in his sweater and coat in one of the two folding plastic armchairs, he would tune the transistor radio, searching for the morning news from Radio Cairo.

Light filtered through the cracks in the wooden shutters, closed against the cold and Davy, momentarily fascinated, fingered carefully those strips of light on the aluminum surface of the table, before becoming bored and banging insistently for breakfast.

"Coming, coming!" I would promise, stirring up the cereal on the primus.

"*Sabeh el-Khayr*, good morning, ladies and gentlemen," the radio spouted between bits of static.

President Sukarno of Indonesia was in Cairo on a state visit; John F. Kennedy was giving a speech in Baltimore, *Merry*-land, the newscaster pronounced it; Queen Elizabeth and her children were spending St. Valentine's Day at Balmoral Castle; two Russian technicians — it all seemed light years away from our sand dune village, where I spooned cereal into Davy's protesting mouth, then cleared off the primus and the previous evening's notes and papers and set the table with jam and silverware, dried milk and Nescafé.

"Good morning! Good morning! Good morning!" Bob came in, Mona, and Beryl with Laura Ann by the hand, still in her sleepers and bathrobe. When Saleh brought in the scrambled eggs and brown flat bread, a pot of hot water for the coffee and tea, we would wolf the food, sitting there in our coats, and gird ourselves for the long day ahead.

"Interviews at the school?" Bob would ask.

Karim would nod over the coffee.

Ah, that coffee! Years later, in my centrally heated house, with its electric coffee pot, I can still taste that stale Nescafé (courtesy of Ali from the Sudan). It was superb! The temptation was to sit outside on our porch, warming in the morning sun and have a second cup. This was fatal, for by the time the second cup of coffee was finished, the children's sleepers would be covered with dust and sand and by the time we had cleaned that—well, it was simply not worth it.

We dressed the children, Laura Ann crying, "Cold! cold! cold!" Beryl and I worked as quickly as our numbed fingers would allow. Faces were washed (no fun when the water is icy), but I remembered Naima who had carried the five gallons of water up the hill that morning and tried to be cheerful. Brrrrrrr!

Beryl would take the children off for a morning turn to look at the goats' new kids. Bob and Karim and Mona would set out on interviews, and Saleh would come in to plan meals and do accounts.

This was a more complicated process than it sounds. Erd-Moz had no markets. Everything that was eaten was grown and stored in the village itself, brought by boat from Aswan or on donkeyback from the county seat of Benha, three miles south along the Nile. Saleh's one-legged brother, Abdou, went to Benha by donkey each day, and shopped for us. So careful planning at this particular moment was necessary to assure that we would have enough to eat for the rest of the day, and, hopefully, something reasonably good.

My friends in Erd-Moz planned their meals according to the amounts of dried dates, flour and beans remaining in their clay storage jars. I had to keep reminding myself how lucky I was to have access to the market; it was not always easy.

"Meat stew?" I would suggest to Saleh.

"Probably all the meat will be gone when Abdou gets there," Saleh would reply gloomily. He had once been an excellent chef in the house of Sir William Willcocks, the British irrigation engineer, but that was many years ago. Saleh was getting old, he was getting lazy, he did not obviously care for cooking on primus stoves with limited supplies.

"Well, fish?"

"Fish. Your husband doesn't like fish."

That was true. But it was also true that Saleh did not like to prepare this pulpy river fish, mostly carp, in fact. It was not very good fish, but it was a change in our monotonous diet.

"Tuna? Don't they have canned tuna in Benha?"

Saleh would shrug. "Who knows?"

"Well," I would finally give in. "What do *you* think, Saleh?"

"Abdou can bring some bones, perhaps, for soup, maybe there'll be a *little* meat we could eat on the bones, though I doubt it. And lentils for the soup."

"Take the little meat off the bones and make a curry."

"We have no rice."

"Abdou can buy rice."

"If there is any."

"Vegetables? Fruit?"

Saleh would look disgruntled. "Maybe some wilted spinach, maybe not. And I know there's no fruit."

"No fruit? Not even dates?"

"Well, we have dates here."

"We need sugar."

"Humph," from Saleh. "No sugar till Friday when the boat comes."

I knew Saleh had few resources to work with, but I knew he could do better than he was doing. His soups were always excellent, so we did not starve. Why wasn't the rest of the meal as good as the soup? He refused to make desserts and on this point we struggled long and bitterly.

"Cake? You certainly can make cake," I had said, after my suggestions of custards and puddings had all been pronounced impossible.

"No cake. It takes eggs. Ah those things take eggs."

"There must be eggs," I insisted stubbornly.

"Where?" from Saleh.

"Where there are chickens there are eggs," I had replied, half laughing and proud of the way that sentence had come out in Arabic, like a proverb.

"And where do you see chickens who will lay the eggs?" Saleh had returned, triumphantly. That sentence had sounded like a proverb too, a proverb of poverty.

Where indeed? I remembered Saleh's nephew spent all afternoon, every afternoon, searching the village for enough eggs to provide us with breakfast.

The phrase "subsistence economy," which I had come across many times in my reading, began to have reality for me.

"Here I am, ready to go if you are ready," boomed Abdou at the door, knocking with his wooden leg. His standard morning joke followed and a laugh, the same laugh every morning. I would give him money and approximately the same shopping order I had given him yesterday.

I made one last attempt. "Abdou, Saleh says there is no fruit, but we must have fruit. Aren't there even oranges in Benha?"

Abdou thumped his wooden leg thoughtfully with his fist. He was an odd man, always laughing loudly and raucously, in spite of or perhaps to belie the basic bitterness of his nature. He had lost his leg in a Cairo trolley-car accident. The government-owned company paid his medical expenses and he was entitled to a new wooden leg each time the shape of his stump altered (not more than one per year). Abdou had so far collected seven wooden legs, on the theory that the government, or somebody, owed him something for his loss. He kept the macabre collection in his guest room and was delighted to show off the various models to visitors. It was poor Abdou's only distinction, Karim had suggested.

"Maybe we could get some fruit from Khartoum," Abdou was saying. "The post boat comes tomorrow."

"Khartoum?" My voice rose. The children needed fresh fruit, we all needed fresh fruit. Khartoum was a thousand miles away.

"They might have some in Halfa," said Abdou. "How much do you want? Might take a while to get it."

I calculated quickly, Bob and Karim and Beryl and Mona and me, David and Laura Ann, plus extra for guests, say, ten pieces of fruit per day for ten days. No, more, the oranges would keep.

"A hundred oranges and a hundred guavas," I announced.

Saleh and Abdou regarded me as though I had become suddenly raving mad.

Abdou laughed gleefully. "A hundred oranges and a hundred guavas, let's see, that would be about three pounds, plus tip to Mohammed's cousin, the waiter on the boat who will buy them, three and a half Egyptian pounds! A *lot* of money! Ha!" He cast a side glance at Saleh.

Saleh muttered to Abdou in Nubian; I heard Bob's name spoken. Aha, this large outlay of money must be cleared with a responsible person, i.e., a man.

We had been meal-planning for more than an hour. Now another half hour to track down Bob in the middle of an interview and ask him if he would allow his wife to throw three and a half pounds foolishly to the winds on a hundred guavas and a hundred oranges. Meanwhile, all the good meat in the market would have been purchased and we would dine on stringy leftovers. Annoyance was breaking over me like an allergic reaction and I fought it down.

"Here's the money!" I repeated my order. "If you want to check with my husband, please do so."

"Oh, madame, but a *hundred* oranges?" Abdou limped out, giggling, and shaking his head at the vagaries of the weaker sex. I discovered that evening he did actually check with Bob before setting out. Five days later, a hundred oranges and a hundred guavas came through the palm groves and up the dunes, tied on the back of Abdou's donkey in a bundle of sacking.

Mekki, the boatman, was a traveling peddler, one of several who worked up and down the Nile from Aswan to Wadi Halfa. He would put in to the dock slightly north of the village about once a month, and the word "Mekki's here" would pass quickly from one house to another. Soon a troop of ladies would wind down the path, baskets of dates on their heads, for Mekki did not barter for money, he bartered for dates. Women who did not have dates on hand but who owned shares in the palm trees could still shop with Mekki, and he would write in a black notebook with a stub of pencil how many dates would be owed him at harvest time in exchange for the beans, the cloth, the sugar that he measured into sacks and baskets.

"Mekki sometimes has good *mish*," said Karim one day. "Why don't we go down and see?"

*Mish* was the strong, aged cheese of goat's milk, probably an early ancestor of roquefort, I thought. Why not? It would be a good change.

Mekki cut us a sliver from a great hunk of white cheese reposing in a barrel of salt water on the deck of his felucca.

"This isn't *mish*," said Karim, wrinkling up his nose.

Mekki smiled. He was a Sayyidi, not a Nubian, and had the strong arms and barrel chest of the Upper Egyptian peasant. "No, it's white cheese," he said.

"Doesn't taste like white cheese, either," Karim complained.

"It is though," Mekki asserted and we bought a large slab. I decided it was simply very old white cheese, unlike the soft fresh cakes of goat cheese we bought each day in Cairo, and had accumulated unto itself various and sundry flavors during its long river journey in that cask of salt water. However, cheese was cheese.

We bought some olives, as many as be would sell us. "I have to keep some for my clients upstream," Mekki explained, with another smile. And I bought Laura Ann a plastic bracelet from the tray of trinkets and mirrors, which Mekki left out temptingly beside the sacks of beans and lentils and macaroni, displayed on deck for the two-day stand in Erd-Moz.

"We don't have any dates, sad to say," said Karim, but Mekki took our money and waved us on. We had long ago learned that dates were the real sign of wealth and prestige in Erd-Moz. Date products were used for innumerable things: Fronds were cut down and burned for fuel, the branches were cut into strips for building the walls and roofs of animal shelters; smaller strips were used to weave baskets and mats; women scoured pots and pans with balls of palm fiber, and Bob had even reported seeing woven palm frond bandages on a man's leg.

Dates meant date trees; date trees meant property; and property meant, as it does in every village and city of the world, status, solidity and respectability.

Saleh's chefly soul must have been reminded of past culinary glories in Cairo by the arrival of Mekki, for that day he concocted for lunch an excellent cold Greek-style salad of marinated kidney beans, squash and potatoes, all made more tasty by the wrinkled black olives and the slices of that old white cheese.

Occasionally small peddlers passed by, a man on a donkey who made the round trip from Benha to Abu Simbel with a load of onions or tomatoes, lured by the prospective customers on the antiquities boat at Abu Simbel Temple.

Women peddlers came, too, on foot over the sand, a bundle on their backs, a basket on their heads. One was a Sayyidi fortuneteller, and she wore, not the long trailing gowns of the Nubian ladies, but the shorter, homespun, black garments of Upper Egypt and the Delta. Middle-aged, blue tattoo marks in her chin, eyes narrowed from years of adjusting to the glare of sun on sand, she had a strong face, a face full of life observed and rejected, life embraced and lived, a shrewd face. She measured carefully, she bargained well and she read palms with dramatic lifts of her head toward heaven and casting of her arms to the skies.

We gathered around her on the sand in front of Saleh's house, as she laid out her wares on a length of rough cloth: combs, head scarves, thread, safety pins, small needles mounted on a bit of hammered tin to clean the burners of primus stoves.

"Khadija was there, with Abdul Nasr, and Dahiba and Naima, Hanim Ali, old widow Fatooma, Beryl, Mona, the children.

The woman refused to read my palm.

"I know nothing of this lady and her people," she announced flatly, and gazing upward, intoned, "Allah the most Merciful, the most Compassionate," passing off her refusal very sensibly, I thought, as though it were decreed by high powers.

Beryl bought a packet of needles from her and Mona pressed closer and asked for a fortune.

"Hmmm," remarked the woman, her eyes slowly taking in the quixotic presence of Mona in this village which she must have known well, she had been coming, the women said, for many years. Mona—wool skirt, good foreign shoes, a green sweater, a Nubian head scarf (we all wore them to be polite), an open intelligent face. What was she doing *here*? "Hmmm," she repeated, gazing not at Mona's hand but at her face.

Khadija teased the woman. "*Ya Amina*, here we thought you were a great fortuneteller, but maybe you can only read our Nubian fortunes," she said. "Beeja, all right, she's a foreigner, but Mona is a Moslem like us and an Egyptian."

"She is a Moslem?" asked the old woman.

"I am a Moslem," repeated Mona. "Yes, I certainly am," trying to banter with the woman, who suddenly straightened Mona's hand with a jerk and a nod which silenced us.

"Sickness, death, I see. That is what the fates decree," she drones

"That's all?" quipped Mona.

"Sickness, death, yes," repeated the woman doggedly.

I could not bear the look on Mona's face. "She's already been sick this week," I said lightly. "Give us some new news."

"Yes, yes," chattered the women.

The fortuneteller dropped Mona's hand. "You will marry for love," she announced, but not pleasantly, and began to tie up her bundle of wares.

"Wonderful!" Mona's face broke into a smile. "I shall marry for love."

"Stay for tea, *ya Amina*," Khadija said.

"No, not today, I have some cloth to take to Kemak."

She stood up, shading with her hand the narrow eyes deep-buried in wrinkles, and stared at the river and the sun. "It will be dark soon," and she trudged off across the sand, her bundle under her arm, her basket on her head, alone.

"Sickness, death, marriage for love, some mixture." Mona was trying to dispel with words the mood that had settled on us from the abruptness of the fortune-teller's departure.

'Where will she sleep tonight?" I asked Khadija.

"Maybe somebody in Kemak will invite her," said Khadija, not much concerned.

"Nobody troubles her alone like that?"

"Troubles her?" It was Dahiba. "Who would trouble an old woman in our blessed land, where everyone is honest? In Cairo, yes, in Cairo you let a chicken out of your sight for two minutes and someone has stolen it and cooked it and eaten it, but here . . . here you could leave money in the street, it would sit there until it rotted, because no one would take it."

This was a familiar theme, the Nubians' pride in their proverbial honesty. Khadija chimed in with a story about a shoe that had been lost for three weeks and found; and old widow Fatooma told her version of the five-pounds-in-the-street story.

"If everyone is so honest, why do you lock your doors?" asked Mona, half laughing. The long, pegged wooden house keys went everywhere with the women.

"Me?" asked old widow Fatooma. "Because I can't see the door of my house from here, that's why."

"But if you aren't worried about people being dishonest, why does it matter?"

The women looked at us. "We always carry our keys," said Dahiba. "It's the best way to take care of our houses."

"But—"

"Look, Mona," said the widow Fatooma, "my door's open, my bracelet is gone. I might even think my old friend Dahiba has it."

Dahiba snickered behind her buck teeth, though her eyes were watchful.

"But," continued Fatooma, "if I've locked my door, then I can't blame anybody but myself."

In the afternoons when the children wakened from naps, we had tea. Originally this had been a kind of conference, a time when our group could assemble and discuss interesting problems that had arisen during the day, what might be useful to do tomorrow. But the longer we stayed in Erd-Moz with the friendly Nubians, the more the tea hour became a social occasion rather than a conference. This particular afternoon of the fortuneteller we had not thought of tea until it was too late. Bob and Karim had drunk their tea, and our share had gone to Mohammed, Abdulla and Abdul Majid, who just happened to be visiting. The stove and the primuses were all occupied with dinner, so we nibbled a few dry dates to stave off hunger till evening.

It had been a reasonably good day, I thought, as I fed Davy and Laura Ann mashed beans, dabs of pureed meat and rice. We had had some interesting conversation. Karim had cleaned the water filters; no one had been sick; Bob had gotten the refrigerator working; I had remembered to boil water and mix milk, and Naima had brought the lanterns before darkness fell.

"Let's bundle the children up and let them look at the stars before they sleep," suggested Beryl, and she whispered, "I think Saleh is making something special for Bob's birthday. He got a jar of strawberry jam from me."

The day had been so long and full I had almost forgotten my morning conference with Saleh, if not a cake for Bob's birthday (no eggs), surely he could produce something. Saleh's eyes had flickered, but he had not indicated what, if anything, he could or would do.

At the end of the meal, which was undistinguished, to put it mildly, Saleh banged at the door and Karim stood up.

"Happy birthday!" he cried. "To Bob!"

Saleh brought in a huge flaming platter.

Bob opened his eyes in surprise.

"Happy birthday!" we shouted.

Saleh had made crepes suzette!

"How did he get them to flame?" asked Bob, in between mouthfuls of the crepes filled with Beryl's jar of strawberry jam.

Karim and Beryl looked at each other.

"Karim gave him a jigger of whiskey," she said, "and started to tell him what to do, but he already knew. Apparently Sir William whoever-he-was liked crepes suzette. These are wonderful!"

That evening, we sat around the tape recorder, the faint Bach competing with the hissing of the Coleman lantern. We discussed our own life histories, we talked about politics and music. But we returned always to Nubian life histories, to Abdou and his seven wooden legs, Mohammed with his modern cradle and his superstitious mother-in-law, Sitta and her husband far away in London, that strange mixture of sophistication and simplicity of one culture and several others which we had all observed in our friends.

"Sometimes I feel as though Mohammed is guiding me along when I'm supposed to be interviewing *him*," said Karim, "suggesting a question, and so on."

"Yes, yes," agreed Mona, "it's an odd feeling, as though they were managing us, helping us."

I described our visit to Sitta's house, on the dune behind Abu Simbel, where we were served tea from fine Bavarian demitasse cups and offered cigarettes from a beautifully carved old Damascene wooden box.

"Sitta even told us the milk had been boiled so it was safe for Laura Ann and Davy to drink," put in Beryl. "You should have seen B.J.'s face!"

This was typical of our friends. They anticipated our customs before we had a chance to allow for theirs, a measure of real sophistication.

"And yet," mused Bob, "whatever talent they may have for assimilating other ways of doing things, it doesn't affect their own sense of identity. They are always Nubian, at least those who find their way back here."

Bob was right. No matter how well traveled or how well acquainted with urban life, the Nubians retained pride in themselves and thee own traditions, not confusing a higher standard of living with a better way of life.

Mona insisted on making us a cup of Turkish coffee, and Karim told us the latest jokes from Cairo that had been relayed via Mekki. That evening, when I crawled into my sleeping bag by lantern light, I realized that for nearly four hours my mental landscape had been calm and level. I had forgotten for the moment the social isolation of my daughter, the painful wheezing of my little son.

# Chapter 6

# The Begum Agha Khan's Wedding Present

The Begum Agha Khan, tall, statuesque and kindhearted, drifted in and out of our lives that year in Nubia. I never did meet her, but Bob did and communicated with her secretary for months about gasoline for our motorboats. The Begum's houseboat was often at Abu Simbel with guests who had come from Paris to visit the Begum at her winter home in Aswan, near the tomb of the late Agha Khan. Then, quite unwittingly, she became the catalyst in a drama that was to involve all of us in Erd-Moz. It had all begun some time before with a wedding present.

The family budget of each household in Erd-Moz was, of necessity, carefully and minutely calculated to take advantage of every possible resource, to plan for every possible expense. Only in this way could a family survive. The bushels of grain expected from each foot of arable land, the fruit from every date palm, the number of pieces of dead wood which might fall from the trees to be used for fuel, the number of pounds or piasters which might arrive from relatives in Cairo or Khartoum—all were estimated long in advance. Wedding presents, contributions to help pay for wakes after a death in the family, hours of labor given to help a neighbor replaster a floor, these were noted in real or imaginary ledgers. One good turn required another; reciprocity was a standing rule.

In such a tightly organized situation, any serious loss or any unexpected gain upset the delicate balance and created serious problems. How could the Begum Agha Khan have known this? On a visit to Abu Simbel, she had simply expressed a desire to see a Nubian wedding.

Mohammed and Saleh, who were in the crowd of Nubians gathered to formally welcome the Begum, had stepped forward.

"We are having a wedding in Erd-Moz this week," Saleh had said. "My niece Naima. Her fiance Jalal is here from Cairo."

The Begum said she would be delighted to come and a date was set. Saleh and Mohammed were then faced with the problem of providing a wedding. Saleh's statement that a wedding was scheduled was only partly true. The wedding he had in mind, that of his niece Naima to Jalal, son of Saleh's dead sister, had been in the discussion stages for years, but negotiations had recently struck a snag. Jalal's father, remarried to a woman in Cairo, opposed the match. It was Saleh who continued to push, and very cannily he had seized on the Begum's request as an ideal way to force Jalal to the altar. Since the code of hospitality is sacred in Nubia, Saleh had a strong weapon. Besides, it was correctly assumed that the Begum would be a generous guest.

Jalal, however, said no. He would not marry Naima, he vowed, unless his father agreed.

Relenting a little, Saleh suggested that the contract be written, the feasting and dancing and the singing of the bridegroom to the *diwani* take place, but the marriage not be consummated, the contract not signed until Jalal's father had given his consent.

Jalal was still doubtful.

"We have promised the Begum," Mohammed had said. "She is the widow of a great leader of Islam. Can we tell her that our word as Nubians is not to be honored?"

Faced with a phalanx of his relatives and friends, Jalal could not hold out. He reluctantly agreed to go through a mock ceremony. After all, honor—and money—were at stake.

On a beautiful sunny winter afternoon, the Begum, accompanied by her party from Paris and three archeologists (one of them a French acquaintance of ours), stepped out of a white launch onto the same stone wall where we were later to land with the children.

She was escorted to a little roofed pavilion of palm fronds which had been erected on the dune below Saleh's house, facing the river, in order to receive properly such an honored grest.

The bride Naima, in borrowed finery and gold jewelry, was properly shy (and confused); Jalal, the groom, handsome and brooding in a suitably romantic way (he was very angry). The dancing to the beat of the big flat drums was spectacular, our friend told us later, the music on the flutes and tamburas of the best.

At dusk, when the sun dropped behind the mountains, suffusing the sky with gold and crimson, the happy couple was escorted to their nuptial chamber near the *diwani*, which had been decorated with a magnificent collection of reed plates (gleaned from all the houses in the village). Pleased with the proceedings, the Begum provided a wedding gift of one hundred and fifty Egyptian pounds (about $400) before traveling back to the temple by moonlight.

Jalal returned to his job in a Cairo textile factory. Naima resumed her household duties in her uncle Saleh's house. And the hundred and fifty pounds? The Begum's chance generosity inadvertently caused long-buried trouble to erupt between the family of Saleh and the family of Jalal.

As the eldest, Saleh became the guardian of the money. Abdul Majid, the groom's brother, was the first to object. The money should be left with a neutral party, he said, to purchase household belongings when Jalal and Naima were properly married. Had the money not been given to the couple? Saleh, after all, was the brother of the bride's father and could be expected to take her side if any dispute should arise.

Naima's mother suggested that half the money should be given to her daughter now, to buy jewelry and clothing. For what if the real marriage never took place? Jalal had left too abruptly, people were saying. Was Naima to be shamed before her relatives and friends, her reputation marred for going through a mock wedding ceremony? She should at least have some of the money.

Saleh, enraged, pointed out that the bride was living in his house. Was he likely to cheat a beloved niece by blood on his father's side? Furthermore, he had also raised the groom Jalal and his brother Abdul Majid as his own sons when their mother died and their father had gone to Cairo. Had he, Saleh, and his wife, Hanim Ali, not worked for this marriage for years, believing it to be the best thing for the children they loved?

Abdulla was called in as mediator. His solution was to keep the money intact until Jalal could be consulted. To this, all parties agreed. Saleh said he would give the money into Abdulla's safekeeping until Jalal decided definitely what he wanted to do about the marriage. But Saleh did not give up the money to Abdulla, as promised.

"It's his wife, Hanim Ali!" whispered someone. "She won't let him give it up."

To avoid an open clash, the mediator suggested the matter be dropped momentarily, in view of Saleh's and Hanim Ali's years of devotion to the young couple in question. The men sympathized with Saleh, who had always had difficulty keeping Hanim Ali in a proper wifely position of subservience. Perhaps the women may have sympathized a little with Hanim Ali in her effort to bring Jalal back into the community. It was getting harder and harder, the people said, to persuade the young men who went away to work to return to Erd-Moz and wed their cousins, the proper and expected Nubian marriage.

By the time I arrived in Erd-Moz, the Begum's present and the controversy over the marriage had been sources of fascinating conversation for more than a year.

Jalal gave one excuse after another for not coming. His most recent was that he could not get a three-week leave from his job.

"He needs three weeks to get married?" Bob asked.

"It is the custom," explained Mohammed. "People would not approve otherwise."

But it was easier for Jalal, far away in Cairo. He did not have to listen, day by day, to the gossip. With only seventy households in Erd-Moz, each household knew everyone else's business intimately and had plenty of time to talk. The fact that two of the oldest and largest of the village families were involved only added spice to the discussion.

Further, this marriage raised many basic questions. To whom did Abdul Majid and Jalal owe first loyalty—to their absent father with another family in Cairo?

Or to Saleh, who had raised and supported them in the years after their mother died? This was a theme that touched many houses in Erd-Moz, for Abdul Majid's father was not the only migrant laborer who had gone to the city to work and had left a wife and children behind. Some sent money regularly to support their families. Some did not. What about inheritance, palm trees, parts of plots of land, shares in a donkey, a water wheel?

Talking out Jalal's and Naima's quandary in every possible variation was a good way of lightening one's own burden of sadness, guilt, uncertainty about the future.

"Why is your father so opposed to the marriage?" Bob asked Abdul Majid.

"He hates Hanim Ali," responded Abdul Majid promptly.

"Didn't she treat you well as children?"

"Oh, yes," said Abdul Majid. "She was very good to us, but we respected her, we never loved her. Believe me, Bob, with all my schooling, I haven't the wits to think like Hanim Ali."

Karim pressed on. What was the source, then, of this violent feeling between Jalal's father and Hanim Ali? Hanim Ali was hated simply because she was intelligent? It did not seem logical, said Karim.

Abdul Majid was a tall man, a handsome man, but his short neat beard hid a weak chin. He hesitated before answering.

"My father thinks women like Hanim Ali are bad for men." He smiled, a bit sheepishly. "They take a man's strength, he says, like a scorpion sucks your blood. Well," and he lit a cigarette, inhaling deeply before going on, "and is he wrong? Look at the way she runs Saleh now! You must have women like that in America."

"Oh, yes," Bob answered, "in English we would say it's the woman who wears the pants in that family."

Bob's remark puzzled Abdul Majid, but only for a moment (in Nubia both men *and* women wear long full underpants and long, full overgarments). Suddenly he guffawed delightedly at this new twist which Bob had contributed to the discussion.

The little joke, rephrased suitably to fit its Nubian context, went all over Erd-Moz in the next two days.

"Have you heard that in Saleh's house, it's Hanim Ali who wears the turban?" giggled the staid old widow Fatooma to a teatime ladies' group, and the audience had dissolved in laughter.

What was Jalal going to do?

Abdul Majid went to Cairo and visited his brother. "I don't know," he reported gloomily. "Jalal is spending half his salary on whiskey! He never drank before. My father's hammering him on one side, Saleh on the other, he's so depressed he can't take it much longer. He says he doesn't want to marry anybody, ever."

And what of Naima, the bride? Throughout the months of gossip, she went about her housework unconcernedly. Only once had she spoken of the situation, to Mona and me while we sat together one afternoon in our courtyard, peeling and eating, with pinches of coarse salt, sweet lemons that had ripened on Saleh's tree. "I've known for years I was to marry Jalal," she said calmly. "My aunt

Hanim Ali wants it, and she runs the house. Why should I worry about it? It is not my decision."

Saleh's cow calved; old Aisha, the midwife, went to Cairo for a cataract operation; Ramadan, Moslem month of fasting, was in progress. Each evening before sunset, Abdulla would walk to the veranda of Saleh's house and stand quietly while a few people gathered. He would raise a hand before him while the sun disappeared behind the black mountains, and then he would call, in a strong, full voice:

"God! There is No God but God!
And Mohammed is his Prophet!"

The prayer sigualed the end of the daily fast, the beginning of the *iftar* meal, the dancing, the feasting, the music and the talking which followed late into the night.

Saleh kept the Begum's wedding gift and Jalal did not come.


An Egyptian psychiatrist, trained at the Sorbonne, once declared to me that he longed to live the life of his peasant countrymen, the fellaheen.

"Their life is so simple," he said.

I raised an eyebrow. "Simple? I think it must be very difficult," remembering the crowded Delta villages, the dawn-to-dark toiling in the fields.

The psychiatrist considered. "Physically difficult, perhaps, but emotionally simple. The sun, the moon, the earth, the flooding of the Nile." He sighed. "Just think of it, madame! A wife, a child, a loaf of country bread, some beans, tea, a few peasant customs, of course. What a marvelously uncomplicated life." His dark intelligent eyes in the worldly face were troubled. "No neuroses," he added.

"None at all?"

He shook his handsome head. "They have no real problems, you see. They are swept along inexorably by the rhythm of their magnificently natural routine."

Now, in Erd-Moz, as I watched the maneuvering, the scheming of Hanim Ali as she strove to drive on her husband, threaten her nephew and deceive everyone else, in a mighty effort to reach a single goal—the marriage of Naima and Jalal—I wondered what my psychiatrist friend might say. The sun rose a little earlier as spring approached, it waxed hotter over the plots of millet and wheat, ripening the dates, the mangoes, the pomegranates, bringing the acacias to bloom. Hanim Ali could do nothing about the sun or the moon, either. It rose gloriously, pouring silvery light on the villages behind the temple of Abu Simbel, and during its brief period of ascendancy, dulling the thick stars that filled the wide sky.

The flooding of the Nile? Someone had already begun to change that, without Hanim Ali's help, as the Aswan Dam rose higher and higher north of the first cataract.

But between the rise of the sun and the rise of the moon, while the fields were flooding, Hanim Ali worked hard. She persuaded Saleh to go to Cairo himself to see Jalal.

The women of Abdul Majid's house whispered nastily that Saleh was "doing Hanim Ali's business."

Because we came upon her one day in the back court with the wooden lids off her storage jars, her scales in the center of the room, we knew that Hanim Ali was remeasuring her hoard of dates, figuring out again just how much currency she had to trade at Mekki's boat for the extra sugar, extra tea, extra butter needed for the wedding and the seven days of feasting.

"Hanim Ali has to buy things for Naima's household," explained Khadija, seeing my eye drop to those piles of dates.

But even Fatima, the most kindhearted and easygoing of women, hinted that Hauim Ali, at the prospect of spending the Begum's generous gift, was getting rather inflated ideas.

"She wants Naima to have new pots, new dishes, all right, but a kerosene stove?"

"What if they don't marry after all?" asked Mona.

Fatima explained that the money would have to be divided some way between the two families.

"If the wedding does take place, Naima will get it all?"

"Yes," said Fatima. "For the bride price, the household, and so on, it's the custom for most of the money to go to the bride's family. But who in Erd-Moz has ever had a kerosene stove, I ask you? Primuses were always good enough for us before."

When we visited Abdul Majid's house, Sherifa could barely suppress her rage against Hanim Ali.

"Who cares about kerosene stoves?" she cried when Mona mentioned this rumor. "Hanim Ali" (she fairly spat the two short words), Hanim Ali is ruining poor Jalal's life. Everyone knows he wants to marry my sister and not that nitwit Naima. Isn't that true, Mona? Haven't you heard that, Beeja? Beryl?"

Mona and Beryl and I said nothing. These were the occasions when I was glad for the inevitable interruptions provided by the children. But Laura Ann had disappeared into an inner room and Davy was calmly juggling a few date pits.

"I mean, my sister is no genius either," Sherifa hastened to add, filling the silence which she wrongly assumed meant we were politely not mentioning the fact that her sister was considered not quite bright. "At least my sister is prettier. Naima is so awfully *plain*. Don't you think so?"

"Uh—er . . ." stammered Mona.

"Owwwww! Oooooh! Mama! Mama!"

I could scarcely restrain a smile at that howl from Laura Ann. She had saved us again. Beryl and Mona quickly jumped to their feet.

"What is it?"

"What is it, Laura Ann dear?"

Laura Ann was carried out to me with so much fanfare she was undecided whether to stop crying or continue her howling so that more attention would be forthcoming.

It was not serious. She ran back to play. Meanwhile the awkward moment had passed when we should have made some specific response to Sherifa's angry remarks.

"Who knows what is destined to happen in this world?" asked Mona noncommittally.

"Who knows?" repeated Sherifa. She laughed harshly. "Hanim Ali knows. She *makes* it happen."

What about the magnificent natural routine theory in this case, I thought.

"Jalal is coming soon," Hanim Ali announced brightly, when she went with the women to gather fuel and fodder in the mountains behind the village houses.

"Oh, no, he isn't," said the widow Fatooma. "His father won't let him, Sherifa says so."

Hanim Ali pretended not to hear this kind of remark

"We will have a wedding when Ramadan is finished," she said, when she went down the hill to feed the cow.

People began to believe her. Hanim Ali, I saw, was one of those vital forces in the social mechanism. Bearer of tradition and sometime manipulator of tradition, it was she, more intelligent and forceful than average, who dimly perceived the reasons and uses for the "peasant customs" which were actually a far more complicated web than my Egyptian psychiatrist friend with his good French education would have guessed.

It was not easy to keep the fabric of tradition and order intact, as the marriage in question demonstrated. Familial ties were loosening with the migrations of men away from home; it was hard for children when their fathers were away for years, it was hard for women to be without their husbands. Naima and Jalal were both products of such disrupted families. Jalal's father had gone to Cairo, married there and had not returned; Naima's father had "gone bad" in the Sudan and had never come home again.

"Why," Hanim Ali explained to Mona, "none of this trouble between our families would have happened if the men hadn't stayed away from the blessed land so long and learned the evil ways of the city."

I admired Hanim Ali's determination, but I saw, too, that in the manner of her mending of the family rupture, her doing what she felt had to be done, she was becoming heartily hated by everyone.

It depended whose side you were on, whether you viewed Hanim Ali as a conserver of tradition or, as Jalal's father had said, a scorpion of a greedy, overbearing woman. The munificent gift of the Begum gave her activities an ambiguous motivation, to say the least.

"Naima and Jalal will have a *proper* wedding," said Hanim Ali proudly, as she bargained with the merchant Mekki for a pile of powdered henna leaves to complete the traditional bridal baths. "Someone has to show people so they will remember, in Kom Ombo, how to give *their* daughters proper Nubian weddings."

Understandably, the other ladies on Mekki's deck, waiting their turn to be served, sniffed at this overweening statement. Abdul Majid's wife, Sherifa, even tried a giggle, but Hanim Ali paid no attention. She counted out her dates into Mekki's scales, set the basket of green henna powder on her head and sailed grandly past Sherifa without a glance.

At dinner, Bob and Karim reported that among the men they had found the same air of suppressed excitement: "Will Hanim Ali win? Will Jalal come?"

That night the nearly wornout Bach tape, which Karim faithfully rewound each evening by hand, was superseded by Saleh's announcement with the coffee.

"Jalal is arriving tomorrow on the express boat!"

"Wonderful!" we chorused, but we were not too impressed. For the last five days the word had been that Jalal would be here "tomorrow."

"*Enshallah* he will come!" offered Karim.

"He will," asserted Saleh "He has never broken his word to me."

"Would you like me to take you to Abu Simbel in the motorboat and bring him back in style?" asked Bob.

"No, thank you," said Saleh.

In the morning we discovered he had left by donkey for Benha, the boat's first stop in Ballana province. Saleh was not giving his nephew any opportunity to get off the boat early and shirk his duty at the last moment by disappearing into the desert.

"What will they do *now* if he doesn't come?" asked Beryl.

We all wondered. If, after all this advance publicity, the day of the marriage announcement set and even the henna purchased, Jalal should fail to appear, relations between the two families would be severely strained. Saleh would be humiliated and Hanim Ali's reputation ruined forever. A major squabble was sure to erupt if the Begum's gift would, in the end, have to be divided. Many people in Erd-Moz would not be too unhappy to see proud Hanim Ali brought low and even Saleh, but a serious break between two large families would take years to mend and would be bad for the peace of the entire village.

At teatime Saleh had not returned.

"The boat may be late," said Karim.

But he still had not returned at dusk, and I could feel the tension in Naima herself when she brought the lanterns. After a makeshift dinner, served by Khadija (we did not dare to ask whether Saleh had returned), Mona announced she would go into Saleh's kitchen and make us some decent coffee.

She was back more quickly than it would have taken to light the fire, much less boil the water.

"He's come! He's come!" she cried. "You should have seen! There was Jalal, Hanim Ali with both arms around him, weeping. Saleh was crying too."

"Saleh did bring them both up, after all," pointed out Karim.

"Yes, and obviously they care for him," said Mona. "We pick away at their motives, but think how much this marriage must mean to them, childless as they are."

In the flush of her triumph, Hanim Ali gave in on one point: The *samma*, or marriage announcement, and the cleaning of the grain for the marriage bread would take place, not in her house, but in the house of Jalal's brother, Abdul Majid. This was considered a gesture on Saleh's part, to give Abdul Majid some sense of having participated, in place of their father, in the wedding of his brother.

Three hundred-pound sacks of grain were brought from Saleh's house to that of Abdul Majid. Sherifa, now that all had been definitely settled, swallowed her pride, her dislike of Hanim Ali's bossing, and supervised the ceremony.

In the court lay yellow heaps of grain, shades lighter than the sand. The women and girls in their black garments picked out the big pieces of mud, they tossed the grain on the orange and purple and beige plates, and while they worked, they sang, trilling happily in anticipation of the commg marriage.

"All the married women in the village came except four; two were sick, one was away, and one is very old," said Hanim Ali, pleased.

At lunch Bob asked, "How is the bride-to-be taking all this?"

Mona and Beryl and I glanced at each other. We did not know. No one had asked her. Naima had sat in a corner of the court while the women cleaned the grain, and we had heard Hanim Ali speaking sharply to her.

"She was telling her to be quiet, and not to laugh so loud," said Khadija. "Hanim Ali," and she smiled a bit, "is determined that my sister Naima shall be the politest, quietest, most proper bride ever seen in Erd-Moz!"

"What about the bride's own mother? Doesn't she resent Hanim Ali?" Karim wanted to know.

We had asked about that, for it was well known that the real celebrators and enjoyers of a Nubian wedding were the mother of the bride and the mother of the groom. To cement the always tenuous ties of the family in the ceremony of a good marriage was the mothers' triumph, product of years of child raising and hard work. This was the moment when they were congratulated on their efforts by other members of the community, who brought food for the feast, small presents for the married couple. The mothers had done their duties, helped work to provide gifts for daughters, bride prices for sons, provided some future for children and grandchildren and at the same time assured themselves of a refuge in old age.

"Naima's mother is luckier than Hanim Ali," pointed out Mona. "She has already married two daughters. She's letting Hanim Ali have the pleasure of this one wedding. It will be all she has."

Crack! The shotguns being fired outside meant that the prayers, the promises before the official (the *mazoom*) were finished and the marriage contract was actually signed. The air was filled with the women's ululations and we went next door to congratulate Naima.

"Stay and have sherbet," urged Dahiba.

Saleh brought into the court the suitcase of gifts which Jalal was presenting to his bride and her family. What had he brought? A gift of $100 and two gold necklaces; two black *gargaras*, three cotton dresses, a black woolen shawl, plastic shoes, three head scarves, two bottles of perfume and two new sets of underwear (ruffled pantalettes and slips, blue and green). Presents for Hanim Ali, her co-wife Dahiba, for Naima's sister Khadija, for his uncle Saleh. The pièce de résistance (admired loudly, "*Allah! Allah!*" by everyone) was a tea service: twelve teacups and saucers, a teapot, milk jug and sugar bowl of beautiful white, gold-rimmed china!

At the end of the first day of celebrations, nine and a half pounds of tea and fifty-five pounds of sugar had been consumed, to say nothing of the dates and the sherbet.

"We borrowed every cup and glass in Erd-Moz," Hanim Ali told me jubilantly. "The girls were here washing dishes till almost midnight."

Her head scarf was a bit bedraggled from the long day's work, but her eyes were shining with pleasure and the two coquettish wings of dyed hair were still in place on her forehead, held firmly by the paste of henna.

In the morning, wedding bread was baked in both the bride's and the groom's house, the sisters and cousins bending over the clay hearths, cooking hundreds of flat loaves from the grain that had been cleaned and then ground at the mill in the village across the river. When had they had time to do that? Between afternoon and late evening, it seemed, Saleh had gone over to the mill in a felucca. This was the bread that would be used for the wedding feast and, on the seventh day after the marriage, sent folded to every house in the village.

Mona and Beryl and I walked with the children between the houses.

In the *diwani* Fatima and Dahiba were giving Naima a ritual henna bath, the first of three. Wearing old clothes, Naima sat quietly while the henna powder, mixed into a greenish paste with herbs and oil of clove, was applied like a mud pack to her arms, legs, back, chest, face. Little chips of sandalwood burning in a tiny earthen bowl scented the room.

Laura Ann looked on with curiosity.

"Laura Ann," buck-toothed Dahiba actually smiled, infected with the nuptial excitement. "We will wash it off tomorrow and make her pretty."

"Let's go to Jalal's house and see *his* henna bath," said Mona.

Jalal, slim and dark in his spotless white *gullabiya* and skullcap, was seated on a new mat in his aunt Hanim Ali's house, flanked by his brother, Abdul Majid, his friends Mohammed and Abdulla. A cigarette jiggled between his fingers; between puffs, he joked with the young girls and women crowding into the court to watch this long-awaited henna ceremony.

> "Take up your golden knife
> And cut down the fronds
> Of your grandfather's green palm trees."

His sister-in-law Sherifa had begun, in a low, sweet voice, the very ancient song of the bridegroom, prince of the village for the days of his wedding. The women responded, humming, and Sherifa sang,

> "Mount your white donkey, oh, bridegroom, oh, prince,
> And all of your relatives will follow you with singing."

Hanim Ali stepped forward, the pot of henna in her hand, ready to officiate for Jalal in place of his dead mother. A thumbprint of perfumed green paste on his forehead, a dot under his skullcap.

> "You bask in golden light," sang Sherifa,
> "The bright light of honor,
> The honor of your family. . . ."

> "Your great-grandfather Hamza," chanted the women,
> "Your grandfather Ali Daoud,
> Your father Mohammed. . ."

Hanim Ali bent and placed a handful of henna in each of Jalal's slender hands, and with her gnarled brown ones she closed his fingers over the paste. It would harden quickly. He would hold luck and richness in his hands.

> "Go take your golden knife
> And cut down the fronds
> Of your grandfather's green palm trees."

Jalal smiled nervously, his fists clenched over the henna, nodding at Abdul Majid, Mohammed and Abdulla, the prince bridegroom's courtiers for the wedding.

"Oh, my son!" began Hanim Ali, her brown weathered face puckered with emotion, her voice breaking as she placed a print of henna on the soles of Jalal's feet.

"Oh, my son!" she straightened up and her high, thin old voice emerged,

> "Oh, my son, you are nobler than pashas,
> Oh, my son, you are first among men."

Sherifa scattered grain over anointed Jalal, the good millet fruit of the Nile silt soil. She scattered the grain over the heads of the unmarried girls gathered round, waiting for a bit of the bridegroom's handfuls of henna paste, a bit for good luck, to harden in their hands and bring a fruitful marriage to them also.

In her bedroom, Naima slept in henna, and was bathed in fresh water early in the morning.

This was her wedding day. After the second application of the henna, a small stick dipped in the hot blood of the calf, slaughtered at dawn for the wedding feast, was shown to her.

"From this moment she is a real bride," quoted Hanim Ali with satisfaction, placing a black shawl over Naima's head, as though the sight of the fresh blood was something so foreign to a young girl's eyes that from now on until the consummation of her marriage she would not be allowed to look upon anything else.

This was Naima's wedding day. Her face veiled by the black shawl, her body covered with thick henna paste under her old clothes, she sat in the closed bridal bedroom off the *diwani*. People came all day to congratulate her and to bring presents, which Hanim Ali and Sherifa carefully recorded in their notebooks, but Naima did not look at the gifts: a goat, a chicken, sacks of dates, small gifts of money.

The butchered calf was cooking in brass pots over many fires. The wedding feast was served.

But Naima sat veiled in the bridal bedroom in her henna, after seeing the blood of the slaughtered calf. Only in the evening when the feast was finished, and people had set off for the dancing in the wide plain of sand below the village, when the boom! boom! boom! of the giant flat drums could be heard in every corner of Erd-Moz, it was then, and only then that Naima was brought into the limelight once more.

Old widow Fatooma, one of the few women in Erd-Moz who had made the pilgrimage to Mecca, was brought into the closed bridal bedroom to take the cover from a great copper pot of water. That morning after the slaughter of the calf, the water had been brought from the river by Fatima and Nezla, two respectable women whose first children were still alive. (Harim Ali was determined that each detail of the ritual be observed!)

Old widow Fatooma first sprinkled Naima with the river water, she poured the pot of water over the bride. Naima's body hair was removed ceremonially, with a sugar and water and lemon solution. She was bathed once more, her skin carefully dried and massaged.

"Henna is the best cleanser in the world!" pronounced Hanim Ali.

Naima's skin glowed with a lovely red cast.

"Henna is good for our brownness," agreed Khadija.

New clothes were placed on Naima, the groom's offerings, green ruffled pantalettes and slip, a flowered cotton dress, a black silk *gargara*, a black head scarf, gold necklaces, plastic shoes. A clean white veil and then a black one were placed over her head.

Boom! Boom! Boom!

The drumbeats were louder, the stars winking, the lanterns flickering red in the sand, the brush fires lighted and held up in handfuls to tighten with heat the skin of the great drums. Every night since the cleaning of the grain and the signing of the marriage contract there had been dancing, but this, the wedding night, was the most important, the climax of the ceremony. Every able-bodied man in Erd-Moz moved in the huge circle on the sand. They clapped for the measured line dance, a shuffle back and forth, the circle of men weaving back and forth on the sand, singing as they moved.

The women danced behind, in groups of four and five, in twos and threes, their hands locked together at their sides, red-and-gold-striped silk scarves tossed over their black veiled heads. So measured and controlled was their dance that the loose silk scarves never slipped, but only moved as they moved, to the drumbeat and the singing. Gold gleamed in the firelight, with the fine-boned brown faces, the white teeth, the white drums held high, boom, boom, boom above the white turbans, the white *gullabiyas*, the brilliant silk scarves flashing. The people of Erd-Moz were dancing, dancing on the sand.

> "Go take your golden knife
> And cut down the fronds
> Of your grandfather's green palm trees."

Older women moved through the line, without losing a beat, to dance within the circle of men. The circle broke; rows of girls and young married women formed; they danced toward and away from the singing men.

> "Oh, my son, I would keep you beside me
> Tie you with my necklaces of gold
> Keep you like the red-gold shawl
>       I wear upon my head."

Hanim Ali, I noticed, was dancing by herself.

"She is not from Erd-Moz," explained Fatima. "Hanim's from the other bank

of the Nile, she didn't dance with the girls here when she was young, so she
has no partner.''

Hanim Ali was all alone.

The song, the flares, the dancing, the stars. The moon had risen and set.

Hanim Ali danced on, facing the drums and the light of the flares. She was
old; she complained of headache and racking stomach pain; she would probably
not dance at many more weddings.

> "Go take your golden knife. . . .''

Naima sat in the bridal bedroom off the *diwani*, the white veil and the black
over her head, the women taking turns sitting with her so she should not be
completely alone.

Hanim Ali's face seemed calm in the firelight, without the jubilance I had noticed
earlier in the day. The ideal for which she had worked so long was almost a reality.

Children slept on the sand. Fatima lay down to rest and I sat beside her.

"Oh, God, I'm tired,'' breathed Fatima.

"Why don't you go home?'' I asked.

"Go home? Who wants to go home?''

"Sit then,'' said Mona, "and rest from the dancing.''

"But if I don't dance at Naima's wedding, I can't expect Naima and Khadija
to dance at Gamal's wedding,'' she explained.

"Gamal is only six!'' exclaimed Beryl.

"I know, I know.'' Fatima wiped her sweating face, adjusted her veil, and
rose to her feet. "But Naima will remember, and do you think Hanim Ali would
ever forget?''

She giggled at us, took a deep breath and found her place in the dance line
once more.

We went to bed late, the boom of the drums in our ears, but we were wakened
again by the trilling cries of the women,

> "Go take your golden knife
> And cut down the fronds
> Of your ancestors' green palm trees.''

The bridegroom was being danced to his bride. Ahead of him was Ahmed,
the "forever man,'' who cried, at each step, the name of each member of the
bride's family, the groom's family, alive and dead.

"Hamza,'' "Ali Daoud,'' "Daoud Mohammed.''

The forever man chanted on and on, for Naima's and Jalal's family trees were
long, ancient and well remembered.

To the drumbeat and the chanting the bridegroom was being danced to his bride.

And was it finished? Not at all. The Nubians do not hurry with important
matters, Fatima had long ago explained to me.

"Everything has its time. Marriage is difficult for a girl, and for a man. Things
go slowly. We give it time.''

The bridegroom slept in the *diwani* with several of his relatives and friends.

But the bride slept in the closed bridal bedroom in her wedding finery, her girl friends and relatives around her.

The bridal couple, Jalal and Naima, had not yet even glimpsed each other in all the four days of ceremonies.

Before breakfast, I heard Fatima and Wahiba passing our door. Beryl, Mona and I followed the girls to the *diwani* where they had come to dance for the bridegroom and his friends. This, too, was a ritual, but a gay one, to occupy the eager groom, keep his natural frustration within bounds while the third and final henna bath took place nearby in the bridal bedroom. Naima's dark hair was oiled and combed and perfumed, her smooth brown body was bathed in incense and another set of new clothes donned.

Formal noon prayers in the *diwani* were followed by lunch. The guests departed.

Old widow Fatooma took off Naima's dark black veil; she placed a white veil over the bride's head, raised the girl up. She opened the door and led the bride out of secluded darkness into the sunlight of noon on the threshold of the bridal *diwani* where her groom Jalal awaited her. The reed plates on the wall glowed orange and purple in the sunlight, the mock chandeliers swayed gently, the white shells clacked softly above the new bridal mat, where the groom Jalal sat intensely upright, staring at the threshold where shy Naima on the arm of Fatooma had stumbled and regained her balance.

Hanim Ali brought forward a plate of grain and sweets and handed it to Jalal. He filled his hands with the grain and emptied them into the white-veiled bride's hands, who sat with head bent, her hands over the plate. Seven times he filled his hands with grain and seven times she emptied them back into the plate.

"Grain is good," pronounced Hanim Ali with satisfaction. "It brings luck and sweetness and richness to the bride."

Jalal solemnly scattered sweets and a few coins about the room. Hanim Ali, the bride's mother, Khadija, her sister, Sherifa, her bridegroom's brother's wife, and old widow Fatooma accepted the sweets, congratulated the couple and withdrew. The door was shut, to remain shut until the following morning.

Naima and Jalal were alone.

"Will Jalal sleep with his bride immediately?" Mona asked Hanim Ali.

She looked shocked and pursed her lips.

"Some do, of course," she allowed, "but a good and decent bridegroom waits until night falls, and in the meantime tries to put his bride at ease. Our girls are modest; they are shy being alone with a man for the first time and they resist as long as possible. That is the way we bring them up, and a good thing, too."

In the morning, the bride and groom would take their ritual ablutions after intercourse and wash their faces and hands in river water before being served breakfast.

Hanim Ali and Sherifa took the wedding breakfast milk and butter in an earthen bowl, Khadija carried the fresh-baked bread.

Hanim Ali's face was drawn with tension and fatigue, but her eyes were still bright.

She bristled at me, "These young people! I tried to get Naima to go down to the river and wash as *we* used to do, but she wouldn't. That girl is so *lazy*."

"Of course, in the old days we lived closer to the river," she admitted. "I still remember. . ."

Her eyes looked beyond us, her harsh face softened.

"On my wedding morning Saleh and I went to the river, it was still almost dark, only a little light in the sky."

Her face was open for a moment, open and young, and I saw how she might have been had their marriage been fruitful, not only a determined defender of tradition, but a more personally satisfied member of the community to which she was so devoted.

"Khadija!" She turned from Mona and me and called to Khadija crossing the court, "Don't forget the green palm fronds!"

An edge of irritation was in Khadija's voice. "Yes, *Amitii*, I haven't forgotten, I've already taken them in.

"And you let them burn on the threshold until the fire died by itself?"

"Yes, *Amitii*, yes."

"Why didn't you tell me?" Hanim Ali scolded. "I wanted to see Jalal and Naima step over the burning fronds seven times." She sounded pettish, old.

"It's done, *Amitii*, that is the most important thing," said Khadija in a kind voice.

It was done. More guests were coming to the door with presents for the bride, chickens, pigeons, sacks of flour, trays of dates.

"Where is my notebook?" wailed Hanim Ali. "I have to write down all these presents!"

She was gone.

Five days of ceremonies and feasting, and more to come, but the greater part of the ritual was finished. She, Hanim Ali, had done it, almost singlehandedly, although Saleh and the Begum Agha Khan had helped. Hanim Ali's incipient neurosis, as my Egyptian psychiatrist friend would have refused to define it (peasants have no problems), had been happily averted. Social harmony had been restored. Naima and Jalal were united in marriage. The magnificent natural routine had been re-established once more.

# Chapter 7

# Amulets and Omens, Signs and Wonders

I said, "I don't think I should leave the children."

"Mona and I'll stay," offered Beryl. "We've been to Abu Simbel. You haven't."

"Go, B.J.," urged Mona. "The temple should be wonderful tonight."

I hesitated. Laura Ann was coughing again, yet Davy's wheeze was no worse than usual, and neither child had fever. Tonight Abu Simbel was to be specially illuminated for UNESCO visitors who had arrived that afternoon by private steamer. Abdul Wahad, a famous Nubian singer, had come from Aswan to entertain the party; there would be Nubian dancing, and Mohammed, our friend Mohammed from Erd-Moz, was to play his new compositions on the tambura before the British and Egyptian television cameras.

"Come on, B.J.," said Bob. "This may be your last chance to see Abu Simbel in all its glory. I promised Dr. Zaki faithfully I'd have you back in Cairo a month before the baby's due. You'll have to go soon."

I did not want to leave Erd-Moz, but I had to go while I could still travel without worry. I did not feel as cumbersome as with David and Laura Ann, and for that I could thank the life in Erd-Moz. The minimal diet, the walking on sand, the sitting and squatting had not been easy, but it had been good for my lazy muscles, an excellent, if sometimes unwelcome, antidote to the lassitude of pregnancy. We had been so busy during my months in the village, that, although we had planned to go several times, we had never made the promised private visit to Abu Simbel.

Yes, I thought, I'll go.

Down the shadowy dunes, through the whispering palm groves, we threaded our way to the river. It was a moonless night. The outlines of the mountains on the opposite shore had long ago disappeared into the darkness, and the boundary between land and river was marked only by the vague movement of water against the quiet shore.

"I don't like it," said Mohammed, looking up at the sky where shifting clouds masked the stars. "Smells like a sandstorm, or some kind of storm."

"A sandstorm this time of year?" asked Bob. "That means choppy water, then. Maybe we shouldn't try it, Mohammed."

Mohammed was silent. He wore a newly wrapped white turban, a pale blob before me in the night, and he clutched his tambura under his arm, that five-stringed homemade instrument from which he could coax the most joyous or the most plaintive of music. I knew he wanted to go badly for it was he who had first suggested the trip to Bob; it was not often he had an opportunity to play for an audience such as was assembled tonight at Abu Simbel.

"What do you think, Abdulla?" he asked, passing on the responsibility for undertaking the trip.

Abdulla must have known how much Mohammed wanted to go; he knew, too, the vagaries and dangers of the river in storm.

"We can try, Bob," said Abdulla softly. "But I don't like the sky either," he added as we climbed into the *Susan*.

I said nothing, trying not to imagine how a sandstorm might affect allergic asthma. Mohammed had said earlier it would take at least an hour to reach the temple, three miles to the north. I huddled deeper into my coat, leaning away from the wind which was pulling the waves up into miniature whitecaps and slapping the troubled water against the sides of the *Susan*.

Bob was steering a straight course downstream toward a glow in the sky, a line of light rimming the back of the mountain within which the rock temples lay. While we chugged steadily ahead, the glow gradually widened, the sky seemed lighter, and fragments of music and bits of conversations began to reach us across the tossing water.

"Oh! Look!"

The involuntary cry was Bob's. Rounding the lip of the mountain unexpectedly, in one brief second we had been catapulted from darkness into a blaze of incandescent daylight.

Abdulla and Mohammed leaned forward in the boat and stared at the splendor of the temple which they had lived beside all their lives, but perhaps had never really seen thus as itself before, so much was Abu Simbel a part of the mountain, the colossi of Ramses a rest stop on the dune paths to the river from the villages over the hill, the shaded courtyard beside the acacia tree an oasis between the grazing pastures of goats.

"*Yallah*, Bob!" cried Mohammed. "Let's *go!*"

Bob turned the boat westward toward the pool of light and sound, the only such splendid man-made display in the thousands of miles of darkness which stretched away on all sides of us.

"This is the BBC," a voice kept saying as we docked.

"Over. Radio Cairo. This is the BBC. Roger."

Colored lights were strung along the masts and decks of the moored feluccas; a row of lanterns on the sand outlined the stage before the temple where deck chairs had been laid out, where the cameras and sound equipment had been set up.

"Now aren't you glad you came?" whispered Bob, taking my hand, and I nodded.

We walked up on the bank. Sudden tongues of wind pushed at us, flickering the lanterns on the shore which, like buoys, marked boundaries against the unknown darkness. None of the guests strayed outside the border of artificial light. They sat in their deck chairs like school children to watch the spectacle they had been brought a thousand miles from Cairo to witness.

"Feel that wind? We mustn't stay too long," cautioned Abdulla.

The wind was colder, it was rising steadily and bringing sand. The audience clapped halfheartedly for Mohammed's new composition on the tambura, for Abdul Wahad, whose songs and tone patterns spoke more to the Nubians than to the foreign visitors.

"*Mesdames et messieurs*," the announcer's voice broke through the applause. "A slight wind has come up, and we therefore cut this delightful program short to allow us time to exercise a very great privilege. Thanks to the generosity of the Egyptian Ministry of Antiquities, we may now tour Abu Simbel, which has been lighted tonight both inside and outside in honor of our esteemed guests."

We stood up and moved obediently toward the temple. Around the narrow door, between the pairs of colossi (my head reached almost to Ramses' stone shin) the family of the Pharaoh Ramses stood out, lighted from behind. There was Tue, his old mother; Nefertari, his wife; the three princesses, the pharaoh-prince son, tiny statues beside the towering figures of the king. The guide pointed out on one of the colossi the famous graffiti of the Greek mercenaries. They had written their names, Archon and Pelekos, on the Pharaoh's stone leg while resting during the Egyptian campaign against the Nubian kingdom, in the sixth century before Christ. We passed into the lofty rock temple, into the mountain itself which had been hollowed out by man.

Eight square pillars rose thirty feet to the ceiling of the great hall, and against the pillars stood Osiris figures of the king, flat and dreamlike despite their height, even in that blazing electric light. The artists of the nineteenth dynasty had recorded on all the walls of the eight chambers the triumphs, the sacrifices, the battles in Ramses II's long reign of almost seventy years. It was a superb tapestry in stone. The king stood, before a lion-headed goddess; he dedicated incense to Ptah; the king knelt under the sacred tree of Heliopolis, in the presence of the god Re-Harakhte, humbling himself only before the deities of his ancestors.

In the corners of the smaller halls flakes of blue and washes of dull red could still be seen, fragments of the paint which once covered all of the inside of the temple when it had been dedicated three thousand years ago.

"It must have been very different then," I said to Bob. "More cheerful."

"Cheerful?"

"Color as opposed to black and white."

''A gayer majesty than this,'' Bob smiled, savoring his bon mot. ''A gayer majesty.''

I smiled, too. The flakes of ancient paint were rough to the touch, but patches of the surface still retained some of the former vividness of color.

''Here you see Ramses' campaign against the Hittites,'' explained the guide; he wore a soft hat, but his voice was loud.

The stone shields of the Egyptian soldiers were arranged around the carved camp in a kind of stockade. Now Ramses emerges from the royal tent, holds council of war with his officers. In his chariot, the king dashes against the enemy line; he aims a monumental stone sword against the Hittite chief. Prisoners are brought before him, roped together, pleading for mercy.

''In the sanctuary of the temple, the most holy part, at certain times of the year, the sun strikes its first rays at the very center of the altar,'' cried the soft-hatted guide. ''The rays are red. It is very remarkable, a trick of the pharaoh's architect.''

We stood on the threshold of the empty sanctuary, tiny and bare. A plain block of stone formed the altar where the sun's rays would strike red. That was all there was, except that the air was close, oppressive, and vaguely perfumed here (from thousand-year-old incense?), one hundred and eighty feet into the mountain from the narrow entrance.

I stirred a bit uneasily, remembering the story of the two veteran American filmmakers who, caught by a light failure here, at the entrance to the sanctuary, had been overwhelmed suddenly, they said, by such great unexplainable fear that they had flung themselves to the floor and then bolted, screaming, for the door.

Bob was whispering with Abdulla. We had to leave now, before the storm worsened. It would take more than two hours to get back to Erd-Moz as it was, for we would be returning upstream and fighting the current and the cross wind all the way.

''He thinks it would be dangerous to wait any longer,'' murmured Bob, taking my arm.

A last quick passing look at the battle reliefs and up to the ceiling, with its carved border of flying vultures. I peered into a side aisle, and there the stone ceiling was still bright with golden stars painted upon a blue sky.

Outside the wind struck us, whipping my coat against my legs. While Mohammed, Bob and Abdulla struggled to get the boat off, someone threw the switch and Abu Simbel lay in shadow. A few lanterns still flickered like fireflies on the sand, the tourist boat sent out weak beams of light from all the cabin windows where presumably the UNESCO guests were preparing for bed in their warm cabins.

Nothing lay ahead of us but fields upon fields of black water. How could Bob find his way back in utter darkness? Larger waves struck us, the boat pitched up and down, backward and forward; the *Susan* turned crazily for a few moments, like a matchstick tossed into an underground pool, and I clung to the sides of the boat, frightened but afraid to cry out. We are surely lost! I wanted to shout.

Yet Bob, with Mohammed's help, steadied the boat and turned us straight south, and then for a long time we heard only the wind, the angry slapping of the water, the feeble mechanical chug of our motors. I closed my eyes and prayed I would not be seasick.

"It seems hours since we left the temple," said Bob. "Aren't we getting near Erd-Moz, Mohammed? Shouldn't I begin to cut over?"

Mohammed shaded his eyes (against what, I wondered), stared into the darkness and conferred with Abdulla.

"A little farther," he answered.

The two Nubians obviously had much better eyesight than I, for I could see nothing anywhere except darkness and emptiness.

"Mohammed," called Bob, "don't forget we have to throw out the anchor behind before we get to shore, or the boat will smash against the stone wall."

I shivered. I stared ahead. It was an act of faith on Bob's part, I thought, to even head inland from the safer reaches of the river when there was nothing to guide him but a dim approaching horizon of the tops of palm trees. But then, we could not stay on the river all night. And what about the children?

"Now, Bob!" shouted Abdulla. "The anchor."

"No," contradicted Mohammed. "Not now. Where's the shore?"

"Now!" shouted Abdulla. "Throw it. We're going to hit!"

Mohammed tossed the anchor into the water, at the same moment the prow of the boat whammed against the unseen wall, and Bob, clambering quickly out to grab the prow before it cracked on the stone again, caught his leg between the wall and the banging side of the boat.

"Ow!" he hollered. "Damn it!" and it took all three of us, pushing the boat away from the wall against the force of the wind, to free his leg. Thankfully, it was not broken, only badly bruised.

By the time we had climbed the dune, we were exhausted.

Beryl was waiting up for us by lantern light.

"Both children seem very hot," she said.

They had fevers of 103, 104. Davy, wheezing, cried out in his sleep. Laura Ann's cough had deepened and she rattled with each breath.

"I think I *must* go back to Cairo this time," I said. "The sandstorm will make everything worse."

We stood in the open court, shivering in the wind as the tourists had shivered outside the temple of Abu Simbel.

"We'll see," Bob said brusquely. His leg was paining him a great deal, I could tell. "I'll go for the doctor in the morning if we can get the boat off."

"But I must leave," I repeated. "I *must*. Don't you see?"

"Yes, yes." He limped into our room.

Through the wall of the children's bedroom, the wheeze reached us, one wheeze, Laura Ann, another wheeze, Davy.

Beryl said, "We better all go to bed, B.J."

Next morning, while we dressed the children, a great commotion arose outside. Women were hurrying past the house and Khadija, with Abdul Nasr on one arm, banged on our door.

"A child of Fatima's has just died," she cried. "I don't know which one. I must go to her. Are you coming with me?"

"Khadija, I can't now," I answered.

She looked at me briefly before joining the crowd of women who were emerging from the streets on the lower dunes, from doors all along our street, and with black head scarves hastily thrown over their heads, were heading for Fatima's house.

"B.J., you must go, too," said Bob. "Khadija is right."

I stared at him. I knew that in Erd-Moz the obligations after death were rigid; one must appear at the house of the deceased as soon as possible. Fatima was my friend, but this morning how could I go to her? I was needed here.

Bob said sensibly, "While you're condoling with Fatima, Beryl can watch the children, and I'll take the boat with Karim and get the doctor from Benha."

"I don't care what he says, I'm going anyway."

"Don't be silly, B.J. You might do the children greater harm by leaving."

"Really?" I cried bitterly. "Really, do you think they'd be better off here in these drafty rooms than in a cabin on the boat?"

"Shhh! People are staring."

"I don't care." My only instinct was to do something, anything.

"We'll abide by the doctor's decision," Bob said firmly.

To my surprise, I burst into tears.

"Go on!" Bob practically shouted at me. "Fatima lost a child this morning. Think of her instead of yourself for a change."

"Let the children sit on the sunny side, out of the wind," I said to Beryl, wiping my eyes on her proffered handkerchief, "although," I added, "I don't know why I'm telling you, Beryl, since you suggested it in the first place."

"Never mind, B.J., go on, they'll be all right."

Mona and I set off together, down the street to the familiar green door where Fatima was receiving mourners outside her house.

"Fatima!" Mona and then I embraced her, a ritual act after death.

I drew back. Fatima and I stared at each other. She was dry-eyed, that appealing, always laughing mouth firmly closed. It was the malformed baby with the lolling head that had died; already the three-year-old boy was pulling on his mother's hand again, whining to be picked up.

"I'm sorry we're outside," said Fatima matter-of-factly, "but Aisha is sick this morning, and the noise would be too much for her."

She took her little boy's head on her lap while she sat with the friends and relatives who had come to keep her company in her mourning. She did not cry, but patted the child on the back, slowly, rhythmically, until its eyes closed, its whining ceased.

The rows of women talked in low tones. They held their head scarves in place against the gusts of wind which stirred all the sand in the street except where the women's garments lay heavily upon it in black patterned whorls and circles. The wind had been blowing all morning, and a fine screen of sand veiled the sky and the sun.

"Where are your children, Beeja?"

It was old Shemessa, eyes narrowed. This morning those eyes seemed like malevolent slits to me, although I knew in another part of my mind that she was simply, like all of us, keeping her eyes nearly closed to protect them from the moving shifting grains of sand.

"Your children, they must be very ill," she went on. "You don't have to tell me. I know."

How did she know?

"The twins, on the other hand," continued Shemessa, "are fine this morning, thanks be to God."

"Ahhhhhh" cried Wahiba, Fatima's daughter, sitting down beside us, and arranging her dress around her. "Ahhhhhh! Beeja! She died in her sleep, poor thing. Ahhhhhh! Shemessa! We didn't even hear her cry."

Shemessa was staring at me, I knew, but I kept my eyes on Wahiba, who seemed much more upset than the dead child's mother. Her weeping was perhaps pretty much form, I decided, since babies are not mourned as greatly as adults, but Wahiba's grief for her dead baby sister was not all assumed.

"Her father and her uncle took her to the mountain this morning to bury her," wailed Wahiba, covering her face with her black scarf.

"Ahhhh!" murmured the women.

Widow Fatooma's face crumpled, a tear rolled from her whitened sightless eye, she buried her head in her hands.

I could hear our motorboat on the river. It would take them a half hour to get to the doctor's, longer to get back against the wind.

Shemessa moved off down the row to speak to Nezla.

"Only a few stones to cover her, she was so small," cried Wahiba.

"Ahhhhh!" murmured the women.

"Mona," I whispered, "Shemessa asked me about the children. How did she know?"

Mona shook her head.

Nezla came up. "Beeja!"

"The twins are well?" I murmured.

"Not bad."

I looked at her face, puffy with fatigue, and I knew they *were* bad. (Like Davy and Laura Ann, the dreams whispered.)

"This is for the boy," she said, slipped something small and smooth and round into my hand and was gone.

"She died in her sleep, poor thing, we didn't even hear her cry," began Wahiba again.

"Poor thing!" repeated Sherifa, who had sat down beside us.

"They took her to the mountain this morning," wailed Wahiba, "her father and her uncle."

"To the mountain," repeated Mona.

How long had the boat been gone? I had no idea.

"Only a few stones to bury her, she was so small," cried Wahiba.

"Ahhhhhh!" I replied.

Was that buzzing above the wind the boat?

"She died in her sleep, poor thing," said Wahiba, her voice cracking.

I heard the buzzing again, louder.

It *was* the boat.

"Ahhhhhh!" returned Mona. "B.J., when you hear the motor stop, get up," she hissed from behind her scarf. "I will stay for a while, and you can send Beryl in your place."

"We didn't even hear her cry!" wailed Wahiba.

But I had already risen, paid my respects to Fatima and was walking toward my house. Bob and Karim and the doctor were climbing the hill, the river behind them dark and pebbled with the roughnesses of the wind.

I opened my hand. There in the dusty sunlight lay a bright blue bead with a dirty string through it, a present from Nezla, a charm to ward off the Evil Eye.

The doctor said Laura Ann had pneumonia; Davy had only a particularly bad asthma attack. Only. He gave us antibiotics.

"Six times a day for the girl," he prescribed. "For the boy his regular dosage of cortisone. The antibiotic won't help."

"I'd like to leave on the express boat tomorrow for Aswan," I said quickly before Bob could stop me.

A glance passed between the men. It was obvious they had already discussed this.

"I do not advise it, madame," said the Egyptian doctor. He was middle-aged, with a tired face. "Getting away from the sand in this wind might help the boy, but any change will be dangerous for the girl. Keep them both warm and quiet, and give them lots of hot liquids."

"Is that all I can do?"

"If you build up the boy's bed with pillows so his head is lower than his feet, I think you will find it will help the mucus to drain out."

Lay him on a slant. Give him tea. Wrap his head. Medicine won't help. Nothing will help. Travel will make Laura Ann worse. So there was nothing I could do, except pray.

Mona came in with Mohammed, who asked if the doctor would look at the twins. They were very bad, he said, the same look on his face that I felt must be on mine.

I shook hands with the doctor. He and Bob and Mohammed headed down the street where the women still sat in rows on the sand crying and marking themselves with dust.

The children lay quietly on their beds; they were too sick to fuss.

The blue bead was in my hand. Almost without realizing what I was doing, I took the string and tied it around one of Davy's bed posts. The glass bead knocked against the palm wood.

Beryl watched.

"Nezla gave it to me," I said lightly. "A present for Davy. What else can I do with it? I can't very well throw it away."

"What did you give her in return?" asked Beryl. "For the twins, I mean?" What indeed?

"I, I haven't—yet, I mean I don't know what to send."

"The plastic ducks," returned Beryl promptly. "The ones you pull on a string." Now it was my turn to stare at Beryl.

"Yes," she said. "That's the thing to do. Mohammed's children have always loved to play with that toy, and so even if the twins don't improve, the others will enjoy it. And Nezla will be pleased.''

I still stood there with my hand on the blue bead string.

"Well, B.J.?"

"You're absolutely right, Beryl, why didn't I think of it myself?"

"It will be a good omen for them," Beryl smiled, and she set off down the street with the duck pull toy wrapped in a towel, holding her own black head scarf across her face to keep the sand out of her eyes.

In the morning, Laura Ann's fever had risen to 104.6. She was flushed and panting. Davy coughed and coughed, almost without pause. Beryl and I had taken turns holding him up at night, but discovered the doctor was right, he seemed more comfortable lying on a slant, his head down.

Hanim Ali came, Hanim Ali with her hard bright eyes, her magic odd rings. "I have written for your son a sura from the Koran," she said.

Khadija came, bringing cumin tea.

Cumin tea. Sugared black tea. *Kharkaday*, the red tea of the Sudan, brewed by Dahiba. Every hour we tried to get some hot liquids down those rasping little throats. The wind was still blowing the fine sand through the crack between the roof and wall and into the bedrooms.

A second sleepless night passed. Between turns with Davy and Laura Ann, I stood in the dark court and looked up at the stars, dimly visible through the film of sand. In our room, Bob was trying to get Laura Ann to sleep.

"Oh where, oh where has my little dog gone," he sang. His voice was hoarse.

The second morning Laura Ann's fever was down. The antibiotic was working. One-legged Abdou brought her a shriveled orange from the market. Our hundred oranges had disappeared long ago.

"The boy?"

"Worse."

I dared not look at Bob directly. I was not too certain what he might do, but I was afraid that I might, at any moment, weep. Laura Ann's crisis had passed, but Davy still struggled for every breath.

"You take Laura Ann into our room tonight," Bob suggested to Beryl. "Maybe you can both sleep. B.J. and I will stay with Davy in here, and spell each other."

At dinnertime the wind blew harder, and Saleh predicted a storm.

"But isn't *this* a storm?" I said. "It's been blowing for four days."

"I don't know what to think," said Saleh. "It should have stopped by now. Maybe a big sandstorm is coming from the western desert." He furrowed his brow and seemed to listen to the wind.

"A big sandstorm?" Bob's voice rose. He tried to clear his throat.

Beryl, Karim and Mona looked into their coffee cups.

"Many children are sick in the settlement," said Saleh sternly. "God sends us only what we can bear. God knows best."

I felt dried and drawn, like one of the desiccated okras that hung from strings in Saleh's summer kitchen.

Later, I tried to stay awake on one bed while Bob dozed on the other. The wind banged a shutter, and Davy wheezed in, out, in, out. Bob, in his sleep, held a muffled conversation with himself. Bang, went the shutter. BANG!

In the ceiling above me, pinpoints of light winked in the roof beams, the eyes of tiny mice, crouching there, staring down.

Davy wheezed in, out, in, out. The shutter banged.

I shook myself awake. I must have fallen asleep, I realized, for though it was still dark, the wind had dropped. Inside the room it was quiet and peaceful. But something was wrong. Something was different. It was—no, no! There was no wheeze, no cough, nothing.

"Davy!" I shouted, springing up. "It's Davy! Oh, no!"

I found myself standing beside his crib and shouting, convinced that my son had died in his sleep while I, his negligent mother, had dozed nearby.

"What's the matter with him?" Bob, his hair standing up all over his head, had lifted Davy up and the child cried at being wakened so precipitously.

Beryl banged in, in her robe. Mona was behind her with a lantern.

"Is he—?" she began.

"He's just fine," said Bob as firmly as he could. "He's breathing perfectly normally."

And then we all looked at each other in that fitful yellow light as the full force of what Bob had just said came over us. *That* was what was different. Davy was breathing perfectly normally. He had not breathed like that for six months!

"B-but," I stammered, "just a few hours ago, when I put him down . . ."

We listened again, and in the quiet, Davy calmed in Bob's arms, his eyes drooped, he was asleep. He breathed regularly, in and out. The wheeze was simply not there.

"Well," remarked Bob profoundly, "let's all get some sleep."

He laid David in the crib, and caught the blue bead string on his elbow.

"What's this?"

"Oh," I said hastily, "Nezla gave it to me. Maybe she was trying to say thank you for the medicine I gave the twins, or something. She said it was to protect him from the Evil Eye."

Bob looked at me. "And you tied it on his crib," he said.

"Yes, well, I didn't want to hurt Nezla's feelings, I mean, we gave her something in exchange."

"You gave her something in exchange," Bob repeated slowly.

"Yes," said Beryl, "the duck pull toy. They liked it always. It seemed like a good omen."

"A good omen," Bob repeated, still more slowly.

"It wouldn't have been proper to throw the blue bead away, would it?" put in Mona. "I mean, it's a sign of affection, to give someone else a blue bead, it means you feel the person's worth protecting."

"And Nezla will feel the same way about the duck, I'm sure," added Beryl earnestly.

Bob seemed speechless. For a moment I thought he might cry, and then I thought he might be close to uproarious laughter. He bent his head, so as not to look at us directly, three women clustered around his son's bed, and he turned the blue bead over and over in his hand.

"A plastic duck on a string," he murmured. "Even exchange, you think, Western magic for Eastern magic?"

The three of us stared at each other, at him. We smiled, a little uncertainly.

"Well, that's a bit of an exaggeration, Bob," said Mona.

"We were only trying to return Nezla's good will," said I.

"We just had to," said Beryl positively.

A little voice at the door interrupted. "Mama! Mama!"

Laura Ann stood there in her sleeper, rubbing her eyes. "Why everybody up?" she demanded. "Up in the dark? I'm *hungry*."

As the news of my son's apparently miraculous recovery spread, we were besieged by visitors.

"You see," said Khadija, "the date honey helped."

"It was the *kharkaday*," pronounced Dahiba. "We should have thought to give it to him before."

"Wrapping his head," said the widow Fatooma. "I told you so."

"Newspapers on his chest," Sherifa reminded me.

Hanim Ali nodded wisely, and said that a sura from the Koran was the greatest help in distress she had ever found.

"I prayed, too, Hanim Ali," I pointed out to the old woman.

"We all pray," she allowed. "What else can we do?"

Fatima came, rather surprisingly, I thought, because I knew that ordinarily after a death one does not go out of one's house for forty days. But Mona said that the death of the malformed baby had in many ways proved a relief for Fatima, who had nursed it faithfully for the ten months of its pitiful life, even while feeling hopeless. The entire community felt that in this case God had acted for the best; and it turned out the period of mourning for an adult was often not observed in the case of babies.

"I'm happy for you," said Fatima simply. "Aisha sends you her blessings, and says she couldn't have done a better job herself, although cupping might have helped." She almost giggled, but contained herself. The time had not yet come for laughing again.

Nezla arrived too. The twins were some better, she told us, and smiled meaningfully. For a fleeting moment, I wondered how she had used the duck pull toy.

"Shemessa had to stay with the babies," she added, "or she would have come to see you too."

I'll bet she would have, I thought venomously, but not as venomously as usual. Shemessa had her own ways of fighting evil and uncertainty and it was hardly her fault that I in some way seemed to personify the enemy.

When the doctor came, I asked him what could have cured Davy.

"Do not use the word 'cure,' madame," he cautioned. "The condition may recur when you go back to Cairo. Chronic allergic asthma is seldom *cured*, but it is relieved like this sometimes, suddenly, after a period in a dry climate. That is why I come to work at Abu Simbel every winter, so that my wife, who also suffers from asthma, may have some relief.''

"But, Doctor," I persisted, "for the first time in more than six months the child is eating well. His fungus infections are actually drying up.''

"That is a good sign. Even a temporary recession will give the child's system an opportunity to restore and strengthen itself.''

I nodded. "And Laura Ann?''

"Much improved. The pneumonia is gone. The element of allergy in her cough seems to have disappeared temporarily. But I repeat, do not expect miracles.''

"Thank you, Doctor," said Bob. "We are very grateful for your trouble.''

"I haven't done much," asserted the doctor. "The climate, the system, the improved weather, the hot tea, who knows what has caused this great improvement in both your children!''

Who, indeed?

Bob looked at the doctor for a second. "The women tell my wife it's the blue bead they brought her which has warded off the Evil Eye," he said matter-of-factly.

The doctor looked at me, but he did not smile. "It is amazing to think that an American would use a blue bead," he said. "Superstition is stronger than I would have thought!''

I felt myself bristling to the defense of my friends.

"They were trying to help," I insisted. "I think anyone, any mother anyway, would do anything she could, *anything* that offered even a possibility of help for her child. Don't you agree?''

"Even cauterizing with red-hot nails, scarification, circumcision, madame? They are all quite common home remedies in this area.''

"I didn't quite mean . . .''

The doctor nodded at Bob. "Your wife's argument is all right, but one can go too far," he said. "Ignorance, how I fight it—every day.''

"Ignorance!" I felt terribly angry suddenly, as the strain of the last days began to slip away into ordinary fatigue. "Isn't that just another word for helplessness? Do the Nubian women have antibiotics? Motorboats to fetch you when their babies are sick? They do what they can—which is a comfort to the living at least and hardly matters to those who die.''

After the doctor had gone, Bob regarded me tolerantly.

"He does the best he can, too," Bob pointed out. "He's a stranger in Nubia, just like we are, yet this is his country, and he's reacting to the women's behavior partly in a way he thinks we'll find appropriate.''

"Well . . .'' I temporized.

"He didn't create the situation either, B.J.," went on Bob. "He can't change it all by himself.''

Nor can we, I thought, though I had to admit that my mind had been more on my own children these past weeks than on anything or anybody else.

"And," Bob added, smiling a bit, "the poor doctor didn't count on how similarly *all* women react when their children are in danger.''

He was teasing me again, I knew, the first time in months, a sign of his own sense of relief at Davy's unexpected improvement.

A few days later we made our second official visit to the *omda*, who suggested sweetly to Bob, in my hearing, that really I should remain in Erd-Moz now, even though my third delivery might be difficult.

"After all, Dr. Bob," he remarked pleasantly, between small puffs of his English cigarette (today in a silver holder), "you can easily find another wife, but remember this child is your first-born son. If he is doing so well here, why take him back to Cairo and risk making him sick again?"

I merely nibbled another nice, plump date and found I didn't care a fig (or a thistle or a date) what the *omda* thought. For these days I watched Laura Ann beginning to run with Gamal, shrieking down the sand dunes, accepted at last it seemed, by the Nubian boys and girls as just another child, not a strange plaything. I saw Davy pulling himself up and standing alone, the discontented frown on his face replaced, quite often now, by a smile of genuine pleasure.

1. *Woman weaving basket.*

2. *Men gather in palm grove after Friday prayers.*

*3. Nubian water wheel.*

4. Men mending fishing nets.

5. *Woman operating a* shadoof, *a device for raising water from the Nile to irrigate the fields. Village in background.*

6. *Weighing meat in village market.*

7. *Man cultivates land near river.*

8. *Woman carries fuel.*

9. *Nubian man.*

10. Woman filling zirs, clay jars which filtered and cooled water.

11.  *Nubian woman wearing gold coin head band.*

12. Woman on village street.

13. *Retired Nubian man.*

14. *Women grinding grain.*

15. *Woman decorating house. House construction was done by specialists, mostly men. House decoration, both inside and out, was a woman's specialty.*

16. *Two women preparing vegetables.*

# Chapter 8

# A Farewell Picnic

The river was calm for our last trip in the *Susan*, a pleasure excursion to visit Mohammed's brother. Ali Daoud taught school in Zingahoor, a small village several miles north of Erd-Moz. Because the day was so beautiful and it was nearly my last in Nubia, we went a few kilometers out of our way to look once more at the temple.

Around the knees of the colossi, clusters of khaki tents, like gardens of giant flowers, were pitched on the sand near the acacia tree, to house the engineering consultants from Italy and Germany. These technicians were busy laying ropes, measuring, preparing plans to save Abu Simbel.

"What do you think, Bob?" asked Karim. "Can they really raise the temple above the level of the lake?"

"Who knows?" Bob was at the wheel today, wearing a wrinkled white sun hat like Karim's.

Mohammed sniffed. "It's ridiculous," he said. "No man can raise the temple. It must go when our land goes, it is part of it. If they raise the temple, why not raise the land and the palm trees?"

The people in Erd-Moz discussed their coming move as though it were centuries rather than a single year away. Yet only last week government agricultural extension agents had registered the small date trees that could be moved, had dug them out of Nubia's ancient soil and wrapped them in damp cloths to send to new settlements in Kom Ombo.

When the barges pushed off from shore with their cargoes of trees swaddled in white, some women had run along the banks of the river, wailing as they had at the death of Fatima's child.

"Dates are the basis of Erd-Moz' wealth," pointed out Karim. "When they go, the people know their change is near."

But today the move to Kom Ombo seemed centuries away to me also.

"It will be a pick-nick," Mohammed had explained, using the English word.

So in our picnic clothes we had set off, except for me, still wearing the trusty maternity jumper, bulging now in its final innings, that button threatening to pop again. Let it hold together till we get to Cairo, I thought.

Davy wiggled with joy rather than discomfort and climbed vigorously up and down Beryl's lap; mine wasn't of much use to him these days. We had Gamal along, Laura Ann's friend, and he sat solemnly beside Mohammed, deaf to the teasing of Laura Ann, trying constantly to escape from Mona's grasp.

It was early March, a beautiful Nubian spring day. The gentle sunlight fell on the dark mountains, stretching away in their basins of sand to the Red Sea. Along both banks of the river tiny squares and strips of ripening winter millet formed an irregular tracery of green in the miles of bronze sand.

"Isn't that Jebel Ada?" asked Karim.

"Yes," said Bob. "Where Nick's going to excavate next year, if his money comes through."

Near the white-pillared porch of the *omda's* riverside guest house, women filling cans of water straightened up and shouted to us across the water.

Beryl waved. She sighed. "We should stay, B.J., it is so lovely, why must we go back to Cairo?"

She trailed her fingers in the wake of the boat and looked around her at the open sky, the imposing quiet of the landscape. White foam rolled over the watery reflections of the towers of Jebel Ada, the white houses, the black-garbed women, the mountains, the patches of growing grain, turned the reflections, blurred them; water broke over the reflections in gleaming black ripples, golden-edged.

We spun on. The landscape gradually emptied of people and houses, the mountains lowered, the river turned and narrowed.

"There! We turn there!" cried Mohammed, indicating a hillside, which looked at first like any other empty hillside among the hundred we had passed in the last half hour, but nearer, we could see it was distinguished by the marks of man. An old-fashioned water lift, or *shadoof*, stood close to the bank, its long-angled beam dangling a rope tied to a bucket by which water was raised to irrigate the land above.

The hillside itself was an irregular rectangle of intensive workmanship between the river and the sky, a cultivated quilt thrown down on the floor of sand and rock. Terraces were shored with rows of stone, so neatly and carefully placed they might have been stitched into the hill. Green shoots of young barley sprouted in the terraces, with vines of peas, climbing runners of beans, froths of *kashrengegg*, the Nubian alfalfa. A few whitewashed houses were spread about on the angles of the hilltop, each open-shaded porch placed to benefit from an unobstructed view.

"The last hill almost to climb, B.J.," whispered Beryl, the only one who still remembered my doctor's strict orders not to climb hills under any circumstances.

On the flagstone terrace we were greeted by the women of Zingahoor, for this *was* Zingahoor, the one terraced hillside and the handful of houses. Laura Ann, enveloped in a fulsome embrace by Ali Daoud's plump wife, Halima, responded with fervor, touching and then fingering carefully the hammered pieces of heavy gold which formed the necklace of the laughing lady of the house.

"Pretty," said my daughter thoughtfully.

"It is yours, my girl, take it," smiled Halima, making the classic offer of an admired object to a guest, an offer she knew would be refused, but which was nevertheless perfectly sincere.

Mohammed clapped Bob on the back. "You've got to watch your daughter, Bob," he said. "She's learning about gold too young. How will you find a rich husband to satisfy her?"

Mohammed could joke and so could Ali Daoud, for they were happy in their marriages, they had children, they had enough land and trees to assure them and their families of a livelihood. When a man is satisfied with his life and does not look beyond to a second or third marriage, he buys his wife gold to show her his love and his appreciation. Hanim Ali had explained it so.

The children were fed in the court, rice and yogurt and an orange and put down for naps.

"Mohammed says you and Beryl and Mona are to have lunch with us," said Bob.

Mona and I looked at each other. "We should eat with the women," I said.

"Yes," agreed Mona.

"It will be easier for the women this way," Mohammed said. "They won't have to serve you separately. You're saving them work."

Mohammed had figured us out long ago.

On the shaded terrace a table had been set with a white cloth and thick white linen napkins. We waited and looked at the tranquil river.

What followed was a gourmet meal, one of the best I have ever eaten anywhere, an al fresco luncheon above the Nile, twenty miles from the nearest neighbor, one hundred miles from the nearest city.

We began with soup, clear broth seasoned with lemon and some delicate herb I did not recognize. The pasta course followed: buttered and spiced rice, served with a side dish of chopped livers and kidneys, in sauce with tiny new onions.

Hot flat bread came fresh from the hearth, wrapped in a spotless napkin, to be eaten with roast lamb, creamed spinach, potato puffs. Fresh mint sauce accompanied the lamb. Salad of thin cucumber slices and *gargeer*, the pungent Middle Eastern water cress, had been dressed with oil and vinegar.

"The food is certainly excellent," murmured Beryl.

"Mmmmm," answered Mona.

"They're amazing, the Nubians," said Bob. "The longer I know them, the more I admire them. Have you noticed, Karim, they are the true gourmands, picking and choosing among the motley cultural traditions of Cairo and Alexandria and bringing what they like back to Nubia."

Silence. Karim of the delicate stomach was enjoying his lunch.

"Don't you agree, Karim? It will be interesting to watch how they adjust to resettlement. Karim!"

"Yes, yes, certainly, you are right, Dr. Fernea," nodded Karim and helped himself to more salad.

Ali Daoud startled us by saying in English, "You like the food?"

"Delicious!" we chorused.

"Who cooked it?" I asked.

"My wife's uncle Sayyid," smiled Ali Daoud. "Sayyid is retired and lives here now, but he used to be a chef in a very important pasha's house."

"I wonder what he can produce for dessert," I muttered quietly, thinking of the egg shortage and my battles with Saleh.

We nibbled some more little bits of bread, wiped our mouths and waited, like greedy children, for another treat.

We were not disappointed. Persian cream arrived in a low bowl of antique Royal Doulton china—Persian cream served with mango slices. The mango was an inspiration, giving the dish an entirely new taste.

"Maybe Persian cream was originally served with mango, in some shadowy time in Isfahan," I murmured. "And Fanny Farmer had never heard of mango, or at least she couldn't get it in Boston, so guess what, she substituted canned fruit cocktail!"

No one was interested in my musings on the origins of Persian cream. They were all taking turns scraping the bowl, politely, but still scraping.

Oranges and ripe bananas from the trees on the hillside were placed on the table. And finger bowls.

"Couldn't we meet your uncle?" asked Bob, as we sat back in our chairs to rest from feasting. "We'd like to tell him how much we've enjoyed the lunch."

Ali Daoud smiled and nodded. In a moment Uncle Sayyid, an old man with a carefully trimmed gray mustache, came out on the terrace with a tray of Turkish coffee.

"Sit down, *Ammii*, I will serve the coffee," insisted Ali Daoud, and Uncle Sayyid did sit down, after shaking hands formally with each of us.

"*Ya* Doctor, welcome!"

"*Ustaz* Karim!"

"*Um* Daoud! (that was me, mother of David).

"Mademoiselle Mona!"

"Miss Burl!" (that was Beryl).

Uncle Sayyid was a small man, but he carried his turban proudly and his eyes were clear and direct under gray brows, trimmed neatly like his mustache.

"It was nothing," he kept insisting while we praised the food. "Nothing," but he enjoyed the praise. "I'm out of practice, but if I had been in Cairo, I could have prepared something more suitable."

"The Persian cream with mangoes was excellent!" I said.

"You liked it?" Uncle Sayyid smiled and placed his hand on his heart to acknowledge the compliment "I had hoped to offer you a chocolate soufflé, it used to be my specialty, but I could not find enough eggs. What the chickens can lay the children need."

We sipped our coffee.

"How long have you been away from Cairo?" asked Bob.

"Three and a half years."

"You don't miss it?" I asked.

"No," said the old man. "I lived in Cairo for thirty-six years, but my heart always remained here with my family, in the security of my own country."

We looked with him at his view. From our hilltop luncheon table the slight curve of the river was clear, the curve north to Aswan beyond the low mountains, and south toward Abu Simbel and Erd-Moz, the village I was soon to leave.

On the opposite shore lay low hills, the foothills of the old dark table-topped mountains I saw each day opposite our house in Erd-Moz

"It is very beautiful," said Mona.

"Yes," agreed Uncle Sayyid.

"And how are your children, madame?" inquired the old man politely, turning to me. "I hear your son's asthma has improved greatly."

"Yes," I answered.

"I am not surprised at this miraculous recovery, are you, Ali Daoud, Mohammed?"

They shook their heads.

"Not surprised at all. You see the scene before us. Now smell the air."

We obliged.

"It is pure, my friends, no dirt, no germs."

I would have liked to agree with him, but I could not. Free of germs and dirt? Well, not entirely, I qualified to myself, thinking of the constant dysentery from which Mohammed's twins suffered, the eye and ear infections that plagued the children, the women who died in childbirth. Uncle Sayyid was right in a way though; people of comparable income were far worse off in the city than they were in Nubia. Perhaps the land *was* blessed for those who could survive its remoteness, its austerity, its rigors of climate. For us, fortunately, it had been blessed.

Karim, who loved Cairo, said, "You don't miss the city at all? I cannot understand that."

Uncle Sayyid considered. "No. You, *Ustaz*, who were born in the city and whose happy moments are associated with the city, you would miss it. But I was born here. Each night when I walked home from the bus in Boulaq, where the streets are so crowded and the children are crying, I thought of this scene before us, and promised myself I would come back. I did."

Bob seemed about to speak, and I had a terrible premonition that he was going to spoil our idyl and ask Uncle Sayyid how he felt about moving to Kom Ombo in the near future. . . . It hardly seemed the moment. But it was Mohammed who raised the issue.

"They say we must leave the blessed land, though, *Ammii*."

The old man sighed.

"Perhaps it will be better," said Ali Daoud, "at least for our children. They can go to secondary school there or to college in Aswan. Education is needed these days. Do you want your grandsons to work as cooks and servants?"

Uncle Sayyid shook his head. "I have heard that argument!" he said. "It is only partly true. Any work is good if the workman takes pride in it. Here we are our own masters. We have our own land and it is beautiful. What more can we want?"

"*Ammii*," Mohammed spoke now, urgently, "it is not good for families to be apart. You know that. It is not good for the women to be without men for years, the children without fathers. Did you enjoy living alone in a room in Boulaq? My father didn't. In Kom Ombo the families can live together again. We can be happy together, we can get better jobs."

"And there are doctors and a hospital," said Ali Daoud, who was known to suffer from liver trouble.

"Let us not talk of it." The old man waved his hand. "*Ustaz* Karim, there is only one thing I miss about Cairo." He smiled. "I am sure you can guess what it is."

Karim smiled back. "The coffee shops," he answered without a moment's hesitation.

Beryl, Mona and I joined the women of the house for tea when Laura Ann and Davy wakened from naps.

"I hear," said Ali Daoud's wife, Halima, "that Saleh and Hanim Ali spent nearly two hundred pounds on Naima's wedding. Is that true?"

"I think so," answered Mona.

"It must have been some wedding! Was the dancing good? And the food?"

"Oh, yes," said Beryl. "The dancing went on for days. It was a marvelous wedding."

"And now there's no living with Hanim Ali, I'll bet," said a shriveled old woman in black, without gold, without a single ornament, not even a ring, who was introduced as Uncle Sayyid's wife, Sekina.

"You know Hanim Ali well?" from Mona.

Sekina sniffed. "I knew her. Grew up on this bank. I remember her well. Stubborn, hard-headed, too proud of her family name, she was. I knew her all right."

"She took on airs," put in a second old woman, Sekina's widowed sister Radiya. "Sounds like she's still doing it. Wedding presents from the Begum Agha Khan! Hmph!"

"Oh, I don't know," said Mona. "Most of the Begum's present they spent on the wedding. And Hanim Ali isn't well, she has bad stomach pains all the time."

"Who doesn't?" retorted Sekina, resting her chin on knobbed and work-worn hands. Deep lines of discontent and worry ran from her nose down past her set mouth.

"You stayed here all the time your husband worked in Cairo?" I asked. I was almost certain of the answer, I found, from the bitterness in her dark old face. After all, I thought, while Uncle Sayyid cooked and tasted chocolate soufflés in the pasha's house, this woman had endured Zingahoor's burning hot summers and chilly winters for thirty-six years! Hadn't she been lonely, lost children in fever and childbirth, suffered unknown diseases and missed her husband?

Sekina narrowed her eyes at me, black and bright still, though nearly buried in the folds of her sorrowfully wrinkled face.

"Hmph," she answered rather rudely. "Hmph," and was silent.

"Oh, *Amitii*," fluttered Halima. "*Um* Daoud is our guest!"

What was going on? What had I done by asking what seemed a perfectly innocent question?

"I've been out, my girl," Sekina finally volunteered. "I could have left. I've been in Arwan a dozen times. I spent a winter in Cairo, a summer in Alexandria after my first son was born."

"A good change," offered Mona, looking around at the women, puzzled too, I could tell, by the turn of the conversation.

Sekina snorted. "Good change she says. Oh, yes, the climate was fine, but I couldn't stand the cities. Filthy places! Filthy people!" She spat the words. "I was glad to get back to my own house."

"And away from her husband," old Radiya put in slyly.

Mona looked carefully neutral. Beryl suddenly was very busy playing "peas porridge hot" quietly with Davy and Laura Ann.

Plump Halima laughed softly, showing several fine gold teeth. "You know how it is, madame," she said meaningfully, "how men get when they've been away from women too long. They can't have enough of their wives."

I nodded.

"You think it's better when they're around all the time, eh?" cackled Radiya, showing one or two broken teeth. "Eh, my pretty?"

Halima tossed her head, sending her head scarf flying and her gold necklace tinkling. Laura Ann drew near, attracted by the noise.

"Yes," she said shortly, "yes, it is, it's much more fun that way, and at least they don't spend their money on *Egyptian women*," with a glance at bitter old Sekina.

The older women were silent. Halima leaned down to me.

"Ali Daoud and I have an arrangement," she said primly. "He always sleeps with me on Monday and Thursday nights. Of course, I don't let on that I enjoy it, or he might think I wasn't a good woman. How is it with you?"

I explained, rather feebly, that in the West perhaps some married couples had arrangements such as hers and Ali Daoud's, but others did not and tended to be more spontaneous.

"You mean your husband sleeps with you now?" Halima was visibly shocked.

"No, no, not just now." I was more than eight months pregnant.

The two old ladies looked at Halima and back at me.

"Of course," said old Sekina, "in America the women sleep with everyone, not only their husbands, and the men don't even mind, just like those *Egyptian women*," she added venomously.

Had Uncle Sayyid enjoyed more of Cairo than just the coffee shops? Had he given Sekina short shrift on feast days, few presents, little attention? This might explain her bitterness.

"We-ell," I said, "what you say about America is not really true, Sekina."

In the breathless silence which followed, I had the curious feeling that Mona was waiting for my answer with nearly as much interest as Halima, Sekina and Radiya.

Beryl rushed in to help. What one saw of Western women was not what Western women really were, in their hearts, she said. "I mean in their appearance," she went on, "just because they don't wear the *milaya* doesn't mean they're not good women . . ." and she trailed off.

With all those eyes fixed upon me, Mona's and Beryl's as well as Halima's, Sekina's and Radiya's, I faltered a little in the speech I launched into. Beryl was right, I said, in explaining that Western women were not necessarily bad women just because they didn't wear the *milaya*. For most Western women, I said, family and husband were very important; Western husbands did indeed mind if their wives slept with someone else and though it was true that a few women might stray from the path of wifely virtue, in general I thought the average Western woman was probably as faithful to her husband as my Nubian friends.

Old Sekina cocked her head at Radiya. "You hear what she says, *some* women *might* stray."

"I heard," answered toothless Radiya shortly.

"And then they want to stop circumcising the girls," said Sekina, in the tone of voice which meant that this speech had been uttered often before. "Can't they see that circumcision is the only way we can help our girls behave themselves?"

"Does everyone behave themselves now?" asked Mona innocently. She and I had both noted that in Erd-Moz handsome Mohammed seemed to receive more greetings from women passing by on the street than did other men, and we had even heard he occasionally drank tea *alone* with a notorious young woman whose husband worked in Cairo.

"Of course," answered Sekina firmly.

"Naturally," averred Radiya, gazing out toward the Nile.

Halima did not contradict the old ladies, and talk drifted to other subjects; Halima's new baby, as rosy-brown and plump as she was; Sekina's excruciating backaches; the Begum's wedding present again and its effect on Hanim Ali's character; and always Kom Ombo.

"I can hardly wait to get out of this godforsaken place and get there," cried Halima fervently.

The old women shook their heads. We were eating melon seeds now, roasted and salted, and Sekina spat out a husk before answering. "You think that now, my girl, but just wait! Those houses! Have you seen any of the houses the government is building for us, madame?"

I said I hadn't, but I had seen pictures of the plans.

"And it's true there are only three small rooms and a court, isn't it?"

"I think so," I temporized. "Some are bigger than others."

"And the animals are supposed to be in the same house with us. What a funny idea! Who thought of that?"

I said truthfully that I didn't know, and reflected that no doubt the architect had been born in the Delta, where the peasants were so afraid their precious animals might be stolen that they insisted on bringing them in at night.

"Yes, yes, *Amitii*," went on Halima, nursing her baby while Laura Ann watched solemnly, "but think of the wonderful markets in Aswan," her eyes took on a faraway look, "the cloth from Damascus, and the cinemas and the gold shops."

Sekina eyed her cynically. "And where will you get the money to buy the gold and the cloth from Damascus, my girl? Or I should say where will Ali Daoud get it? Here at least we can dream, eh, Radiya?''

The two old women chuckled at their good fortune and Halima's foolishness.

"We won't move," said Sekina, biting into a seed. "It's just talk. Men talk."

"Right," returned old Radiya. "We'll never move."

She had no teeth for the seeds, but she took one and sucked it to be comradely, moving closer to her sister as she did so.

"How could they cover this house?" she asked me. "Look how far down the Nile is. It could never come this high."

Was it possible that before another spring came round, the terraced hillside, the whitewashed veranda, the palms and the banana tree would lie beneath the waters of the Nile? The plans being made in Cairo said that it was.

> "The world is charged with the grandeur of God.
> It will flame out, like shining from shook foil;
> It gathers to a greatness . . .''

Beryl was quoting to Karim as we chugged slowly home in the late afternoon light. The sky was strewn with streamers of pale rose-colored clouds, and the river was calm and golden.

"Poetry, eh?" interrupted Mohammed, who had recognized the cadence although he did not understand the language. He smiled brilliantly. "I bet you don't know this, though."

> "Shall I ever meet Buthayna alone again,
> Each of us full of love as a cloud of rain?''

Karim smiled back. "Oh, yes, I do, Mohammed," and he responded with the next couplet of Jamil. Rhythms in Arabic, then in French from Mona, in English from Beryl and me made a kind of counterpoint to the steady chugging of the motors, the soft breathing of the sleeping children as we retraced our course upriver and tied up in the growing dusk behind Erd-Moz.

Love for their beautiful hillside home was strong in the old women of Zingahoor, strong enough to compensate for other things they had missed in life, strong enough so that they could dismiss as obviously impossible any suggestion that it might ever change. For Uncle Sayyid, love for the blessed land of Nubia was strong also, strong enough to have conquered the temptations and delights which other ways of life may have offered to him. He had been restored in old age to his homeland, the reward to which his people traditionally looked throughout years of migrant labor. To what would future generations of Nubians look forward? Or would the Nubian men and women, without a homeland, quickly lose their special identity and disappear as surely as their fields and homes, their magnificent view of the Nile.

We went down the hill, through the palm groves, along the muddy footpath where the lemon and mango trees had bloomed, where the hard green fruit, the last for these trees, was ripening, to the stone wall, where Bob and Karim had the *Susan* waiting. Beryl carried David, Saleh and Mohammed had our bags, Laura

Ann clutched to her stomach a small reed plate of purple and orange, a farewell present from Gamal. Khadija was at the bank with Abdul Nasr; Nezla, Sherifa; Fatima with Gamal, Wahiba, Suffra; even Dahiba and Hanim Ali had seen fit to come down the hill to see us off. Old Shemessa was not there; she was with the twins. I understood that perfectly well. And Naima, the new bride, had to stay in the house for a full forty days after the consummation of her marriage.

"I'll see you in Cairo, though, Beeja," she had told me, "when I come to visit my husband. He has bought me a kerosene stove," she confided.

When we pushed off from shore, the women in their trailing black gowns bent down to the river, dipped in their hands, and tossed after us handfuls of the shining Nile water.

"Come back!" they called. "Come back, *Um* Daoud! Come back, Beryl!"

At my feet was a sack of dates, hand sewn by Khadija, the last crop from the blessed land, a present from our friends. We waved at the cluster of black figures until they had disappeared, become a part of the bank and the palms below the dunes.

The express boat did not arrive until midnight, and to save time the motors were kept running while the few passengers boarded. Beryl climbed up an iron ladder on the side, the children were passed to her, one by one, and I was hoisted up, with much difficulty, by four Nubian sailors, the black water churning below me and the goats bleating in fear in the hold.

"Good night!" called Bob. "Good night, Davy! Good night, Laura Ann!"

"Take care!" shouted Mona.

"Night night, Laura Ann! Night night, Davy!" It was Karim, bidding the children good night for the last time in Nubia. The bell on the bridge clanged its warning, the motors speeded up, the steamer churned toward mid-river.

Davy, who had dozed while we waited, only to be wakened again to board, sank onto my shoulder, asleep once more.

"Night night, Baba! Night night, Karim!" chirped Laura Ann, although Bob and Karim could not hear her. She, too, was nearly asleep, but the reed plate was still firmly clutched across her chest. "Night night, Gamal, night night, Abdul Nasr. Night night, Mona."

"Oh, B.J.," said Beryl. "It's over."

We looked at each other and found we had tears in our eyes as the white steamer of the Sudan Railways pushed down the Nile through the moonlight to Aswan.

Our third child, a daughter, was born in the Coptic Hospital the first week in April. Bob had come to Cairo to be with me and we named the baby Laila to commemorate her Egyptian origins. She had red hair and green eyes and Sister Angelina confided that Laila was prettier than newborn Davy, but perhaps not quite as pretty as Laura Ann. What did Matron Natalya think?

"She iss sound, thanks God, why does have to be pretty?" boomed Madame Natalya.

On the third morning of Laila's life, proud Roushdi bounced in with the telegrams from Nubia.

"Thank the good God you have a healthy child!" signed Fatima, Abdulla, Aisha.

"Congratulations!" Mohammed and family.

"Best wishes on the birth of your daughter!" from Saleh and family.

When Mona returned to Cairo from Erd-Moz, she brought a gift.

"The women want to make sure you're taking proper care of this child from the beginnng," she said, "so I promised I would buy you a charm to keep away the Evil Eye."

It was a gold pin, inscribed with Laila's name and a blessing from the Koran.

"Oh, and B.J., something very exciting happened right after you left, did Bob tell you? On the seventh day after his wedding, Jalal got a telegram from his father in Cairo blessing the marriage to Naima."

"Really?"

"Yes, really! I think everyone was surprised, but Jalal was terribly pleased, too. I was in Saleh's court when the telegram came, and Hanim Ali nearly split my eardrum with the ululatious of joy she managed to produce at that moment. Remarkable woman, Hanim Ali."

"Remarkable," I agreed. "What other news?"

"Old Aisha's eye operation was a success. She's to have the other cataract removed next fall and she says to tell you she'll be ready then to deliver your next child!"

Naima and Jalal were truly wed, with the blessing of Jalal's father; Hanim Ali must be content, I thought. My son, David, was walking, Laura Ann had hung her orange and purple reed plate on a nail above her bed and resumed her social life in the *ganeena*. I had borne Laila, Bob's work on the Nubian project was progressing according to plan. Three years had passed since our arrival in Egypt, and according to our agreement with the university, we were due for a summer's home leave with our families in America. The magnificent natural routine by which my Egyptian psychiatrist friend clocked the life of his peasant countrymen seemed to be working for all of us.

In the spring the flame trees burst suddenly into bloom. Below the Citadel, built by Saladdin, the red-orange flowers blazed against the muted stones of the Sultan Hassan and the Rifai mosques. The single tree outside our apartment house seemed paler, but on the island of Gezira the row of resplendent trees cast a blurred yet fiery stain upon the water of the Nile. Hanim Ali and Saleh came to Cairo from Erd-Moz, bringing Naima to her husband, Jalal. They telephoned to say that they would pay us a call. I had a moment of misgiving. Abbas was a Nubian, too. Could I ask him to wait on his fellow Nubians?

I needn't have worried. As on other such occasions, the Nubians took charge and managed things so that I should be comfortable.

"Beeja!" cried Hanim Ali and Naima at my front door, enveloping me in embraces of black silk perfumed with sandalwood (they did not wear the trailing *gargaras* in the city, Naima explained).

Saleh was already in the kitchen, greeting Abbas and exchanging news about Nubia. Abu Simbel was to be saved, it seemed, raised to stand like a single island in the vastness of the new flood-lake.

"They'll never do it!" predicted Abbas, as he served tea. "How can they put that mountain of stone up?'' (and he gestured to the ceiling with my best teapot).

"Well," said Hanim Ali with some asperity, "everyone said they'd never move us, either, but the people in the Kenuzi area have already gone. From the boat you can see the houses. They took the shutters along to Kom Ombo so the windows are empty. They look awful." She shuddered.

"If they can do that," put in Saleh, "I say they can lift the temple, too."

"Aren't you going to show me around your house?" asked Hanim Ali, after she had examined my teacups carefully from all angles. "You were always asking us to show you around our houses, Beeja. Now it's your turn!"

I nodded, there being really nothing I could say to *that*.

"Ah, you have a nice big bed, the doctor and you." She tested our mattress with the heel of her hand. "Seems comfortable, too. And where do the children sleep? Oh, my," she giggled and Naima echoed her. "You don't have a cradle like Mohammed, do you?" She ran her hand over the rails of the three children's cribs. "He said all foreigners had them. Hmph!" This discovery seemed to give her great satisfaction. "And where are the children?"

"In the park with their nanny." I led her to the balcony where a panorama of playing children, nannies in white and blue uniforms, Czech ladies in homemade spring prints, was spread out before us under the trees in the sunshine.

"A nice view," said Hanim Ali, leaning on the wall of the balcony. "Don't you think so, Naima? And that one flame tree there is pretty, just in front. Aren't you lucky to have a nanny? Hangs the wash out here, does she? Good idea, catches the sun and keeps the laundry out of the way at the same time." She passed through the french doors into the study in a rush of flowing veils, and paused under the round white Japanese lantern which hung from the ceiling.

"Is it made of paper?" she inquired.

"Yes."

"It makes the light of a small bulb seem stronger, doesn't it?"

"Yes, Hanim Ali."

She began to talk to Naima in the Nubian language, and I could almost see her mind working. I would not have been at all surprised to visit Kom Ombo later and find homemade paper lanterns around the electric lights in Hanim Ali's new house. Perhaps she was planning to experiment in Naima's Cairo apartment first. I marveled again as I remembered the Nubians' ability to see possibilities of beauty in the humblest objects, to make their surroundings attractive with a minimum of materials—a quality of mind they shared, after all, with the makers of our paper lantern.

"Have you got your kerosene stove?" I asked Naima.

She nodded. "It has four burners that work all at the same time," she said proudly. Remembering the work required to build one brush fire for tea or coax one primus stove into blazing flame, I appreciated again the luxury of automatic stoves.

"How about your apartment? Did Jalal get one from the company?"

"Yes, he did," interposed Hanim Ali before Naima had a chance to reply. "And it's a very good apartment."

I caught Naima's eye. She had covered the lower part of her face with her *milaya* suddenly, and I suspected strongly that she was smothering a giggle. Perhaps, in time, when she had the security of her own home and children, she, too, would develop the independence of Hanim Ali and insist on *her* daughters having proper Nubian weddings.

## PART II

# Nubians in Egypt
## Peaceful People

*Robert A. Fernea*

# Chapter Nine

# The Importance of the Nubians

The life of the Nubian people, as described in the following pages, no longer exists. The Egyptian government has resettled the Nubians in new communities and on new lands north of the city of Aswan, near Kom Ombo. Waters of the Nile, backed up by the High Dam at Aswan, have covered the houses and flooded the area where these people lived hundreds, perhaps thousands, of years. Yet Nubian culture, developed during a long history, has not been obliterated by the floodwaters. The values and techniques that allowed Nubians to live peacefully in a difficult environment in the past still persist to some extent in the new communities, helping these people adjust to radically different patterns of life. As we shall see, the building of the High Dam and the resettlement of Nubian villagers are only the most recent of a long series of events that have brought Nubians ever more in to the mainstream of Egyptian society. In a world in which people are constantly being uprooted from their native communities, and where their traditional culture seems of little use in their new settings, the Nubian example is worthy of our attention.

Like the Nubians, most of mankind lived during the greater part of history in small, relatively isolated settlements and villages and slowly developed workable variations on the basic themes of human culture. Today the isolation necessary for such creativity is largely gone, and distinctive small communities themselves are vanishing, if not under the floodwaters of the Nile, then at least in the homogeneous mixture we call modern society. Little record remains of the achievements of many of the cultures that have already disappeared: achievements in terms of values; patterns of social relations; techniques for wresting subsistence from varying environments; approaches to expression and communication in pictorial art, in words, in the building of houses, and in the fashioning of the objects of everyday life. These unique manifestations of human capabilities will not appear again, and we are all poorer for their loss. This essay is an attempt, then, to record some of the achievements of the Nubian people while they still lived in their ancestral home.

Who are the Nubians? Western readers may recall that the Nubian is mentioned in histories of Pharaonic Egypt, both as king and slave, and also appears as a character in the tales of the *Arabian Nights*. The foreign visitor to modern Cairo will be told that the tall, elegantly garbed black employees in the best hotels are Nubians, urban immigrants from villages in the southernmost region of Egypt who are famous for honesty and faithful service. But such fragments of knowledge scarcely answer our basic query. To discover who the Nubians are, we must look both to the past and to the present of this ancient population of Middle Eastern people, a people who share much of their heritage with other residents of the Nile valley, but who have retained to the present day a rich cultural tradition that is uniquely their own.

In general, the people called Nubians are those whose native villages extended along the Nile from the first cataract at Aswan south into the Sudan through the region known as Dongola. Because of Nubia's unique position between two competing centers of power, her exact boundaries have never remained fixed. The present border between Egypt and the Sudan, which splits Nubia and divides the population, is the most recent outcome of this situation. Within Nubia itself, several distinct groups of peoples may be identified. Nubians speak two related languages in several localized dialects, and some other social and cultural differences are to be found among the inhabitants of this thousand miles of Nile shoreline.

Historically, the Nubian region has been both an isolated stretch of Nilotic villages and a continuously settled area of land linking sub-Saharan Africa and Egypt. In this unusual combination of circumstances lie many factors that help explain the development and persistence of this special group of people. Nubia, because of its often inhospitable desert environment and limited natural resources, has never become a traffic corridor or a mere zone of transition between Egypt and Africa. River traffic has always been discontinuous, impeded by long, impassable stretches along this section of the Nile and a shore line cut by rocky cliffs and water-filled ravines.

The relative poverty and isolation of the region discouraged colonialism and encouraged indigenous cultural development. Foreigners visited or invaded Nubia from time to time, as soldiers, administrators, and raiders; some married Nubian women, but until recently, when such intermarriage took place, the outsider was more likely to settle in the village community, than to take his bride out of Nubia. Thus, whatever the origins of the foreign fathers, the children of these unions grew up learning Nubian languages and customs. Contact with the outside world remained sporadic, and, as centuries passed, the small number of outsiders was each time gradually absorbed into the local communities.

Thus, the question of Nubian identity in a physical or a genetic sense is as complex as the question of their cultural heritage. Their physical appearance, as a tall dark-skinned people of proud bearing, remains distinctive in Egypt, however, despite their many resemblances to the people of Africa, the Mediterranean world, and the surrounding desert. Though in Sudan the Nubians cannot readily be distinguished from their other Muslim neighbors, in Egypt today the term Nubian still continues to refer to a black minority in the cities who come from a particular region of the country. Today, as we shall see in succeeding chapters, in spite of differences among themselves the Nubians' own sense of their identity is strong.

Like their American counterparts, the Nubians have had to struggle to overcome not only the disadvantages of rural origins but also the social stigma of historical involvements with slavery, involvements that for both groups finally ended in the nineteenth century. Both Nubians and American blacks have been victims of uncomplimentary references and stereotypic attitudes on the part of some of their numerically superior fellow citizens.

But the obvious comparison between these two minority groups must not be overdrawn. The persistence of exclusively Nubian villages, repositories of a distinct culture, has helped this people at all times to retain a sense of who they are. The black American is now attempting to discover a heritage all but obscured by generations of white domination. This is not a Nubian problem. Nor does the modern Nubian face the barrier of discriminatory legislation and racist institutions that have been the lot of American black men. Modern Nubian history is that of Muslims in a largely Muslim society, a society that has never created distinctions within itself through Jim Crow legislation. The Nubian people, without the crippling effects of institutionalized racism, have been able to establish peacefully a place for themselves in Egyptian society. Today Egyptian Nubians compare favorably with the Egyptian society at large by almost every social and economic standard.

The Nubians, like village people everywhere, have been obliged to cope with the problems of a modern world not of their making, a world created and dominated by urban people employing technologies far different from those utilized in small rural communities. For the Nubian population, however, the pressure has been particularly strong and relentless. Since the turn of the century, when the first barrage was constructed at Aswan, the arable lands of the Nubian valley, never plentiful, have been progressively diminished by the reservoirs of ever-higher dams. This steady encroachment culminated with the High Dam at Aswan, which has finally flooded the entire region of Egyptian Nubia and part of Sudan, necessitating the resettlement of those villagers who had not already departed to more prosperous regions of the country. For the first time in many centuries, technology has created an unoccupied zone between Sudan and Egypt; thus, Nubia, as an inhabited region, is now at an end in Egypt and greatly diminished in the Sudan. Nearly a decade has passed since the village Nubians faced the trauma of resettlement in government-built villages south of Aswan, near Kom Ombo, and in Kashim el-Ghurba in the Sudan, and the region we shall be discussing is now under many feet of water.

The sudden and dramatic quality of the Nubians' relocation should not obscure the fact that these people are experiencing, in a more concentrated way, what minorities of people throughout the world have faced: the loss of isolation and cultural independence, which threatens us all with the dreary consequences of uniformity. Traditional cultural differences, those unique variations in the conduct of human life, have for a long time been subject to the irresistible pressures of conforming change; cultural diversity is everywhere rapidly being replaced by the more banal difference of economic class. The effect of mass communication, easy social contacts, and common economic involvements threatens the persistence of all distinctive traditions just as surely as the Aswan High Dam threatened the existence of the Abu Simbel temple and the other monuments of Pharaonic culture in Nubia.

Seen against the larger background, the Nubian achievement has been remarkable. In a few generations, what the Nubians have accomplished is not the sterile preservation of themselves as cultural curiosities (however admirable) but rather a series of social transformations that have sustained their villages and permitted the individual Nubian to find his own footing in the rapidly changing world into which he has been thrust.

The more significant question is not "who are the Nubians" but how have they been able to cope. In 1963, when they were moved to Kom Ombo, the trauma of resettlement was great, and dire predictions were made about the Nubians' future. Yet today, less than fifteen years later, they dominate local elections to the Egyptian National Assembly; their children have demonstrated amazing success in the Aswan public schools; and they have renovated many of the houses provided by the Egyptian government, to make them conform more to Nubian ideas of space and comfort.

What are the particular qualities of Nubian culture that have enabled these people to face, with such courage and success, the change and uprooting to which they have been subject? Is the development of social means of resolving conflict and avoiding violence within their communities the key to their achievement? Has the central position of women as the guardians of cultural continuity provided a special strength? This essay is an effort to challenge, with new myths, the old myths about the Nubians derived from the tales of Scheherazade and the Pharaonic wall paintings. I use the phrase "new myths" advisedly, for Nubian river life of more than a decade ago, like the days of Scheherazade, is now a thing of the past.

The new myths that I will attempt to set forth are based on studies of Nubian history, culture, and society before resettlement. The substance of these new myths hopefully may help us understand some of the problems faced by comparable groups everywhere, perhaps by each of us as we attempt to deal with a world that so little resembles that of our parents.

The increasing loss of cultural, social, and economic autonomy and the often subsequent breakdown of social order that cultural minorities throughout the world have had to face cannot be avoided by creating artificial reservations that lack adequate and appropriate means of subsistence. We know this only too well from the disasters of our national policies toward the American Indians. The Soviet creation of ethnically and linguistically based "states" lacking political and economic autonomy may also prove, in the end, to have been a futile gesture. The problem is not how to avoid change but how we can accept it and survive, not only in the physical sense, but also in terms of the self-respect, sense of personal worth, group identity, and peaceful cooperation with one's fellow man that makes life worthwhile for the individual.

Thus, while the essay that follows is a picture of a way of life that has largely ceased to exist since the High Dam was built at Aswan, it is also a study of the cultural heritage of a people who have found ways of adapting to drastically changed conditions of life.

Of course, the key to the Nubians' success is to be found partly in the nature of Egyptian society, which has made many alien minorities a part of itself throughout its long history. But most importantly, the success of the Nubians rests, I believe, upon the nature of their own unique society. What kind of people created Nubian society? This is the central problem to which this essay is addressed. Even if the answer remains partially obscure, it is here we must search to understand something of the conditions necessary to the survival of us all in a changing world, which our plans cannot anticipate nor our minds fully comprehend.

# Chapter Ten

# The Nubian Past

Over several millennia, Pharaonic, Christian, and Muslim kingdoms rose and fell within or adjacent to the land we call Nubia. But until the middle of the twentieth century, the history of the Nubian people could only be dimly perceived within the chronological events set down in the written records of neighboring states and in the accounts of foreign travelers. Recent archaeological work and research in Arabic archives are now adding new perspectives to this framework, from Pharaonic times to the Christian period (from the sixth to the fifteenth century), and in the later Muslim era.

The many excavations of sites within Nubia that took place before the land was flooded by the Aswan High Dam have yielded a great deal of new information, including written documents, previously unknown, from the Christian period. "The known time range for old Nubian documents is from A.D. 795 to 1484. By far the greatest mass of this material (none of it yet published) has come from Qasr Ibrim; the majority of it is official and private letters, legal documents, and the like. . . . In fact, the material from Ibrim shows clearly that Old Nubian and Arabic were the secular written languages of medieval Nubia and were very widely understood, while Coptic and Greek were employed almost exclusively in religious texts."[1]

The Nubians themselves have as their heritage, in addition, an oral history, a rich, undated treasury of artifact and myth. For centuries these people were born and matured in a land filled with the monuments and ruins of past civilizations. Remnants of the Christian and early Muslim eras are part of the landscape, and folk traditions persist from both periods. The more spectacular temples and statuary of Pharaonic times, which have been part of the daily lives of the Nubians for as long as four thousand years, have also been the source of tales and legends.

128

In the twentieth century, the temples partly inspired an architectural renaissance in Egyptian Nubia.

However, this brief historical survey is not designed to claim, for example, that Pharaonic Egypt contributed only archaeological inspiration to modern Nubia, or to indicate what specific influences were added during Christian and Muslim eras. The threads of these historical experiences are woven so tightly into the fabric of contemporary Nubian culture that specific debts to the past can scarcely be identified. We can only examine some known events and conditions and try to infer what might have been the consequences of such events and conditions for the people of the time.

Egyptian Nubia has always been a relatively isolated area, somewhat poor in the resources that might have encouraged permanent colonization for agrarian purposes. The cataract at Aswan was a natural barrier to river traffic long before any dams were built, and the scorching deserts on either side of the narrow Nile valley discouraged both entry into and exit from the settled area. The arable land consisted of small amounts of alluvial soil deposited annually by the Nile. The size of such deposits varied according to the flood, and the soil shifted with the wind and water erosion. Beyond the alluvium lay sterile sand and rock, and the Nubians ventured into this barren area only to bury their dead or to gather the grasses and plants that sprang up spontaneously after an occasional rain.

On the other hand, until Nubia became a Muslim land, it was an important source of slaves for the Middle Eastern world. At different periods in its long history, Nubia also accumulated considerable wealth as an intermediary in trade between African and Mediterranean regions. It was therefore a target for numerous invasions and raids until this century.

The introduction of the water wheel to Nubia in Roman times was a significant contribution to the local economy. In peaceful years, the villagers utilized the water wheel to enlarge the area and extend the period of cultivation. But in troubled times, investments in irrigation equipment and arid terraced lands were not possible; the Nubians then must have survived by planting quick-growing crops like millet on the riverbanks, crops that could grow while the soil was still damp from the annual flood. The date palm trees brought a spurt of prosperity to some parts of Nubia, but these seem to have been introduced as a source of cash crops only during the nineteenth century. In general, the environment placed ironbound restrictions on the economic growth of the area; it could only provide a subsistence economy for a limited number of people. Given the meager resources, no population centers of any great size could develop. The entire population of the Nubian valley probably never numbered more than a few hundreds of thousands, and then only when peaceful conditions prevailed.

The conventional histories of this region must be examined, then, with the ecological background in mind. For example, we read that in the sixth century Nubia became a Christian land. The Empress Theodora sent missionaries from Constantinople who converted the local leaders, and shortly thereafter the entire thousand-mile area from Aswan to Dongola was united under one king. This achievement seems almost incredible if, that is, we view the Nubian conversion to Christianity and the subsequent statehood in anything like the modern sense.

For, as we have already stated, much of the Nubian region consisted of rocky shore line, and the settlements were sparse and widely separated. The obvious difficulties of communication must have limited considerably the contacts for both administrative and religious purposes. Postrevolutionary Egyptian officials tried, with modern technological means, to "integrate" Nubia into the centralized administration of Egypt. Yet, in 1960, few officials had penetrated this riverine land, and inhabitants of most of the villages could not remember that any outsiders had come to their communities before preparation for resettlement began. Probably, the Nubian communities, linguistically diversified and widely separated, were united and administered only enough to permit the more powerful centers of the region to collect tribute from the weaker, a pattern found elsewhere in the Middle East during this period.

The limited archaeological evidence from Christian times suggests the emergence of a wealthy clerical hierarchy, probably with considerable secular authority. On the walls of the rare Nubian churches found and excavated during the sixties, enormous frescoes were discovered, picturing ecclesiastical figures, dressed in the rich regalia of the Eastern church. Despite eyes somewhat distorted and enlarged according to the iconic style then in favor, the figures are undoubtedly Nubian.

Very likely the church of Theodora's time re-created in Nubia, on a reduced scale, the same hierarchically organized theocratic structure then existing in the Byzantine Empire. The claims of the church on the lives of the Nubians can be inferred from the presence of a few large public buildings, the cost of which would probably have been a burden for the average villager. The importance of the clerical hierarchy may have been limited in the more isolated settlements, yet the contribution of this religion to Nubian culture finds testimony in names, customs, legends, and folk art motifs, which have persisted in contemporary times. Furthermore, the Christian hierarchy of Nubia reinforced a structure for formal leadership and helped give the outside world an authority with which it could deal.

In the seventh century, the new Arab ruler of Egypt, ᶜAbdallāh ibn Saᶜd, invaded and conquered Nubia. But, instead of pressing the claim of Islam, he quickly withdrew and concluded a treaty with the Christian Nubian king that became the basis for relations between the two regions during the next six hundred years.

According to the treaty, an annual tribute of 350 slaves was sent to Cairo, following the custom in relations between a Muslim state and a subordinate Christian state. In return, the Egyptians were to send gifts to Nubia of food, horses, and cloth, which may well have been an important source of income for those who received and distributed this benefice. The treaty also suggests to us that Nubia was to remain open to Muslim traders, who were not to live there, but for whom a mosque was to be provided. Clearly, it was in the interests of Egypt to have, on its southern border, a friendly, technically independent buffer state with which it could trade.

Islam, however, was an important force in the lives of the Christian Nubians long before the final collapse of the Christian states and the eventual conversion of the population. To the north lay a powerful Muslim neighbor, Egypt, and the nomad tribes in the surrounding deserts were largely Muslims, as well. In the eleventh century, the Rabīᶜa, an Arabian tribe from Yemama who had first entered Egypt in the ninth century, forcibly settled in the Nubian region around Aswan, and at this time the first general conversion of a part of the Nubian population is likely to have occurred. The Rabīᶜa brought their religion and tribal political organization with them, but they adopted the language and presumably much of the culture of the villagers as, over the years, they intermarried with the local population and came to be called the Beni Kanz, and later the Kenuz, a name for this group of northern Nubians that survives to this day.[2]

The history books provide no further indications of mass conversion from Christianity to Islam until the final conversion of the local Nubian elite, some five centuries later, made it a matter of official state importance and thus worthy of recording. The Arab historian, Ibn Khaldūn, notes that in the fourteenth century southern Nubians in positions of authority, who needed to consolidate their ties with the more powerful Arab tribes occupying neighboring deserts, married their sisters to Arab sheikhs. In giving their women to the Arabs, says Ibn Khaldūn, the Nubians also gave away their princedoms, since not only did the children of such marriages become Muslims according to Muslim law, but also, according to Nubian custom, titles and lands were passed from sister's brother to sister's son.

If matrilineal inheritance was the Nubian custom in Christian times, the Nubians' vulnerability to Arab domination becomes clearer. Intermarriage, a famous instrument of diplomacy among Arab tribes long before Islam, transformed the Nubians into Muslims without the necessity of full-scale conversion. Again, however, it must be remembered that, whatever the father's origins, the child learns to speak from its mother and begins the discovery of himself generally within her domain. Thus, the southern villages of Fedija Nubians, like their northern Kenuzi neighbors, retained their own language and, we presume, much of their traditional culture. That this culture resembled that of other Nilotic villages more than that of the distant world of Byzantium seems safe to assume. Then, as now, this traditional culture, incorporating whatever elements it may have absorbed from other sources, was transmitted by the women of Nubia, in an almost unbroken sequence, to succeeding generations.

Around the beginning of the sixteenth century, the last Christian Nubian kingdoms passed from recorded history, and our knowledge of the local populations becomes even more limited. The villages of Nubia, lacking any centrally organized diplomacy and with very limited military strength, were left to deal with nomadic populations as best they could. As in other times and places, some of these villages surely placed themselves under the protection of specific tribes and came to be regarded in some instances as settled branches of the same tribal group.

The disappearance of the last active Christian church in Egyptian Nubia is recorded as having occurred during the sixteenth century, though most of the ecclesiastical organization had collapsed before this. Historical studies generally refer to Nubia as an Islamic region by this time. However, conversion to Islam could not at first have been universal, nor did it have uniform results for all Nubians. Chronicles of medieval times show that some Nubians, recognized as Muslims, were listed as free men in the labor forces of Lower Egypt. But at the time, Nubians were also taken in slavery, because they either were not Muslims or were not recognized as such. The northern Kenuzi Nubians would not seem to have been subject to enslavement, because of their earlier conversion and their proximity to Egyptian Muslim influence.

But many Nubian communities, particularly in the south, even if once converted to Islam, had little means of maintaining the practice of their new religion. With the collapse of the church-based administration, no central authority existed that could support local centers of learning, and the occasional presence of alien armed forces must have drained off any economic surpluses the area produced. Without provision for the continual propagation of the religion, conversion meant little to the convert, for Islam, particularly among non-Arabic-speaking people, needs literate men who can read the Quran, lead prayers, and supervise the religious education of the young. Therefore, if any of these Nubians are enslaved by Muslims, it must have been largely because, unable to demonstrate their beliefs, they were not regarded as true Muslims.

The issue of conversion to Islam and recognition as Muslims is thus extremely important to our understanding of the Nubian past, not only because of the great legacy of personal belief and social institutions that Islam provided for the Nubians, but also because recognition as Muslims ended the dangers of enslavement: Islam expressly forbids one Muslim to enslave another Muslim.

As a people, the Nubians were never totally enslaved, and the present generations are for the most part not the descendants of slaves. The latter qualification is needed only because Nubians, no less than other middle Eastern groups, owned slaves, as part of their household labor forces, while this practice was permitted and when they could afford to do so. As elsewhere, the slaves were absorbed eventually into the population and strengthened the African contribution to the Nubian community. Those Nubians who were themselves unfortunate enough to be taken and enslaved (young boys were preferred) were lost to their villages forever. Often they were castrated, thus eliminating even the possibility of descendants outside Nubia.

But association with slavery, in whatever form, has left a common legacy among Nubians, expressed today in their determination to refute any accusation of inferiority, by demonstrating their devotion to Islam and by striving to advance through the channels of social mobility that are as open to them as to all other Egyptians. For, unlike black Americans, black Egyptians never have had to face the social and economic barriers of racist institutions, which have remained an obstacle to equality of opportunity in the United States long after the institution of slavery was outlawed. Being recognized as Muslim conferred formal equality, and this has had a formative influence on Nubian life in the last century.

The collapse of the Christian states in Nubia and the conversion of the population to Islam coincided with the long period of Mameluke rule in Egypt. The Mamelukes were a military slave elite who ruled Egypt from 1250 to 1517 and then administered it until their power was decisively ended by Mohammed Ali in the early nineteenth century. Relations between Egypt and Nubia during this long period varied between total lack of interest in Nubia to the establishment of military garrisons near the present southern border of Egypt. As we shall see, these garrisons became the basis for new ruling aristocracies in the region. In the final overthrow of the Mamelukes, their survivors fled south, attempting to escape Mohammed Ali, and ravaged many Nubian communities.

Troubled conditions persisted in much of Nubia until the latter part of the nineteenth century. Again, the situation varied, as European travelers of the period have attested. James August St. John traveled in Nubia in 1832, and at some points in his journey up the Nile south of Aswan he found a desperately poor people, living half-naked, in make-shift houses, having been reduced by Mameluke raids, apparently, to the most meager levels of subsistence:

> . . . in all of these villages there is no bread to be obtained. Milk and butter are generally found, however, but these, together with eggs, — when they can be procured — are considerably dearer than in Egypt. . . . [the Nubians] appear, at present, to entertain no hopes of a political change, though the slightest reverses occurring to Mohammed Ali, would again, I make no doubt, awaken their ancient love of anarchical independence. If we assert, with Burckhardt, that the villages of the Nubians are built of stone, a wrong idea of them will certainly be conveyed; yet I scarcely know what other terms to employ. The huts of which they consist are, in many cases, merely so many low circular walls of small loose stones, piled rudely upon each other, and covered above with dhourra [millet] stalks; they are so frail that the smallest force would be sufficient to destroy them. Twelve or thirteen of these huts, often fewer, huddled together among heaps of ancient ruins, or on the shingly slope of the mountains, constitute a village, or hamlet, which might be easily passed without notice, particularly in the dawn or twilight, being exactly of the same hue as the surrounding rocks.[3]

Yet, despite the poverty of the Nubians, St. John records with admiration their industry: in other areas of the country, he notes, "every day we saw fresh proofs of the industrious character of the present inhabitants. The perseverance they exhibit in watering their fields, when prevented by poverty from erecting *sakia*[s] [water wheels in Egyptian Arabic] is exemplary."[4]

The above observation can be contrasted with the description of Nubian activity near Aswan, closer to Egypt, in the area where Islam had been longer established. Just south of the First Cataract near the temple of Philae, St. John reports that he saw the following:

> . . . to enlarge the extent of their fields, the industrious inhabitants construct long walls, or jetties, of large stones, running out at right angles with the banks to a considerable distance into the stream, narrowing its course, and allowing the mud, which quickly accumulates behind them, to harden into solid land, which is immediately brought into cultivation. I have observed a similar practice on a smaller scale, upon the banks of the Rhone, in the Upper Valais; where, in fact, much land might thus be gained, had the Valaisans half the industry and energy of the Nubians. The skill, neatness and enterprise of these people, who, having for ages enjoyed more freedom, are superior in vigour and hardihood to the Fellahs, excited our admiration.[5]

As he moved once more farther south, into the Fedija area, St. John noted still other developments:

> The inhabitants of Derr are supposed to be the descendants of a number of Bosnian soldiers, established in Nubia by the Sultan Selym; and still in a great measure preserve their comparatively fair complexion and European features, though in many instances, it is clear, from their physiognomy, they have intermarried with blacks. In the morning several decently dressed lads passed by our boat on their way to school, with the wooden tablets, on which they are taught to write, in their hands.[6]

The areas around Derr and around Ibrim had prospered to some degree despite, or perhaps in part because of, the foreign garrisons sent by the Ottomans to Egyptian Nubia, the southernmost outpost of their empire. Not only Kurds and Hungarians, but also mercenary soldiers from many distant regions of the Oriental and Occidental Turkish world, came to Nubia, where they perished, departed, or intermarried with the local population and settled there. The mixed origins of these Nubians' forebears are still reflected in such local family names as Magari and Kurdi. During this long and obscure period of foreign intrusions into the southern region of Egyptian Nubia, a succession of hereditary Muslim overlords, entitled Kāshifs, became established. These men, absorbed into the Nubian community, had brought with them the education and literacy of the wider Islamic congregation. Under their supervision, mosques and Quranic schools were built, which served to indicate to the world at large that here indeed was a congregation of Muslims—a community thereby excluded from predatory slave raids.

The Kāshifs of Ottoman times were replaced by Mohammed Ali with his own administrative officers, also called Kāshifs. Their rule was often tyrannical.[7] Through intermarriage, however, many Fedija Nubians trace descent from these men, as well as from Ottoman Kāshifs, and it is still a source of some prestige. Even after the advent of British colonial administration, Kāshif descendants retained considerable local authority in some Nubian communities.

When, in 1811, Mohammed Ali struck down the Mameluke leaders in Cairo, many Mamelukes fled south and caused much destruction; there is little doubt that they were responsible for some of the desolation reported by St. John. Some Mamelukes, upon reaching Nubia, attempted to challenge the position of the Kāshifs appointed by Mohammed Ali and establish themselves at Qasr Ibrim among the Fedija Nubians. These last invaders of Nubia failed to secure their position, were driven from Egyptian Nubia, and were finally captured and returned to Lower Egypt.

Between 1880 and 1900, Great Britain assumed control in Egypt and the Sudan and finally ended the slave trade along the Nile. Kāshif rule also was ended. For the first time, the Nubians were left free to attend to their own affairs without the interference of a local aristocracy and without fear of slave raids. According to one Nubian, "During the period of British authority we were like the man in the middle in bed between two others. Although the man on each side of the bed pulled the blanket back and forth, the man in the middle was never uncovered, and remained warm and secure."

Several points emerge from this brief survey. First, it seems improbable that Nubia ever was a highly integrated or complex society. The topography of the region and its meager resources generally limited such development. Only the richest communities could support a stratified society; the number of such communities fluctuated with the prosperity of the region, and they were probably not larger than small market towns. Throughout history, Nubia remained primarily a long, narrow, and irregularly spaced succession of villages along the Nile; except in Dongola, no other more cohesive form of settlement was possible. Christian and Muslim hierarchies could thus rise and fall, and their effect on the majority of Nubian settlements was largely absorbed by the stronger and more persistent patterns of village life.

Invasion and colonization in Nubia resulted in intermarriage and assimilation. The invaders were always men, and the Nubian women thus remained a stable and permanent force in the society, passing on their traditions to their children. Finally, over many centuries, slavery touched the lives of Nubians, though this experience varied within the area. The major effects of slavery on Nubian society were twofold. At various times, it created dangerous insecurity in most communities and prevented them from developing their own resources. Second, slavery prejudicially affected social attitudes toward Nubians in Egypt and elsewhere in the Middle East. Obviously, however, the Nubians of today are not the descendants of slaves; those unfortunate people who were victims of the slave trade were, as we have said, lost to their own communities forever.

Entry into the modern world in the nineteenth century as Muslims ended the long period when Nubians were often at the mercy of more powerful neighbors. As Muslims, they had the freedom to develop their own villages again and were permitted to travel to the cities of the Middle East, as free men, to seek employment. The period of ignorance in Nubia was at an end, the Nubians' status as members of the Islamic community assured. This was a time of great development, a golden age of Nubian culture.

### Footnotes

[1] William Y. Adams, personal communication.

[2] Beni Kanz and Kenuz were terms derived from the title "Kanz el-Dawla" bestowed on a chief of this group in late Fatimid times.

[3] James August St. John, *Egypt and Mohammed Ali, or Travels in the Valley of the Nile*, I, 380-381.

[4] Ibid., pp. 386-387.

[5] Ibid., p. 366.

[6] Ibid., p. 438.

[7] A tale from Ballana illustrates the high-handed ways of the Kāshifs, even after loss of official recognition: The wife from a rich and powerful Kāshif family used to reserve the right to go through the luggage of Nubian labor migrants who returned to Ballana villages with presents from the city for their families. She took for herself the items that pleased her before distribution to the family could occur. This is said to have happened to the grandparents of older Nubians near the turn of this century.

# Chapter Eleven

# Nubian Origins

The relationship of the present Nubians to the ancient populations of Egypt and Sudan and to the Nubian kingdoms of Kush has yet to be fully established by archaeologists and historians. However, we do know that contemporary Nubians are a mixture of many peoples. The African, Arabic, and Mediterranean contributions to the population may be surmised from the Nubians' appearance and have been recently demonstrated in studies of blood types. Some tentative explanations of how this process occurred may be inferred from the more recent history related in Chapter 10. Here we are concerned with linguistic and geographic evidence, to help identify the major groupings within the Nubian people before resettlement. Language distribution is also relevant in examining relations between the Nubians and their neighbors, particularly those of Upper Egypt.

Upper Egypt, home of the Saᶜīdī peoples, conventionally is defined as the area from Asyūt south to Aswan. On the outskirts of Aswan, the Nubian villages began and extended south along the Nile past the Egyptian Sudanese border to Khartoum. If, however, we accept the Nubian view of the location of their people, Nubians are also to be found north of Aswan town, in the rich agricultural areas around Esna, Edfu, Daraw, and Kom Ombo. The inhabitants of many villages in the region look Nubian, being somewhat darker than other Egyptians. Members of an old Upper Egyptian tribal grouping, the Gaᶜafra, these people are generally considered to be Saᶜīdīs like their neighbors, and it would be difficult to make a clear-cut separation between the various groups in the area. However, many Gaᶜafra believe they are related to the Nubians, a belief reciprocated by the Nubians themselves.

The Fedija, Nubians of the South, have described the Gaᶜafra people as ''Arab Egyptianized'' Nubians with whom they feel at home and share similar attitudes and life styles, even though they no longer share a common language. The

136

Ga^cafra apparently feel somewhat the same way, for, during the years of the British Mandate, many young men from these villages reportedly chose to serve not in the regular divisions of the Egyptian army but in the Hagana, the Sudanese border unit, which contained a large percentage of Nubians.

Aside from the possibly related Ga^cafra, few Nubians lived north of the Aswan Dam until their total resettlement near Kom Ombo in 1963. However, some villages had been relocated north of Aswan in the early part of the twentieth century, after they had been displaced by the raising of the earlier dam. The first principal all-Nubian villages, before final resettlement, were found south of the Esna-Kom Ombo region, across the old dam and the First Cataract. These were Kenuzi settlements. The existence here of the Kenuz, occupying approximately one-third of Egyptian Nubia south of Aswan, continues to be a major puzzle for the student of Nubian history. The Kenuz speak a Nubian language that is understood and shared by the people of Dongola, in the Sudan, more than a thousand miles to the south. Yet nothing in the oral traditions of the Nubians or in historical accounts tells us when or how the geographic division took place between the ancestors of the two populations. The close similarity of their speech suggests, however, that it occurred not too many centuries ago.

If, as we presume, the Kenuz and the Dongolawī were once one people, who separated from whom? The Dongolawī people are much the larger of the two groups and lived in the most fertile and ample region of the Upper Nile, whereas the Kenuz in Egyptian Nubia are a small minority of approximately fifty thousand persons. The best evidence, however, that the Kenuz were immigrants from Dongola is probably linguistic, in that there is historical evidence of a language boundary at the southern border of Dongola (where it is today) as early as the late tenth century, whereas Old Nubian documents record no dialect boundary in Egyptian Nubia at that time.[1] Nubians have suggested that perhaps the Kenuz were originally a trade colony, sent by a Dongolawī kingdom to look after trade and shipment at the First Cataract at Aswan, the old port city that marked the boundary on the Nile between Egypt and the ancient Christian kingdoms of Nubia.

In Pharaonic times Aswan produced, not grain, but granite for sculptures; but it was also a rich and important entrepôt and border station and continued to be so in medieval times, long after the Muslim conquest of Egypt in the seventh century. The region between Dongola and Aswan was occupied by several often independent and mutually antagonistic political entities during much of the Christian era. Thus, it seems plausible that, for both commercial and political reasons, groups of Dongolawī may have clustered under the protection of the Egyptian border station at Aswan, their business being to facilitate shipments of goods between Egypt and Dongola. Camel caravans, assembled south of the First Cataract, could avoid contact with the ancestors of the Fedija Nubians, immediately south of the Kenuz, by traveling overland. This transport history might explain the Kenuzi domination of most of the commerce that (until recently) took place between Aswan, the Kenuzi villages, and the Fedija Nubian villages all the way to Wadi Halfa.

Until half a century ago the large commercial sailboats plying the Nile were almost all owned by Kenuz, and up to the time of resettlement, Kenuzi merchant boatmen regularly traveled up and down the river, peddling their wares in the villages of Fedija Nubians, far from their own homes. Kenuz often seek employment on Egyptian and foreign ships; in fact, some Kenuzi men spend a lifetime in maritime service abroad. The Kenuzi reputation as travelers and tradesmen thus would seem to support the "trade colony" theory of their background.

To see the Kenuz as being of recent, intrusive origin, separating the historic Fedija people from the Ga$^c$afra and the rest of the older Sa$^c$īdī population of Upper Egypt, also helps us to understand the existence of the cultural line between Nubia and Egypt, which has been conventionally drawn at Aswan. Over many generations a grey zone probably existed between the two historic groups, a zone neither totally Sa$^c$īdī nor totally Fedija, created by frequent social contacts and by intermarriage. The districts north of Aswan town, mentioned above, comprised this zone, a region from which the tough, handsome Egyptian Sa$^c$īdī has emerged, a mingling of Egyptian, Nubian, and Arabian over the last thousand years.

The coming of the Kenuz, a people without historic ties to the other inhabitants, may have created the first sharp division at Aswan, effectively blocking contacts between the older settlers, north and south. Agricultural resources were always very marginal along this stretch of river near the First Cataract and could support in the best of times only a relatively small population. Possibly, the Dongolawī ancestors of the present Kenuzi people, dependent primarily on trade rather than agriculture, had become numerically and linguistically predominant by the time the Beni Kanz came from the desert and overran the area in the eleventh century.

This hypothesis is further strengthened by the somewhat parallel existence of another intrusive population farther south, the small enclave of Arabic-speaking "Nubians" found between the Kenuz and the Fedija, in the Wadi el-Arab region. Many of the men in this intermediate area were descended from members of the Allaqat tribe, which originated in the Nejd of northern Arabia. These Nubians still consider themselves Allaqat and have occasional contacts with the tribe. Their genealogies reveal marriages with both men, and, to a lesser extent, Fedija, but the language has remained exclusively Arabic for most of the men and women in the region. Until very recently these people did not call themselves Nubians at all, and they are now so identified in a political-territorial rather than an ethnic-linguistic sense.

These Arabs explain their presence in Nubia by recalling that they (too) were traders. Situated at a strategic point, where the Nile bent sharply for a brief span, thus making river travel slow and difficult against prevailing winds, the Arabs were able to offer merchants faster and less expensive travel overland. During the days of Kāshif rule in Nubia, from the early seventeenth until the nineteenth century, the ancestors of the present Arab enclave transshipped goods by camel caravan overland from Wadi el-Arab to the towns of the Sudan. Beyond Wadi Halfa, the Second and Dal cataracts made the Nile unnavigable for long stretches; presumably, this natural barrier, combined with the presence of alien forces in the region, made further river shipment impractical.

Thus, by the fifteenth century, when Moslem Arab power had largely, but not entirely, gained ascendancy over Christian Nubia, a Moslem Arab outpost in Egyptian Nubia linked trade partners and kinsmen in Moslem Arab regions of the Sudan by caravan routes. In just this way the Christian ancestors of the Kenuz may have been linked to Christian Dongola, also bridging an alien population in an earlier era.

Beyond the Arab enclave, south of Wadi el-Arab, lay the first villages of the Fedija Nubians.[2] The term *Fedija* raises problems; historically, these people used no term of self-reference other than *Nubi*. *Fedija* is in fact a Kenuzi word that means fellah (peasant), a term that has less than complimentary connotations. The historic relations between these two groups have not been particularly warm, and the fact that the Fedija have begun to refer to themselves by this term no doubt reflects the several generations of peaceful contact that have passed between the two groups.

Contact between the Fedija Nubians and the Mahas and Sukkot groups farther south was inhibited by the rapids and barren cliffs of the Batn el-Haggar, a thinly populated region that extends from the Second Cataract south of Wadi Halfa to the Dal Cataract. The Fedija share their language with Mahas and Sukkot Nubians, and the house types and other readily observable aspects of their culture are similar. After the Dal Cataract the Nile Valley south to the Third Cataract (the Abri-Delgo Reach) became fertile and supported many large villages of Mahasi-speaking Nubians on both sides of the Nile.

The linguistic boundary between the Mahas-Sukkot peoples and the Dongolawī occurs a few kilometers south of the Third Cataract of the Nile. However, the Third Cataract was neither a great natural obstacle nor an important historical or political boundary and therefore does not explain this linguistic division.

Dongola, with its broad fertile shorelands and islands of rich soil, south of the Third Cataract, is still occupied by people who to some degree identify with the heritage of the ancient kingdom that flourished there, in the cities of Kerma and Old Dongola.

Dongola was beyond the scope of our study of Egyptian Nubia. However, according to one authority, the people of this region "are really Nubian only in speech (which is rapidly disappearing); in all other respects they are as thoroughly Arabized as their cousins, the Shaiqiya and Jaᶜaliyin, and they generally deny a Nubian identity. . . . On the other hand, the Mahasi retain, at least up to now, a definite sense of their special identity and history. Consequently, I would say that the Mahasi of the Abri-Delgo Reach (i.e., those that were not displaced by the Aswan Dam), rather than the Danagla [Dongolawī], represent the probable last refuge of distinctly Nubian culture and traditions."[3]

With linguistic divisions and a long history of shifting political boundaries and alliances, how appropriate is it to speak of an autochthonous "Nubian" people? Anthropologist William Y. Adams, who has made the culture history of Nubia an object of extensive archaeological research, has provided an authoritative observation in this regard." There is very little doubt that until three or four centuries ago (i.e., until the Arabization of the Shaiqiya, Jaᶜaliyin, etc.) Nubians formed a solid linguistic and cultural bloc extending along the Nile from Aswan in the north at least to the junction of the Niles, and probably to Sennar, in the south, and perhaps westward into Kordofan and Darfur as well. How long they may have been in this habitat is uncertain, but I think it was certainly long enough to qualify them as 'autochthonous.'"[4]

The questions as to how long the people we call Nubian have lived in this region, where they may have come from originally, and their possible relationship with the ancient civilizations of Kush, which once occupied much of Nubia, must await the results of recent (and future) research. The forthcoming study of Nubian history by William Y. Adams will undoubtedly add much to our understanding of these problems.

Use of the term *Nubian* as a self-referent has only become general among the Egyptian Nubians in recent years; a sense of identity has developed as the construction of the High Dam has made Nubians the object of national attention and has presented them with a crisis of overriding importance. At the same time, the construction of the High Dam has permanently divided the Nubians of Egypt from those of Sudan through resettlement. The Nubians of Egypt are no longer a Nilotic people, and the patterns of life developed along the river must now be adjusted to a radically different environment in much closer association with the peoples of Upper Egypt. Before discussing this problem of adjustment, we need to look at the traditional circumstances of Egyptian Nubians in what they refer to as their "golden age," those decades just prior to resettlement.

### Footnotes

[1] William Y. Adams, personal communication.
[2] Elsewhere the term *Mahas* has been used to refer to the Fedija and their language, but Mahas also refers to a Sudanese Nubian group immediately south. The two groups are closely related, but to avoid confusion I utilize only *Fedija* throughout this book.
[3] William Y. Adams, personal communication.
[4] Ibid.

# Chapter Twelve

# The Nubian Polity

Nubians speak of their native land as *balad elaman*, a land of safety and security, a place where people and property were secure and where one could live in peace. To those of us who, as outsiders, have lived in Nubia, the claims as to the blessed quality of life do not seem exaggerated. One cannot associate violence with this land and people. Nor were the more subtle patterns of factionalism and hostility so evident here as they sometimes are in village life elsewhere. This fundamental impression of the nonviolent, peaceful quality of Nubian life can only be explained or made plausible if we understand what I have chosen to call the Nubian polity. Polity, in this sense, involves economy and ecology, as well as the kinship organization, and the values and attitudes associated with these basic conditions of everyday life.

Social organization in the traditional Nubian village was simple in the sense that no special officers existed who made executive decisions or judged conflicts. The same patterns of association between individuals that sufficed to carry on the work of cultivation managed to resolve the conflicts that are everywhere a part of human relationships. Whatever the political institutions of the past may have been during the Christian period, for instance, or during the days of Turkish Kāshif rule, these were largely forgotten by the time of our studies. Until the building of the High Dam and the consequent resettlement, Nubians, though technically subject to the administrative authority of Cairo, remained largely free of outside interference. Many villagers we visited by sailboat and donkey could not remember when a stranger had last approached their shores. The occasional administrators from the central ministries in Cairo confined their visits largely to the *omda*, the locally selected, but government-appointed Nubian who acted as liaison between the villages of his district and the outside world. The Nubian villages, poor in resources, and of slight political significance, had little interest for the national government. Only after the Nasser revolution of 1952 did a more benevolent form of interference begin to appear in the form of schools, subsidized staple foods, fuel, and occasional medical services. But these comparatively recent developments had still not touched the lives of all the villages prior to resettlement.

Although the Nubian villages were tied to cities hundreds of miles away through a pattern of labor migrancy we shall discuss later, in terms of their everyday life they were isolated far beyond the degree characteristic of many peasant communities, where trips to the city market regularly break the seasonal routine. The desolate environment behind the villages tied the people more closely to the edge of the Nile than most peasants are tied to their communities. Movement from village to village was difficult; boat travel was slow where it existed at all, and moving along the Nile by donkey from one village to the next took time and effort. Cities of any size were hundreds of miles away — so that until this century little contact existed between Nubian villagers and the outside world.

When peaceful conditions permitted the Nubians to live in their villages and cultivate with some security, efforts were made to cultivate all of the very limited arable land. Irrigation was necessary, and in some areas local conditions made practicable the construction of water wheels (*eskalay*), an invention introduced in Roman times, which, at that time, significantly increased cultivation. Where shore condition or the paucity of exposed alluvium did not justify the expense of water-wheel construction, a second device, the *keeyay*, or water-bucket lift, was used, although the *keeyay* conveyed only a small fraction of the water that an *eskalay* could handle. Since the land irrigated by either device was likely to be strictly limited, it is not surprising that the word *eskalay* means not only water wheel but also the land cultivated by means of this mechanism.

In the Fedija area, where water wheels persisted until he resettlement of 1963, construction of an *eskalay* required a concentration of wealth often beyond the means of those owning the adjacent land.[1] The wooden piles that had to be driven into the muddy shore of the Nile, the complex wheels that dipped an endless chain of clay buckets into the water, the platform on which a pair of cows turned the mechanism, and the hollow logs that carried the water to the farm land were all individually valued, different families taking responsibility for the construction of these expensive parts. The total cost was more than a single household might accumulate in a lifetime.

The Fedija Nubians point to the great expense of the *eskalay* to explain the mixture of families in some villages. Any man who could share the investment necessary to build a water wheel acquired a right to a share of the produce of the *eskalay*; this in turn might encourage him to settle a son near the *eskalay* through marriage with a principal landowner, for a Nubian bride customarily brought with her a certain amount of land, which the bridegroom added to his own inheritance as the basic resource for the new family. The Nubians of Ballana remember that the Kāshif often obliged Nubians to give them a daughter in marriage in exchange for an interest in an *eskalay*.

Water wheels were land-water-machine complexes instituted by means of shared investments. The principal means of avoiding excessive division of the complex through inheritance was marriage. Marriage linked the co-owners of the wheel and the land, and subsequently their offspring; since Nubians prefer marriage between relatives, especially paternal cousins, these unions frequently rewove the strands of kinship between descendants and co-owners. As married couples, the intermarrying cousins in effect added together the same inherited interests that their fathers, as brothers, had divided.

Nor was this pattern of kinship networks and shared economic interests limited to the *eskalay*. Palm trees were another important example of the same phenomenon. The initial ownership of a palm tree was usually based on a three-way partnership between a landowner, the owner of the palm shoot, and the person (usually a woman) who watered the shoot constantly over the many months before it got its growth and could draw sufficient moisture through its own roots. As a result of these investments of labor, real estate, and "capital," the ownership of the palm tree was divided three ways, but, as the shares were subsequently divided between heirs or given to children as wedding gifts, the rights to the fruit of the tree became widely diffused and each Nubian was likely to be involved in many such minicorporate marriage and descent networks, no one with exactly the same composition as the next. At the time of the date harvest one saw groups sitting under the trees, the fruit from each tree being divided and subdivided into little piles of dates, usually under the general direction of the old women who best remembered the complicated rights of ownership involved.

Cows, also, were corporately owned and were an essential source of power in the traditional Nubian economy, being the only creatures used to turn the heavy water wheels. Without these animals, the wheels stood idle and the fields untilled. Yet, cows, subject to death and sickness, were a rapidly depreciating investment, somewhat redeemed by the possibility of calving. Following the general pattern of shared resource ownership, most farmers had interests in several cows, a "leg," or one quarter, of the cow being a common share. The person who sheltered and fed the cow when it was not working was entitled to its milk and calves as compensation (though these arrangements varied); each of the other co-owners had to feed and water the cow during the twelve-hour shift that the animal worked on their *eskalay*. Each *eskalay* had a piece of land set aside for raising feed for the cows when they worked a shift at the wheel, thus eliminating arguments over dividing responsibility for feed among the various owners of the *eskalay*.

Buying shares in a cow was a relatively high yielding if somewhat risky investment for the Nubian with extra cash. He could buy cow or calf shares up for sale, leave the animals in the stables of the other owners, and collect rent on their use (a share of the crop being irrigated), since he then owned more right to cow labor than he needed himself. A study of cow ownership by Abdul Hamid El Zein reveals a very complex stock-market-like situation with price fluctuations, marginal buying, and monopolistic potentials. Cows sometimes became a source of social discord, and thus it was probably well for the peace of the Nubian society that *eskalay* and palm shares, after the initial investment, were never sold or traded like cow shares, but only inherited or bestowed upon the young as gifts.

The significance of the system of shared ownership goes well beyond economic considerations. An annual trip to a neighboring village to collect a few handfuls of dates clearly had more social importance in terms of maintaining relationships with the collateral ranches of the family than in terms of the actual material value involved. "We know the family is still together," said one Fedija Nubian, "when it gathers to divide the produce from land or date trees owned by our great-great-grandfathers. When the shareholders say 'I don't care; help yourself,' then we know the big family is breaking up."

In the case of the *eskalay*, one or two men usually cultivated the land as part owners as well as sharecroppers for the frequently numerous other shareholders. Many of the shareholders might be away working in the cities of Egypt or the Sudan, having relinquished their rights to the produce of the *eskalay* for years. The important consideration was that the absent villager owned shares that were remembered and that could be activated should he or other members of his immediate family return for a visit or settle again in the village. The basic resources of Nubia not only served to sustain the families that actively utilized them, but also helped to maintain social ties with the large percentage of residents who lived and worked elsewhere. In such ingenious fashion the villages and extended families of Nubia managed to hold the loyalties of many more individuals than the strictly limited resources could support.

Without recognized rights to land and palm trees, the individual migrant's tie to the village had no substance; claiming or retaining rights to a share of the village produce was tantamount to public recognition of membership in a descent group represented in the village. If one has recognized kinship in a Nubian community, then one must by the same token have some claim to the community s resources. Cow shares are sold and bought, but other property rights become available only as gifts at marriage or through inheritance and, of course, can only be disposed of in the same manner.

In peasant villages and urban settings throughout the world, the inheritance of property is both the greatest threat and the greatest source of strength to bonds of kinship. How many families are irrevocably divided because of quarrels over inheritance? How many claim the loyalty of their members because of a persistent interest in family property? I have suggested that Nubian society would be threatened with total extinction if its economic resources were not used because of disputes over property ownership; this theory still does not explain why such disputes do not generally occur. The reasons for such an unusually peaceful state of affairs lie partly in urban attitudes and values and partly in the Nubian kinship system.

The Kenuzi and Fedija Nubians differ significantly in their systems of kinship, for the influence of the Beni Kanz Arabs on the natives of what is now the Kenuzi region transformed that society into a segmentary tribal organization not unlike that of Arab tribes found elsewhere in the Middle East.[2] Tribal groups were distributed over a number of villages divided into maximum lineages, subdivided into secondary lineages, and finally separated into individual families—all reckoned on the basis of descent from a common ancestor. In the past the tribal system of the Kenuz may have been closely linked to property rights, but our evidence for this is limited. At the time of the Nubian Ethnological Survey, much of the land in the Kenuzi region had disappeared under the waters backed up by the dams constructed before the High Dam at Aswan. Neither palm trees nor *eskalays* existed in the Kenuzi village at the time of our studies. Only in the saints' shrines that dotted the area did the tribe actively share a common interest with common responsibilities at certain specific times of the year during the *moulid* celebrations (these will be discussed in more detail subsequently).

The Fedija Nubians, on the other hand, were still able to cultivate much of their ancestral land in the southern most districts of Ballana and Adendan and were generally better off than their Kenuzi neighbors to the north. As late as 1962, the large stands of date palms in the Ballana, Adendan, and Abu Simbel districts were still an important source of income for the villages. Thus, it was possible, at the time of the survey, to see something of the way in which kinship organization controlled the peaceful and sustained exploitation of the meager natural resources.

The Fedija refer to all units of family membership as *nog(s)*.[3] A man's first *nog* is his household, the group of people for whom he is economically and socially responsible, including his wife, or wives, and children, as well as any other relatives who live in his house and are dependent on him for support. (Few Nubians have more than one wife, but those who do feel it is desirable to support the wives in different houses—this is the only situation in which the man's first *nog* will encompass more than one household.) In other contexts, all of a man's dependents may be referred to as his *nog*. Only with marriage does one acquire the *nog*, or responsibility of an adult; the *nog* is the primary group that pays a man respect and is obedient to him.

The best definition of the second *nog* is also a function of how it operates; the second *nog* is comprised of those relatives with whom one still divides the products of land and trees, no matter how small the shares may have become. Therefore, most men have two, largely overlapping *nogs*: the *nog* of one's father, wherein most of the household property is shared, and the *nog* of one's mother. The matrilineal *nog* is often very close in composition to the patrilineal *nog*, since, by preference, many marriages are between men and women who share patrilineal ancestors. Yet, a mother is likely to have received some shares of property from a relative who did not provide property for her husband, and the children will be involved with both sets of people. Where a man has made an exogamous marriage, the mother's *nog* will, of course, involve her children with another largely different set of people.

The bilateral *nogs* are not only of economic importance to the child. "Mother's relatives" remain a separate and important category even when mother and father are paternal cousins. As one Nubian explained it, "My mother's relatives were those men [and women] whom I met while they were in the house with her; my father's [male] relatives were men I met outside with him." Although in Nubian society social segregation of males and females is not nearly so rigorously practiced as in many traditional Arab settings, men do not ordinarily venture into the private quarters of a house unless they are the brothers, fathers, or husbands of the women of the house, or are kinsmen who, through family tradition, have long been intimates of the household. Thus, even in this society of endogamous marriages, the child's world is divided into two sets of relatives: the indulgent, loving group around the mother with whom one can behave with great informality, and the group surrounding the father—those who represent the family in society, who care for its honor, and who must be accorded respect lest a son blacken the reputation of his own kinsmen by appearing not to care about his father's dignity.

The child owes less to the matrilineal *nog* and, materially, is likely to receive less. Yet, many Nubians mention being taken by their mothers some distance from the home village to attend a division of dates among the mother's relatives. Many Fedija men can recite the maternal lineage of their mother almost as readily as that of their father, going back seven or eight generations, and a number of Nubian men carry the mother's rather than the father's name as their own second name. For example, instead of being called Abdulla *Hassan*, the name of his father, a man might be called Abdulla *Fatooma*, the latter being his mother's name. Abdulla Fatooma would not officially be the man's name, but it would be the name by which he was called.

In a number of ways, the Nubian kinship organization resembles American kin systems more than that of most Arabs, who much more exclusively emphasize patrilineal descent and relationship. (I, for example, am ''Alta's boy'' in some situations and ''George's boy'' in others.) However, as the child moves to the most inclusive and public kinship group to which he belongs, the emphasis on paternal descent is reasserted. The largest *nog* includes a large number of smaller *nogs* spread over a number of villages and districts and is defined as these men (and their household *nogs*) who bear the same family name.

While the members of the largest *nog* presumably share a common paternal ancestor, though he may be ten or twelve generations in the past, the largest *nog* does not usually carry the name of that ancestor, as is characteristic among the Arabs. Rather, the name of the *nog* often refers to some quality or outstanding event in the experience of the group. One important *nog* of this largest type is the Fagirob, who are found in several districts and many villages near the Sudanese-Egyptian border. The Fagirob trace their ancestry eleven generations back to a man named Sharif, but the group's name (Fagir, i.e. Fakir) came into use because, it is said, the men of this group at one time were religious teachers of the Sufi persuasion; many Fagirob still claim a particular interest in religion. This use of an adjectively derived name, rather than a specific ancestor's name, gives the system considerable flexibility. Family identity may be maintained among the widest possible group of people, not only those directly descended from the common ancestor, and permits movement into the group as well as movement out of the group through migration and loss of contact. For example, descendants of a man married to a Fagirob woman might eventually call themselves Fagirob, particularly if the property they inherited was from the mother's people.

A man's largest *nog* is thus not strictly divided into lineages, as in Arab tribes, but rather consists of smaller *nogs* composed of men who share property. The *nogs* are overlapping, in the sense that a man may own shares in several different groups, not all of which are his closest kinsmen. This feature is very important, for, unlike the Arab tribe, the Nubian *nog* does not split easily into opposing segments of kinsmen.

While the Fedija Nubians know of the Arab feud, they have no memory of such a custom, and indeed, given the nature of their *nogs*, it is difficult to see how the feud could have developed; feuds usually require sharp definitions between "us" and "them," which hardly seem possible in the flexible Nubian kinship system we have described. To pin on the Fedija kinship system the conventional classificatory terms used by anthropologists (which largely depend on the way in which descent is reckoned) is to unduly formalize the system.

Because more individuals have rights to shares of village harvests than could possibly subsist from them if all the rights were exercised, and because many individuals must find their living in the cities and help support their dependents in the villages, the precise composition of any given *nog* is impossible to predict, whether it be a household *nog*, where one survey revealed twenty different combinations of relatives living under the same roof, or the larger *nog* composed of all people sharing the same family name. A Nubian village is not only a place where a minority of men can live and work as farmers, cultivating their own and other's shares of land; it is also a place to which the widow returns from Cairo to find a home with a brother, a place to which a migrant returns temporarily to marry or to rest between city jobs, and particularly a place where women and children stay with the head of their household *nog* when no room can be found in the city. To reiterate, all the villagers, both absent and present, have rights of their own in their villages that have been relinquished to others in their absence but that, if contacts have been maintained with their kinsmen, may be resumed once more when and if they return to their ancestral homes. The demographic facts of a high birth rate and limited resources must also be kept in mind if one is to understand the relationship between the ecology, the economy, and the kinship organization of Nubia. Kinship bears a close relationship to the Nubian polity and particularly to the remarkable absence of violence and serious quarrels found in Nubian communities.

With other peoples of the Middle East, Nubians share a strong sense of responsibility for helping others resolve their differences. Strangers inevitably crowd round a street quarrel, add their voices to the argument, comment on the merits of both sides, separate the principals if violence seems imminent, and offer suggestions to resolve the difficulty. Whether within the family or on the street, the Middle Eastern ethic is the exact opposite of the Western practice of "staying out of other people's business." When a non-Arabic-speaking American sees a group of people gathered on a street surrounding two men on the point of serious fighting, the Westerner fears a street brawl and rushes away; if he could understand what is being said in the crowd he would realize that an ad hoc process of conflict resolution is taking place and the protagonists are being offered honorable ways of withdrawing from the contest.

When quarrels occur among relatives, however, the case is somewhat different. Such quarrels are regarded by most Middle Easterners, and particularly Nubians, as extremely dangerous. Every effort must be expended to resolve these situations within the family and to do so as quickly as possible. Why? Quarrels weaken and divide the only group of people on whom an individual can depend, one's own relatives. Factionalism divides kin groups, reduces the number of individuals involved in mutual assistance, and can result in leaving one alone and exposed to the hostility of strangers, too weak to maintain a position in the economy and the society. Until the last few decades, the idea of turning one's back on kith and kin to find independently a job, or a wife, or a residence was quite alien to Middle Eastern society.

Obviously, the Nubians' sharing of resources could be a prime source of conflict as well as an integrative force. Relatives of several household *nogs* (who together constituted the intermediate *nog* sharing kinship and rights to *eskalays* and palm trees) must agree on the ways in which these resources are to be utilized, on the individuals who are to benefit, to subsist from the resources, and on who is to retain only residual rights to them. How did the Nubians decide who should stay in the village and farm and who should immigrate to the city, who should remain in the city and who should return home? The question is partly answered in our forthcoming discussion of Nubian marriage, but it seems still a logical source of contention, just as the many divisions of crops that each harvest brings forth might be the subject of serious quarrel; how is it that these divisions are regarded as celebrations of family unity rather than sources of disagreement?

The real danger of quarrels over harvests and resource usage lies, of course, in the possibility that the *eskalays* might fall into disuse. But many men, extended networks of kinsmen, have sentimental and material interests in the *eskalay* or the palm trees. The resources are the symbol of the kin's unity and their tie with grandfathers long dead, as well as the source of their daily bread. Therefore, an ample number of kinsmen would be linked to both sides of a dispute among relatives, ready to mediated differences and reconcile antagonists. No matter what the exact relationship between the disputants might be, intermediaries, the *wasta*, or ''go-betweens'' found in many Arab communities, can and do come forward to carry messages back and forth between disagreeing groups to find a compromise and, if necessary, to help shame the principals into reconciling their differences.

The fundamental Nubian conviction that each adult man or woman has a basic responsibility to intercede in quarrels between those kinsmen and neighbors with whom one shares some identity of interests is well illustrated by a Nubian anecdote of apparently recent origin, a combination of an old story and a new one.

The old story concerns two men who were constantly quarreling over the division of water provided by an *eskalay* they shared. To irrigate both pieces of land that the two men owned, the water had to be channeled first into one ditch and then into another. One of the men was always accusing the other of taking more than his share of water until their uncle overheard the two men arguing. The uncle thought about the situation briefly and then walked away, only to return in a moment with a stone, which he placed in the middle of the canal, thus effectively dividing the water into two streams and putting an end to the source of contention.

The new variation of the story involves the nationalization of the Suez Canal in 1956. During the brief military conflict between the British and the Egyptians, several Nubians hurried back and forth between fields and villages to listen to the latest news on a shortwave battery radio. Along the path over which the men hurried, an old man sat under a palm tree. He would struggle to his feet to ask what was happening, only to have the men pass by quickly in the opposite direction. Finally, in frustration and annoyance, he grabbed one of the younger men as he rushed by and demanded to know what the commotion was about. ''Grandfather,'' the young man said, "the British and the Egyptians are fighting over the Suez Canal!" The old man reflected on this for a moment and then asked, "What's the matter with them? Couldn't they find anyone to put a stone in the middle?"

Putting a stone in the middle is a political art at which the Nubians are extremely skilled and that they take very seriously. Most frequently, quarrels between kinsmen are resolved quickly by a third, usually older relative. If more kinsmen become involved in the dispute, or if the quarrel concerns a serious matter not amenable to private diplomacy, the Fedija Nubians may call a family council of the larger, property-sharing *nog*. Then all the resident kinsmen gather—not only men, but women and children as well. An elder kinsman presides over the council, one who has come to be accepted as a spokesman or this extended group of kinsmen, the intermediate *nog* referred to commonly, for example, as "Hamza's people."

The leader of "Hamza's people" is expected to hear both sides of the argument, to let all parties present their cases, and, finally, to make a judgment that he senses will receive support from the majority of third parties present. One well-known Fedija leader commonly settled matters by relying on the fact that, in most quarrels between men, one man was very likely to be somewhat older than the other. In this case he would make the younger man kiss the elder person's head, asking his forgiveness because he had not respected a person older than himself. Then the leader would oblige the older man to embrace the younger in front of the family gathering, asking his forgiveness for having tempted the youth into showing disrespect to his elders by quarreling with him!

Conflict resolution takes a more serious tone in violent offenses, such as physical injury, rape, or murder. The news of such offenses is kept from women and children, the matter is not discussed publicly, and only the men of the *nog* gather to hear the case. The sanction in such cases may be social death for the offender, who would then be required to give up all his possessions and property rights and leave the community forever. If the culprit refused, the men of the village would refuse to speak to him until complete social and economic ostracism would oblige the guilty party to leave.

On the other hand, should a defendant take his problem to the police, he would receive the same treatment as the offender! For violence not only threatened the moral standard of the community, but also exposed the village to the peril of outside intervention in community affairs. Crimes would then be punished according to alien laws in ways that could be far more detrimental to the general welfare of the village than the consequences of the original mistake. The greatest protection of the weak is secrecy, a fact known to peasant villagers throughout the world and one that the Nubian has learned well. Egyptian police on duty in Eneiba, the administrative center of Ballana, in the Fedija region, often complained of boredom in their position; aside from minor smuggling, they said, there was no crime in Nubia. Researchers in the area had an identical impression. Yet, if crimes of violence had occurred, no outsiders, in accordance with Nubian standards, would ever have known of them.

No feuds, no fractious disputes over shared resources, no pervasive factionalism in the villages, no violence—even if this picture is not entirely a true one and appears to be so partly because of an outsider's ignorance, it is a fact that this is the Nubian's image of his own society and one in which he takes great pride. Within the closely woven fabric of kinship and economics, ample numbers of peacemakers can be found to resolve every quarrel, and other conditions of Nubian life also complement this situation by reducing possible sources of tension. Migration is one such condition.

By the middle of the twentieth century almost every Nubian male had spent part of his adult life working in an Egyptian or a Sudanese city, and in recent years wives accompanied them in increasing numbers. Even though a migrant in the city was not hidden from his other migrant relatives, the urban setting unquestionably provided greater privacy of action and freedom from social constraint than did the village in Nubia. The village was the conservative end of this bipolar world, a place to be revered in the conversations of the migrant, to be honored and idealized — but hardly the place for a young man who wished to explore the pleasures of alcohol and women and to publicly carouse occasionally with age mates. Migration was thus an outlet for high-spirited and adventurous youth, and more than one dignified elder, who appeared the soul of respectability in his village retirement, was whispered to have been quite a rake in Cairo in the old days. The most discontented villagers were the young male schoolteachers, who, although scarcely libertine themselves, felt rebuffed and constrained by the excessive conservatism of their natal community. In a number of villages, for instance, the older men, allying themselves with younger religious conservatives, periodically attempted to forbid dancing at weddings, a pleasure the younger people much enjoyed. Such discrepancies in attitude between young and old were as serious a source of tension in Nubia as in any other small community. For Nubian villages, like many other Middle Eastern communities, were places where formality, respect, and constraint characterized the relations between generations. Nearly all informal, voluntary socializing and recreational activity was confined to gatherings of peers.

Kinsmen of one's father's generation were treated with the respect accorded one's parent: no lounging about, smoking, or casual conversation was permitted in their presence; when passing by on a donkey, one should dismount and greet such men. Young married men not working in the city constituted another, very important clique in most communities. Since marriage was the mark of adulthood, this energetic group pushed to play a role as men in their community, sometimes in opposition to their father's peer group. In another category were the young unmarried men and the grandfathers of the community who found themselves in a similar position, one waiting for the days of social importance and the other having passed them, as in the song the Nubian musician Hamza El Din sings, of the grandfather visiting with his grandson, both ignored by the rest of the family and glad for each other's company.

In societies without more specialized institutions governing the community, the differences in rights and duties based on age are almost as important as those based on sex. The respect for elders drummed into the Nubian child was a strong weapon for the older man who needed to force a reconciliation among his sometimes quarrelsome younger kinsmen. When affairs of common community concern were discussed after the men's Friday prayers at the village mosque, it was generally the younger men who proposed, the older who disposed. But the strains between young and old that this age-grading sometimes exacerbates were greatly relieved by the possibility of labor migration, the alternative between city and country, which many men believed lay open to them.

Another factor contributing to the peacefulness of Nubian life was the definition of misfortune in these communities. Just as in parts of the world where witches are found, human beings in Nubia were sometimes considered the agents of others' misfortunes. The difference was that Nubians believed that these "other people" were not personally to blame for the catastrophes. Rather, they were the unfortunate, but impersonal, possessors of the evil eye. Every village had one or more men, women, or even children known to have the "eye." Animals fell sick, children got fever, men broke their legs, water jars cracked, and house walls collapsed, all as a result of an envious or admiring glance from a person with such an eye. The only protection was to be inconspicuous, to not draw attention to good fortune, and to ward off the evil eye and render it impotent by using blue beads, Quranic inscriptions, or a charm in the form of a hand. (The latter is known throughout the Middle East as the Hand of Fatima, daughter of the Prophet Mohammed.)

The evil eye then, despite its location in a human being, is an impersonal force in Nubia, a much more humane attitude than that projected by the scapegoat theory of the witch. A man with the "eye" cannot help himself; he has "something missing" in his personality or his life that makes him envious of others' good fortune. This is a Nubian explanation, combining a certain psychological perspective with a view of human destiny and fate. Nubian insistence on the impersonal nature of this force, on the principle that the individual possessing the "eye" is not to blame for the consequences of his glances, is very strong. But people with the "eye" are also expected to be careful with it as much as possible. Men, sitting with a person who is known to have the "eye," will sometimes shout suddenly at him when he absentmindedly falls to staring at something or someone, somewhat in the same way as we do when trying to frighten someone out of the hiccups.

The dangers involved in trying to use the "eye" willfully to harm someone are nicely illustrated by the Nubian story of the farmer who quarreled with his neighbor and decided on what he considered a perfect revenge. He brought an old man with the "eye" to the edge of a dune overlooking the field where his neighbor's cows were pastured. "Look, look down there at those fine cows," he said. "Where?" asked the old man, whose sight was failing. "Down there, under that palm tree off by itself on the left," said the vengeful farmer. "My! What fine eyes you have," said the old man with the "eye."

Attempting to use the evil eye to one's advantage inevitably exposes one to its dangers. This is quite different from using others as scapegoats for individual or collective misfortunes. The Nubians may well be fatalists, a term loosely used to describe many Middle Eastern people, but their fatalism does not prevent them from journeying to Cairo for medical treatment when they are sick and seeking scientific ways of treating their sick cows. It does, however, help keep each personal sorrow in a community from becoming the source of rancor and dispute among people who must live together and share the same resources if they are to survive.

I have tried to outline the social and economic features of Nubian life that help maintain the apparently low levels of factionalism and the high levels of accord in the community. These conditions are not, of course, subject to exact measurement and are unquestionably subject to variation in time and space in ways that cannot be fully taken into account here. They also grew out of need. Shared ownership of resources—palm trees, land, cows, and water wheels—was obviously required in Nubia so that the community might survive. Spreading relationships and kin ties more broadly over all sections of the community, through the series of flexible social units (*nogs*), kept feuding and quarreling to a minimum. These relationships were also necessary for the community's survival, as was the development of conflict resolution to a fine art.

The threat posed to the survival of the villages by the high levels of migration must also be acknowledged. Many women and children would have been unable to exist without the subsistence increments provided by urban migrants in the form of thousands of dollars' worth of small postal orders delivered every few weeks on the eagerly awaited post boat. In villages where over half the population was female, few women would have had much hope of marriage were not the absent migrant men sufficiently tied to their village and kin to want to return and marry their cousins and neighbors. Once again, the Nubians improvised ways of dealing with the possible loss of the men of the community. The shared resource base and the kinship system have already been mentioned. But, in addition, the importance of the city-to-village tie is expressed in other ways. Many formalities, for instance, are associated both with leave-taking and with arrival. The wife is the first to say good-by to her migrant husband and the last to greet him when he arrives, as he takes leave of every village household before his departure on the Sudanese post boat and greets each house when he returns via the same boat. A man living in Cairo is expected to send telegrams of condolence when a death occurs in the village and to pay a call at the household of his deceased relative or neighbor as soon as he returns to the home village.

Death ceremonies are, in fact, occasions at which attendance is most stringently required. During the three-day mourning period, all the members of the smallest, intermediate, and largest *nog* visit the home of the bereaved. Sailboats may arrive from districts several miles away, bringing together members of the largest kin group, who may not have seen each other since the last member of the *nog* died. Women gather inside the house of the bereaved, while the men sit together in temporary structures constructed outside especially for the occasion. Of course, attendance at mourning ceremonies varies with the age and importance of the deceased; young children bring together only kinswomen and the men of the immediate family, while an important elder may require the attendance of hundreds of people and bring dozens of telegrams from all over Sudan and Egypt. Still, whenever a death occurs, women will pass the news on from village to village, dropping whatever they may be doing and flocking to the home of the dead person, often bringing food to help care for the visitors who may be coming from greater distances and spending one or more nights. Once more, the system of *karray* exchanges (to be discussed later) is invoked and utilized. The person who fails to carry out the expected pattern of behavior on such occasions, who does not do for the bereaved family what was done the last time a death occurred in *his* family, will suffer the disapproval of the entire community. A migrant who fails to send condolences is often spoken of as dead himself—indeed, an accurate expression, since neglect of this fundamental social duty is tantamount to a public declaration that the offender is no longer interested in his village or kinsmen, and has parted forever from his Nubian community.

Well over half of every Nubian village lived away in the city; the household economy of most families depended on some support from absent members as well as on the shares of land relinquished in absence. This was one of the most fundamental facts of Nubian life before resettlement, and, lest the peacefulness of village life in Nubia seem to be a romanticized notion, one should remember that a great deal of that life was, in effect, lived hundreds of miles away. Unlike villages elsewhere in the world whose boundaries are finite and who can offer no alternative to the inhabitants, the villages of Nubia were easy to leave and the efforts of the remaining inhabitants were mobilized to retain ties to their absentee members. The basic problem was to see that resources were effectively used at home while the migrants made their way to the city, mindful of their responsibilities and ties to their native land.

One must still give the Nubians great credit for devising careful, nonviolent solutions to the problems of limited resources and of migration, a cultural approach they have also brought to bear on their life in the cities.

### Footnotes

[1] For more detailed information about the *eskalay* and its operation, see Abdel Hamid El-Zein, "Socio-economic implications of the water wheel in Adendan, Nubia," in *Contemporary Egyptian Nubia*, ed. Robert A. Fernea, II, 298-322; and "Water and wheel in a Nubian village," M.A. thesis, American University in Cairo.

[2] Since his manuscript was written, Dr. Charles Callender has published with Fadwa el Guindi *Life crisis rituals among the Kenuz*, which should be consulted for further information about the Kenuz.

[3] I am indebted to Bahiga Haikal El Ghamry, who first brought the importance of the *nog* to my attention.

# Chapter Thirteen

# The Fedija Marriage Ceremony

Nubians, in explaining the nature of their "blessed" society to outsiders, often begin by describing the marriage ceremony. As the various steps of the marriage arrangements unfold, other networks of relationships within the society emerge, expressed somewhat differently than in a formal economic analysis. Drawing heavily on customs of the Fedija area, let us look at Nubia in this way for a moment.

Agreements to marry, according to the Nubians, may be made while the principals are still infants; some women are said to marry off children even before they are born! One day, of course, the bride and groom must themselves agree to such a union, but resistance to a long-standing family decision is difficult. In other cases, a boy may know a girl and wish to marry her but leave the arrangements to his parents, after he has first persuaded them of the wisdom of the decision. But since shareholdings and family relationships are basic considerations underlying all decisions about marriage, in general it is the adults who tend to initiate marriage talks.

The woman in question is also a basic consideration, and problems of shareholdings do not preclude visits by women of the boy's house to the house of the girl's family, particularly if the families do not already know each other well. Not only the girl's appearance, but also her manner and behavior are scrutinized. Nubians particularly appreciate grace and poise in a woman, and the bridegroom's family notes carefully the girl's ability to serve visitors with dignity and without nervousness.

If all goes well, the engagement, *firgar*, is formalized by a visit to the girl's home by the boy's closest relatives. A meal is served and the bride-to-be's father

154

announces the reason for the occasion. The oldest or most respected man present asks God's blessing upon the prospective marriage, following which all the people recite the Fatiha (the first sura, or verse, of the Quran). Often a reciprocal visit to the groom's house by the bride's family takes place, which helps facilitate the many arrangements that must be made before the final ceremony.

For the public announcement of the engagement, the bride's father will slaughter an animal (*gojir*). All members of the villages and the *nogs* of both the bride and the groom are invited, indeed obligated, to partake of the feast. Failing to attend such an occasion is not as serious as neglecting to offer condolences upon a death, but it is a very grave insult, nonetheless. The father of the groom reciprocates with a second feast for the community.

These occasions are made possible by another level of reciprocity that is of fundamental importance in Nubian society. Each household, each adult, is linked to others through favors received and favors owed. The exchanges, *karray*, serve to mobilize the community's resources for private ceremonies. Each woman for whom the bride's or groom's mother has done simple favors will bring some contribution for the feast: her best cups, perhaps, or some tea, sugar, or loaves of bread. Every married woman, it is said, has her own private stores from which she takes contributions on such occasions. Unmarried young girls, who do not yet have household stores at their disposal, will offer services, to fill the *zirs*, or clay jars, with river water, for example. The partners in the exchange are usually members of the same extended *nog*, but similar gestures are expected among neighbors in the village, whatever the exact kinship.

The evening before the wedding itself is the time for *kofferay dibbi*, a party similar to the *layla elhenna*, or night of henna, in Egyptian marriages. The bride and groom are both treated to an elaborate toilette, he with his friends at the river, she in her house, though she may also visit the bank of the river briefly. Henna is applied liberally, and the bride and groom, dressed in their wedding finery and attended by their friends, become the object of entertainment, affection, and teasing. On this evening the couple is considered to be both vulnerable to the evil eye and yet possessed of a special *baraka*, or grace, which sets them somewhat apart and makes them the center of attention and concern. *Kofferay dibbi* is really a kind of sanctification ritual, not unlike the preliminary ceremonies of many Christian weddings, and altogether it is a happy occasion, marked by singing and dancing at the respective houses, in company with most of the guests who will attend the coming wedding. Since it is also the last night the boy and girl will spend as part of the largely unmarried set that is paying them court, *kofferay dibbi* has some of the bittersweet nostalgia of a graduation, a leaving behind of the familiar for a new status, as yet unexperienced.

Culminating the long days of parties, wedding announcements, and arrangements is the *bale dibi* (or actual wedding). All neighboring villagers and members of *nogs* within traveling distance assemble for the ceremony, which begins after the prayers at sundown and continues often through most of the night. The marriage contract (*ʿaqd*) is written and signed (*katib el-kitab*) before the local *maʿzoun*, a government-appointed, but locally selected village official. The *maʿzoun* also asks for the consent of the bride and of the groom and officially registers the union.

Then comes the bestowal of gifts, which, in Nubia, is of special importance. At this time the boy receives shares in land, water wheels, date palms, cows, and even houses, as well as smaller gifts (*karray*). Gifts are given not only among the groom's new peers, the married men, but also by the older men, so the exchange relationship is established across generational lines. The sum of inherited shares and gift exchanges will determine whether the groom can support his new household *nog* in Nubia or must go to the city to supplement his income.

For this ceremony, the groom sits in a circle of men, and a man with a book sits next to him to register the gifts. First the gifts of family heads are offered, the act marking the young man as now able to reciprocate in this adult activity and tying him ceremoniously to a pattern of reciprocal exchanges from which he may never be free as long as he remains part of the community. After the gifts of neighbors and less closely related members of the *nogs* are recorded, the father of the groom will stand up and ceremoniously declare what he is bestowing on his son. "I give my son my share in the Fagirob *eskalay*," he may say. This will have been a matter of previous discussion, for often the father of the bride is then prepared to say, "And I give my daughter my share in the same *eskalay*." Following this exchange, the bride's brother may return a small share in the same *eskalay* that he received when getting married. A maternal uncle may say, "I give my sister's son a quarter of such and such cow." Even a house no longer in use may be given a groom, though this is less usual. Hopefully, the new couple will receive enough to begin life as a *nog*. More importantly, the groom is henceforth a man. Even if his father continues to enjoy authority over his son, the new groom, say the Nubians, "feels differently now about the land he tills; it is his own."

While the men are offering their *karray* outside, the women gather in the house for a similar ceremony. The shares in water wheels, land, cows, and houses are echoed in the jewelry now bestowed upon the bride by her mother and by others of her mother's generation who love her and are close to her. Ideally, most of the gold worn by a married woman should come to the bride from her groom, but the groom's mother, the bride's mother, and the bride's maternal aunts are expected to make generous contributions. No Nubian bride leaves this prenuptial party without enough personal adornment in gold and silver to signify that she has reached adulthood. Gold earrings, ankle bracelets, pendants, necklaces, and hair ornaments are presented; the pieces that the groom offers may be new, but the gifts of the bride's mother, mother-in-law, and aunts are often older pieces, the legacy that one generation of women passes on to the next, not as a blind inheritance but as a gift at the time of attaining adulthood. The jewelry is a gift given in such a way as to remain, like the communities' agrarian resources, active and in use, not put away and neglected because inherited by a woman who has left the community to live an Egyptian life in Cairo. The jewelry, which is the bride's personal property, may save the woman or her children from disaster in the extremities of financial hardship.

The bride also receives small gifts of money, food, and such household objects as woven colored plates as *karray* from her sisters, her brothers' wives, and her friends, as well as from her mother's friends and neighbors and from distant female relatives of both bride and groom. These *karray* serve to establish, for the bride, those ties of reciprocity by which she, too, will be bound as long as she lives in the community.

After the ceremony of the bestowal of wealth and *karray* the dancing and singing resumes. At some point later in the evening the groom leaves the guests and is danced to his bride, who, dressed in her marriage finery, waits in the *diwani*, or marriage room of her own home, which has been specially decorated for the occasion. Heading the festive procession (*seefa*) is the village chanter, or "forever" man, who, accompanied by drums, sings an ancient marriage song; between stanzas, the "forever" man will intersperse long lists of the bride's ancestors and the groom's ancestors and will recite couplets in praise of the families now being united.

At the bride's house, the procession disperses and the guests return to the dancing and singing. A few children may remain behind to peer through cracks in the roof and try to observe the contest of wills inside the *diwani*.

The groom, as in other parts of Egypt and most of the Middle East, is expected to keep giving his new bride small presents to persuade her to speak to him. When the bride speaks for the first time, the children leave and the couple may then proceed to consummate their union; occasionally a midwife's assistance is necessary, for the practice of female circumcision makes initial sexual experience very difficult. This particular custom seems inexplicably cruel in a society notable for its lack of cruelty. Yet it is practiced by women on their young daughters and they believe that it is necessary to the proper raising of a girl, helping her, the women say, to act with a degree of self-control that saves both her and the community from trouble. Small wonder, however, that the marriage night is a very tense period for many couples.

The belief that a bride should come to her husband untouched by other men is as strong in Nubia as in neighboring lands. Yet, if a Nubian bride is discovered not to be a virgin, no violence erupts as is sometimes the case in Arab communities; Nubian society takes care of the problem in other ways. Among Fedija Nubians, a girl who brings this social misfortune upon herself and her family must quickly be married by a paternal cousin, even if he is already married. The cousin must be someone who will care for the girl and will agree never to mention the reason for their marriage or taunt the girl with her past mistake. This is stated as ideal behavior; killing or mistreating the girl in any way is neither expected nor condoned.

A man is married in his bride's home and, throughout Nubia, spends some time there, depending on local custom; forty days is frequently reported as the average period. After the first seven days, when neither the bride nor the groom are supposed to leave the *diwani*, the groom may visit all his bride's neighbors briefly and take his ease in her community. During this time the wife theoretically learns how to serve her husband; she has long ago acquired the skills of cooking and housekeeping, but managing a husband is a new task, which, the Nubians say, must be learned individually, for it is different with each couple. The bride is better able to develop ability in this realm while she is in the accustomed familiarity of her own home; better, too, for her to become acquainted with her new husband in the security of her own territory, rather than in that of her mother-in-law. After this initial honeymoon period, the couple usually goes to the groom's father's house, sometimes to live there for months, sometimes for years, depending on a great many economic and social circumstances. Studies of current household composition show that most nuclear families have their own house, but some say this was less true in the past.

Shortly after returning to his home with his new bride, the young groom may have to go to Cairo or another distant city to earn his living and support his new family. Many Nubians divided their energies, spending some years as farmers and some years as urban employees, but opportunities to return to Nubia and earn a living in agriculture were few, particularly if a man lacked the means or desire to begin his married life in this way. Men who returned either brought an income with them from outside the community (savings, a pension) or were accepted as dependents in the home of a kinsman.

Marriage, then, economically, socially, and ceremonially, is the most momentous occasion in the life of a Nubian man or woman. Rich and elaborate in detail and execution, the ceremony involves the entire community and serves to focus and reemphasize the basic needs and values of the family and, ultimately, the community.

The practice of bestowing wealth on the groom at the time of marriage has social as well as economic significance and serves also as a tension-reducing aspect of Nubian culture. In many peasant communities, the father's stranglehold on land appears to be the cause of much hostility between generations; the sons are often deprived not only of a home of their own, but also of the means of subsistence until they are middle-aged. Even when the father dies, the eldest son usually inherits the greater portion, and the other sons are left with inadequate land; troubles between brothers over inheritance are commonplace. But in Nubia, the issue of the patrimony is settled at the outset of a man's adulthood; in a large family, one or two sons may be provided for, and the remaining sons know early that they will be obliged to leave and work in the cities. Thus, the bitterness is kept to a minimum. Some property retained by the father is, of course, inherited and subject to the equal division among heirs prescribed in Shari^c^a law. But this may involve no more than the family house, since the rest of the property has already been assigned to its next owner.

Only if a father feels doubtful about the seriousness of his son's marriage is he likely to avoid giving him much property. Such a public statement of doubt is itself unsettling to a marriage and may eventually be a self-fulfilling prophecy. Older men do keep a hand in their son's agricultural activities, but only, say the Nubians, through custom and with respect; the community considers shameful any failure by a father to bestow on a marrying son as much of a share in the family holdings as seems practical and possible at the time.

Flexibility, then, is inherent in the Nubian system of sharing the ownership of resources. Flexibility is also evident in the system of dividing the ownership of land between generations. A man, by giving land to his son or daughter, unites shares and creates a large enough holding to support or help support a new family group. Only by such rational manipulation of resources can control of the land be managed in order to assure continual use. By choosing young men with serious intent and apparent attachment to Nubian values and society, and by bestowing land upon them at the time of marriage, the society assures that the *eskalays* and the palm trees will not fall into disuse either through arguments about ownership or because too many heirs, with too small interests, are unwilling to cooperate in arranging for the land's management and utilization, No arbitrary rule of inheritance could guarantee this result as well.

The Nubian marriage illustrates still another dimension of social relations between members of the same community—the dyadic, reciprocal relationships established among men and women by the *karray*, or exchanges of gifts and material assistance. Through these dyadic exchanges among peers the resources of the community can be further employed to provide for the particular, often sudden crises in the lives of individual members. Through *karray*, the houses are replastered, the fields are harvested, and banquets are provided for large numbers of guests. This relationship is explicitly recognized and clearly stated; those who fail to assume their responsibility in such tasks are ostracized. Thus, while the individual is doing his duty toward someone to whom he is obligated or whom he wishes to obligate, the cumulative effect is of general consequence, since this is the manner in which the community mobilizes its efforts to produce ceremonies and to complete difficult tasks that involve everyone.

The Nubians, in their very conscious willingness to accept the privileges and obligations of exchange relationships with many other people and for many purposes, are utilizing one of the most potent forces for social unity to which we have recourse. In many societies today, exchanges are no longer an effective force in neighborhood or community affairs, being sporadic and individual rather than organized and general. The Nubians have perhaps gone a step further in reciprocity and added a ceremonial component to such behavior.

"We are all attached to each other like the links of a chain," said one Nubian, "and at the moment when something must be accomplished, the links are pulled tightly together." The circles within which the links are pulled together may involve neighbors, members of the village, members of the household *nog*, the intermediate *nog*, or the largest *nog* of extended kinsmen. Friendship is the least formalized circle and may be the smallest. "If my neighbor comes without being asked when my roof must be replaced," says the Nubian, "that is how I know he is my friend." The largest circles of reciprocity are stated in the wedding ceremonialism when the *karrays* are carefully recorded in lists and in public announcement. But, small or large, formal or less formal, the fundamental principle of the circles of exchange relationships remains the same—one of compelling and total reciprocity.

# Chapter Fourteen

# The Kenuzi Saint Cult

T he Kenuz of northern Nubia, who comprise nearly half of the total Egyptian Nubian population, have adapted their culture to conditions of extreme scarcity of village resources. At the same time they have preserved a form of social organization that no longer has the important economic functions that were presumably once a major raison d'être. Fortunately, the anthropologist Charles Callender lived in a Kenuzi Nubian district for nearly a year with a group of research assistants. Here I largely depend on information from his papers and those of his assistants.

Earlier, I mentioned that the social structure of the Kenuz differs from that of the Fedija. The Kenuz are organized in patrilineally determined tribes closely resembling those of the nomadic Arabs. While adherence to a genealogical model involving calculations of descent from a founding ancestor is of greater apparent concern to the Kenuz than to the Fedija, the differences between the two groups on this basis should not be overemphasized. "In theory, a Kenuzi tribe is a patrilineal lineage descended from a single ancestor. The tribe, or maximal lineage, is divided into major lineages descended from sons of the ancestor. A major lineage in turn reproduces the structure of the tribe itself through divisions into minor lineages, which tend to develop minimal lineages." However, says Callender, "much of this structure is simply a convention."[1]

The proliferation of lineage segments is counterbalanced by the incorporation of individuals and even whole lineages into another lineage through intermarriages and common residence. Thus, like the Fedija nog, the Kenuzi gabila, or tribe, is composed of permeable units into which individuals, unrelated by common descent, can pass. Their descendants will eventually be accepted as blood kinsmen. Basically, the Kenuz differ from the Fedija in their greater preoccupation with the ideological aspects of patrilineal descent, rather than in the social reality of their kinship organization. The strength of a Kenuz's dedication to and involvement with this subtribe is not affected by the fact that the genealogy determining this membership is at least as much ideological as genetic. Unlike the Fedija, tribal leaders among the Kenuz are formally recognized at the various levels of tribal division, and disputes are formally adjudicated according to the tribal relationship between the individuals involved. This degree of formal segmentation is missing among the Fedija, and disputes are not so apt to divide the communities into opposing camps on the basis of lineage divisions.

The strength of the Kenuzi tribal organization is dramatically illustrated in the activities of the *moulid*, or saint cult, which is highly developed among the Kenuz but totally lacking among the Fedija Nubians. While serving religious and personal ends, such cults also help to articulate and symbolize the tribal organization and its component parts.

In the Kenuzi district of Dahmit approximately 150 shrines of various importance were located among a resident population of less than fifteen hundred persons. Some of these shrines, physically no more than a pile of stones, were the object of attention by a family, a single woman, or sometimes even children, who would imitate their elders by acting out cult activities as a form of play. The most important involved the entire tribe, while the lesser cults were associated with minor lineages of much more limited membership. Dr. Callender offers the following description of the major saint cult associated with one entire Kenuzi tribe.

> The Mehannab sheikhs are Hassan and Hussein, regarded as the tribe's ancestors even though descent is traced only to Hassan — an irregularity probably connected with the prevalence of twins as the objects of tribal cults in East Dahmit. Their shrine, a small two domed building, stands on the outskirts of Jama [a village], next to a dancing ground and adjoining the tribal graveyard. The association of cemetery and shrine, reinforcing the ancestral motive prominent in tribal cults, formerly characterized other tribal shrines in Dahmit and can be seen in the ruins of the old Jama flooded in 1933.

> Some aspects of the cult of Hassan and Hussein continue throughout the year. Women vow gifts to the sheikhs if their requests are fulfilled; grooms visit the shrine during the wedding procession, and visits are made by persons leaving for Egypt. This annual climax of the cult is the *mulid* [saint's day celebration] held on the 15th of the Islamic month of Shaaban. This celebration is financed and produced by the tribe. Rather complex in nature, it combines such essentially secular activities as dancing and a feast with a minimum of ritual centering on the replacement of the tomb covers, which are carried in procession to the Nile for washing, and then paraded through the Mehannab villages. Women present gifts to the shrine in fulfillment of vows made during the previous year, or for the privilege of dancing [although dancing may also be in fulfillment of a vow]. This mulid is the major tribal undertaking. Its integrating functions are clear: this event involves all the Mehannab in Dahmit [about 250 persons] and many of the migrants, some of whom return for the occasion or send gifts for vows made in Cairo or Alexandria.[2]

As is the case with many of the saint shrines of Nubia, the actual bodies of Hassan and Hussein are not presumed to lie buried at their cult tomb; rather the shrine is only symbolic of the burial place, even in the case of the minority of holy men who are presumed to have died in Nubia. The rising waters of the Nile reservoirs covered most of the area where shrines had been built before this century. The shrines of the more important saints often consisted of a whitewashed room with a dome on top, all constructed of stone and mud brick. Inside might be found an empty coffin with incense pots and candles, a fragment of an old antiquity, or a few slabs of rock. But whether elaborate or simple, the shrine sites were established on the basis of an *ishara*, or sign, often in a dream, to a person resident in the village.[3] The *ishara* indicated that the *baraka*, or blessed virtue of the deceased saint, might be manifested as miracles if a cenotaph were to be constructed at some particular location. Such dreams sometimes encouraged adults to take seriously the play shrines constructed by their children, and similar dreams dictated where shrines should be rebuilt after flooding. In every instance, however, the shrines are apt to disappear and the cults abort them, unless they become the object of special interest of a particular tribal lineage or sublineage. Thus, of the 150 shrines found in Dahmit, only 12 had staffs appointed to care for them and only 7 were the object of saint's day celebrations.

While any shrine could be the object of a private vow and therefore of personal significance, the celebration of a *moulid* was usually the special responsibility of a lineage. Members of the lineage would provide food, in fulfillment of vows made on condition that some special wish be granted. In addition, money was collected to help buy animals for the feast; these were the contribution of the entire tribal group.

Each important shrine had a *nakib*, or custodian, whose function was to collect and distribute to the needy the food left at the shrine, to oversee the planning and execution of the *moulid*, and to tend to the maintenance of the shrine. Such a prestigious position was usually passed from father to son and often was filled by the sheikh of the particular lineage involved. His female counterpart, the *nakiba*, was, however, usually selected by the *nakib* from among the needy women of the community. For her work in cleaning the shrine, lighting the candles, and filling the water jars outside the door, the *nakiba* was rewarded less by honor and more by material assistance through access to the food left at the shrine throughout the year.

In the earlier days of Nubian migration, when men had more freedom to come and go, Nubian migrants would return in large numbers for the *moulids* of their tribes, in some cases bringing new tomb covers with them, perhaps in imitation of the official Egyptian pilgrimage to Mecca each year, which involved carrying a new cover for the *ka'ba* (the Sacred Black Stone of Mecca). *Moulids* were, then, occasions when the urban and village components of the tribe united in support of a common enterprise. Friendly competition existed between the major tribal groups to see which one could produce the best feast and attract the most visitors, for, while it was the duty of the Kenuzi tribesman to attend and support his own *moulid*, it was his privilege to attend, as a guest, those of the other Kenuzi tribes. By the same token, vows could be made at any shrine, regardless of tribal affiliation; indeed, some shrines were specialized in the kind of *baraka* they offered, as in the case of one that offered special protection against scorpions in an area where they were thought to be particularly numerous.

The degree to which the saints' shrines served as the focal point for the rituals of lineage is illustrated not only by the inclusive joint celebration of the annual *moulid*, but also by the number of more private acts associated with the shrine. In addition to vows, which could be made at the shrine at any time of need, a bride visited the shrine on the morning of her wedding, often leaving an offering; each wedding procession stopped at the shrine, to leave a gift for the *nakiba*, together with white flags dipped in henna, similar to the flags often placed over the lintel of the new bride's room. Pieces of such flags could later be used as charms, along with some dust from the shrine, by other mothers who were hoping for a marriage for their own daughters.

Just as a Fedija Nubian ceremoniously takes leave of each household in the village when he leaves for the city and greets each household when he returns, so do the Kenuz visit their shrine, say a sura from the Quran for their revered sheikh, and leave a small offering. This visit is considered necessary because the *baraka* of the saint is believed to protect those absent from the village and working in the cities far away.

The great annual *moulids*, however, those joyous celebrations that involved the larger community, were held only at those important shrines among the Kenuz that are symbolic of the burial place of a founding ancestor of the tribe or subtribe. Colorful processions from shore to shrine, offerings of food, prayers, dancing, singing, and feasting were all to honor the founding ancestor, to seek his blessing and protection. In this sense, the saint cults are also ancestor cults, both lending symbolic importance to the ideology of tribalism and reinforcing tribal unity through providing a focus for joint rituals. With such minor exceptions as burial grounds and tribal guesthouses, this is all the Kenuzi tribe or its divisions can share, since water wheels and palm trees have almost disappeared and most of the agricultural land was under water much of the year from the beginning of the Aswan dams in 1901. Callender reports that, of the Mehannab tribes, about 1,000 members lived in Alexandria, 350 in Cairo, perhaps 100 in Aswan, and a few were scattered elsewhere; only 226 Mehannab were resident in Nubia at the time of the study.[4] How appropriate, then, to have as a symbol of tribal unity and a focus of tribal activity a saint whose *baraka* is limited neither by time nor by space!

What of the conditions in the Kenuzi districts before the first dam began to flood the region? Callender emphasizes the importance of tribal ownership of property stressed in the reports of the old days by his informants. "Land and water rights in a *saqia* [water wheel] development, acquired by an individual, eventually passed by inheritance to a lineage, whose rights were ultimately conceptualized as ownership by the tribe, even though most Mehannabs had no rights in the saqias."[5] One wonders whether such corporate ownership would not eventually have had effects on the tribal lineage system not unlike those described in the case of the Fedija *nogs*. Ownership passes to individuals and in passing, through the random accidents of birth and death and the more deliberate acts of marriage, moves across lineage lines, involving men in lineages other than their own as determined by patrilineal descent. Unless property rights were totally corporate, belonging to the lineage or the tribe with no inheritable rights of private ownership, it is difficult to see how those property rights could have continued to conform perfectly to the strict tribal constructs that now prevail among the Kenuz.

Tribal membership among the Kenuz was also used as the basis for the formation of urban clubs, which, as we shall see, were of great importance in helping the migrant Nubians adjust successfully to life in cities. As Callender notes,

> Labor migration among the Kenuz preceded the building of the first dam at Aswan, although its earlier extent is uncertain. It may be a very old practice. Possibly the tribal system, or some of its aspects, may represent a means of adjusting to unsettled conditions; and perhaps the Kenuz should be viewed as practicing a form of nomadism, represented today by labor migration and formerly by riverine trade through which small settlements were often established in other areas. But an important element of stability during at least the past two centuries has been the role of Dahmit and the other districts as the tribal center, which it has held in spite of increasing depopulation.[6]

When we ask why a greater emphasis on tribalism is found among the Kenuz than among the Fedija Nubians, why the saint cults are celebrated in Kenuzi Nubia and not in the Fedija area, we are confronted with a problem familiar to students of human societies. Is it because the Kenuz were tribally organized by an Arab tribe centuries ago? Is it because saint cults keep tribal divisions strong, replacing, in a sense, property rights that might have had contrary effects? Or did saint cults with elements of ancestor worship develop among the Kenuz because they already possessed a strong tribal ideology? Historically, tribal shrines were found throughout Arabia long before the advent of Islam and were one of the manifestations of polytheism that the Prophet Mohammed attacked and destroyed when uniting his pantribal followers under one God. Yet one must remember that such worship conformed well with the conditions of a nomadic life, providing foci of common activity and belief for an otherwise dispersed population.

We do not need to choose between history and economic conditions as *the* primary cause for the development of Kenuzi saint cults and tribal institutions. We may merely recognize that these social institutions have served the Kenuz well in their struggle to replace their village resources with urban incomes, while enjoying the relative security of remaining part of something greater and more enduring than either the individual or his immediate family.

## Footnotes

[1] Charles Callender, "The Mehannab: A Kenuz tribe," in *Contemporary Egyptian Nubia*, ed. Robert A. Fernea, II, 186-187.

[2] Ibid., p. 204.

[3] Nawal el Messiri Nadim has most interestingly described the origins of these shrines in her M.A. thesis for the American University in Cairo, "The sheikh cult in Dahmit."

[4] Callender, "The Mehannab," p. 183.

[5] Ibid., p. 207.

[6] Ibid., pp. 214-215.

# Chapter Fifteen

# Migration and the Urban Experience

T he period from the end of Turkish rule until the construction of the first Aswan Dam constituted a brief golden age of Nubian culture. However, beginning at the turn of the century, Nubian lands were progressively flooded by the reservoir of the Aswan Dam, which had been heightened several times by the British and the Egyptians. The newfound security, which probably resulted in a growth of the Nubian population, was undermined by a decline in the resource base, and ever greater numbers of Nubian men were thus obliged to seek employment outside Nubia in the cities of Egypt and the Sudan during the first half of this century. This pattern of migration was not totally unprecedented, since ample evidence exists to show that Nubians had sought urban employment before the twentieth century. What is remarkable is the way in which the Nubians managed to adapt to the economic necessity of migration and divided communities and still maintain the fabric of their society.

The way in which the Nubians found a footing in Egyptian urban society and in effect saved their rural villages from starvation, the way they were able to maintain their homeland when it was no longer able to maintain them, is intimately related to the nature of nineteenth- and early twentieth-century Egypt, a society then in transition from slaveholding to free labor. Although the British formally outlawed the slave trade in Egypt in 1880, the manumission of slaves took many years, and, informally, the social status of slave did not disappear until well into the twentieth century, when the last of the legally freed slaves died as retainers in their ex-masters' households.

While slaves were used for agricultural labor at various times and places in Egyptian history, in general the Egyptian agrarian economy depended more on sharecropping than on slave labor, as contrasted to the American South. In Egypt slaves were more usually a feature of wealthy households, a mark of distinction between the rich and the poor, the aristocrat and the common man. Even today, a Nubian doorkeeper is a sign of prestige among well-to-do Egyptians, even if he is shared with a dozen other families in an expensive apartment house; this standard seems to have been established during the period of slavery.

Raised in Egyptian households, the Nubian boys captured in slave raids were lost to their own culture. While the memories of slave raids are kept alive among Nubians today through frightening stories told by grandfathers, no tales are recorded that describe the restoration of a slave to his own family. Villages with many black inhabitants supposedly are found on the delta today, near Tanta, for example. Yet, little contact takes place between the contemporary Nubians and descendants of freed black slaves.

The first waves of migrants from Nubian villages, then, did not gain access to their initial posts as servants through the influence of slave ancestors. More likely, the middle- and upper-class Egyptian discovered that paying a black man, newly arrived in Cairo, a small sum to stand before one's door or to run errands was an attractive and logical substitute for the owning of slaves, which became legally difficult and hence far more costly toward the end of the nineteenth century.

This was a period of prosperity in Egypt. The price of Egyptian cotton on the world market increased greatly during the American Civil War, and at about the same time the tourist trade emerged as a source of income for the country. Upper-class Europeans discovered in Egypt not only a promising area for economic exploitation, but also a warm winter spa filled with entrancing antiquities. With the aid of foreign investment and guidance, luxurious hotels and restaurants were constructed to encourage and accommodate this new source of wealth. Egypt suddenly became a favorite stop on the world tours of the fashionable and wealthy.

Upon this scene appeared the first Nubian migrants. Like the blacks in America, Nubians were associated with slavery and servitude in the public mind and were considered particularly suitable for this work. Without special training, with often only fragmentary knowledge of Arabic, they still found ready employment as servants in the strata of Egyptian society enjoying new prosperity. The Nubians provided the trappings of the old aristocratic, slave-owning wealth, but did so as free men who could leave their jobs at will to pay visits to their native villages. Tall, handsome, proud, and dignified, they had not experienced the humiliations of slavery and were hired not only by private families, but also by the new foreign hotel keepers, who provided long gold-braided robes, tarbushes, and snowy turbans for the Nubians in order to appeal to the Arabian Nights fantasies of the tourists and colonialists who thronged to Egypt at this time.

While seeing the Nubians as servants appealed to existing prejudices in Egyptian society, and while the Nubians' imperfect knowledge of Arabic encouraged attitudes of superiority on the part of Egyptians, the fact that the Nubians were Muslim automatically gave them a legal status in the society that could not be denied. The Nubians took care to emphasize the common denominator of faith by observing Islamic religious practices and by taking an interest in religious matters. At the same time, the Egyptian prejudice toward the *barabara*, as they called the Nubians, encouraged the Nubians to work and live together, avoiding all but the necessary social contacts with most Egyptians. As soon as a Nubian found a position he took care to try and fill the other jobs around him with men from his own community, and, if he left for Nubia, he replaced himself with another Nubian.

The jobs themselves, of doorman or house servants, required little formal skill and could be taken and abandoned with ease. The role of doorman in particular suited the Nubian temperament, for a doorman is frequently a neutral figure on the Egyptian scene and is often called upon to arbitrate quarrels between the other servants in a house or between lesser employees in a hotel. A good doorman comes to occupy a pivotal position in the affairs of a house, an apartment building, or a hotel, even today, after a century of change in Egypt, and the householder or building manager, who is himself frequently absent, counts upon the general knowledge that the Nubian doorman has acquired to help him keep the establishment successful and at peace. The role of doorman was also an excellent way of infiltrating Nubians into other jobs within the household, and the doorman often was instrumental in helping his fellow Nubians gain positions as waiters or cooks or drivers.

Nubians use the term ''adventurer'' to describe their great-great-grandfathers who first went to the cities of Egypt to look for work. Going to the city was, and remains, a great adventure for the village boy, just as for any country folk. The city is a risky place where one may experience great success or crushing failure, where temptations are plentiful and rewards often ephemeral. A young man's relatives in the village always had ambivalent attitudes toward the adventure, for, although the work provided much-needed income, it also offered an opportunity for the young man to meet and marry an Egyptian woman and perhaps disappear forever from the Nubian scene. (In Egypt any prejudice against the Nubian black is largely impersonal in character and quickly becomes irrelevant as soon as one becomes directly acquainted with a particular Nubian; the virtue of a steady job has made many Nubians most acceptable husbands for Egyptian women.)

Linguistic, racial, and cultural differences between Nubians and city Egyptians should not be unduly stressed, however, in explaining the Nubian group cohesion in urban centers; in many ways the Nubians were doing no more than other ethnic and kin groups in the same setting. At all levels of Middle Eastern society, even today, the extended family is expected to help in locating work, and the monopolization of particular jobs by certain religious or ethnic groups is a well-known historical phenomenon.

In establishing themselves in the cities of Egypt in the twentieth century, the Nubians were doubly fortunate. Not only were they replacing in part a labor force, slaves, that had suddenly disappeared, but they also were entering the urban scene just when economy was expanding to create ever-higher levels of demand for workers in the service occupations. Thus, the Nubians did not have to compete for traditional occupations already preempted by other groups, and they constituted one of the few lower-income groups that directly benefited from the new tourist trade and from the expenditures of the new foreign population and the growing Egyptian upper middle class. The Nubians' success in establishing themselves as part of the urban labor force, then, would not be so remarkable except for two factors: the degree to which the majority of Nubians remained associated with their ancestral villages over several generations, and the rapid upwardly mobile movement of their position in the urban employment scene.

The change that has occurred in the Nubians' position in the urban labor market in Egypt is a phenomenon that cannot be easily considered as common to all groups in an expanding economy. Egyptians and resident foreigners still generally believe that Nubians work almost exclusively in the service sector of the economy. Indeed, the great majority of Nubians do, but the last two decades have changed the pattern significantly.

In 1962 a survey was made of approximately 1,000 migrant Nubians who were identified and located on the basis of a survey of households conducted in Nubia itself.[1] The selection was carefully made in order to ensure a representative sample of the estimated 100,000 Nubians who reside outside their ancestral villages. The survey revealed, among other things, that the Nubian employment profile, when compared with the total distribution of all Egyptians in various job categories, was almost identical with that of the population at large. In other words, for the size of their population, the Nubians are represented equally with Egyptians in the professions, in managerial positions, and as white-collar workers. When one considers that the Nubians entered the Egyptian urban economy in force only slightly more than fifty years ago, and that at the time they were illiterate, did not speak Arabic, and had low ascribed social status outside their own lands— their achievements deserve and require some further examination.

The reasons for this rapid upward mobility lie partly in the conditions of Egyptian urban life, as the Nubians experienced them, and partly in the fact of being Nubian. Certainly, the association with foreigners was one such condition. Many older Nubians state a preference for employment in foreign homes or establishments. This action may be partly attributed to a Nubian sensitivity about the Egyptians' attitudes toward him, but it is also true that foreigners, with egalitarian ideas and bad consciences following the end of slavery, may have treated Nubians with greater respect and relied on them more than the ordinary Egyptian employer would have done. In any household or business enterprise in a foreign land, the local employee is far more than simply a man doing a job; he is also a channel of communication between the foreigner and the local environment. The local employee must cope with much that his employer only half understands and must explain why some actions are appropriate and others are not. Enterprising Nubians, who quickly learned at least the rudiments of the foreign employer's language, were local citizens who were able to guide the foreigner through the often bewildering labyrinth of daily affairs, whether it involved food supplies, government regulations, or street demonstrations.

In return, the foreigner paid his Nubian servant higher wages and, prompted by a variety of motives, sometimes helped the man to bring his family to Cairo and to place his sons in school. At the turn of the century the number of foreign schools was increasing in Egypt, schools that often accepted a few tuition-free students, especially if the student's father worked for a foreigner known to the school. Servants' quarters were sometimes large enough to house employees' families, and so Nubians were able to find a place in the city for their children at less expense than that of other rural migrants in similar positions.

Thus, the symbiosis between the Nubian and the foreigner in private homes and public establishments, though by no means the exclusive involvement of the city Nubians, was of considerable reciprocal advantage. Aside from the economic benefits, the fact that the Nubian, like the foreigner, was also considered something of an outsider may have contributed an element of sympathy and understanding to the employer-employee relationship. In strictly economic terms the Nubian was simply a salaried employee, but in a broader context the job was more all-encompassing, even if the foreigner was not always aware of this. The act of cooking and serving food to guests in Nubia, as throughout the Middle East, is an honorable one and brings credit upon the host. For a Nubian to be partly responsible for the well-being of guests, whether in a home or a hotel, was in accordance with his traditional values. The fact that Nubian men undertook kitchen tasks, which in their own homes would have been performed by women, did not upset the Nubian male as it might an American, for instance; whatever doubts the Nubian's have about their masculinity, they are not manifested in this way!

Furthermore, the foreigners' own values did not fail to make some impact on Nubian culture through several generations of relationship. The character of a good man, as defined by a Nubian, is not unlike a description of a proper nineteenth-century Puritan English gentleman. Honesty is very highly prized and frequently mentioned, as is the associated virtue of dependability. It would be absurd to associate these virtues only with Nubians, as a category apart from other Middle Easterners, or to suggest that the qualities developed only through contact with foreigners. However, I cannot refrain from emphasizing that these virtues are *discussed* more by Nubians than by any other group of people I have met anywhere, not only in the Middle East.

By working in hotels and night clubs and in the homes of wealthy foreigners and Egyptians, the Nubians had an opportunity to observe life styles largely unfamiliar to other Egyptians of low social status. The Nubian sons who played with the children of their father's employer, may have aspired to identify themselves in the future with the employer's social group, an aspiration the Nubian fathers were quite ready to encourage. For, although working as a servant is no disgrace in the Middle East, white-collar jobs are more prestigious among Nubians as among other Egyptians, and one seldom encounters the attitude that what was good enough for a father is good enough for his son.

Why, then, under circumstances of increasing social mobility, did Nubians continue to be interested in village affairs? The old ties were there, but they might not have sufficed if new institutions had not been created to reinforce the links between migrants and their home villages. The Nubian *gamaᶜiyya* society, or social club, was the urban institution that, more than any other, played a key role in the Nubians' struggle for a place in the city and in their upward mobility in the labor market. It was the *gamaᶜiyya* that helped the migrants cope with the new problems of city life and assisted them in the task of maintaining close contact with their rural communities.

At one time or another between the end of the Second World War and the 1963 resettlement, more than forty *gamaᶜiyyas* were active in Cairo, Alexandria, and Aswan. The successes of the *gamaᶜiyyas* as well as their problems are reflected in a general history of the Cairo Fedija clubs from Tushka district, which has been reconstructed through personal accounts from many Nubians and especially from Hamza El Din, a celebrated Nubian musician and composer now teaching and recording in the United States.

Clubs like the *gamaᶜiyyas* are at least as old as the mid-nineteenth century when guild lists from the time of Mohammad Ali record the existence of Kenuzi Nubian associations among dock workers at Egyptian ports. Apparently, the Kenuz, armed with their experience at the port of Aswan near the First Cataract, made their way to other Egyptian cities well ahead of the more isolated Fedija peoples. When Hamza's grandfather, with other men from Tushka, migrated to Cairo in the early 1920s, they came by donkey and sailboat, attracted by the high wages and labor demand of the city, for no steamboats connected the Sudan and Egypt, or the villages between.

The *gamaᶜiyyas* grew out of the migrant adventurers' desperate need for a meeting place where they could sit together and speak, in their own language, about their own affairs. Working as servants in European quarters of the city, which lacked suitable coffeehouses, the early migrants had to count on meeting their fellow Nubians in coffee shops near Abdine and other market centers of the city, between daily errands. The first formally organized Fedija clubs began in the twenties. Several men from the same largest *nog*, or maximum group of kinsmen with the same family name, each contributed a few piasters a month toward the rental of a room where all could meet. Similar arrangements persisted for several years, but eventually the basis for Fedija clubs shifted from *nog* to district of origin—the *nahia*, or collection of villages strung together along the narrow stretches of fertile Nile shore. Tribal membership, however, has remained the basis of Kenuzi urban clubs, yet another example of the greater strength of formal kinship as a basis for association among this tribally organized people.

During the twenties and thirties, older members of the Fedija migrant community were beginning to die in the city, and a common burial ground was needed. The men were also concerned at the time with the manner in which Nubian women traveled all over the city to pay traditional condolence calls on the occasion of a death. As we have seen, condolence calls at the mourning ceremonies are a strict obligation in Nubian society on the part of relatives, neighbors, and friends, and the Nubian migrant women took care to observe the custom, although the distances between houses were often greater than in Nubia and the territory through which they passed was not exclusively Nubian.

The men did not like the women traveling freely throughout the strange city, and they tried to stop the practice. The women refused, pointing out that Nubian women, just like Nubian men, needed the opportunity to console each other at the time of death, that they, too, had feelings and emotions, and that, if they were not permitted to visit each other's houses on these sorrowful occasions, they would each contribute money and rent a room for a woman's club! Such an ultimatum on the part of the womenfolk helped the men's clubs make their decision to buy the burial grounds, in the hope that this would be a common meeting place for both women and men. Many clubs purchased plots, which was a source of great relief to the resident city community, for Nubians attach much importance to the graves of their ancestors and regularly place offerings of water at the gravesides on religious holidays.

The clubs were also centers of communication and education. Lessons learned by the grandfathers during their first days in the city were passed on to sons and grandsons. Recipes were exchanged. Kin were recruited to provide extra service for important parties where Nubians were employed. Job openings were reported, and replacements were found from the same *nog* or village, for often news traveled by word of mouth from the villages to the city; the club was a convenient central headquarters at which the newcomers and the older residents could meet.

Teachers were hired in the 1930s and early forties to tutor the Nubian men and their young sons. To the Nubian adult of that period, education meant arithmetic, since the majority of men were faced with doing regular accounts as part of their jobs in private houses or in hotels. However, the sons enrolled in Cairo schools were also at a great disadvantage because of their comparative ignorance of Arabic. Thus, the reading and writing of Arabic was added to arithmetic, and these sessions became, in effect, adult literacy classes as the fathers listened to and participated in their sons' lessons.

"While we were servants at our work," said Hamza, "everyone wanted to be master in the club," and this led to difficulties, since "everyone talked and nobody listened." Sometimes a decision was reached only when, after hours of discussion and argument, the men departed, saying, "It's up to the rest of you." Eventually only the club president would be left and he would do as he thought best.

Despite the arguing and indecisiveness, the clubs in the forties were well enough organized to start food cooperatives, through which shipments of sugar, tea, and kerosene were sent to a number of their home communities. The mechanism of the cooperatives was later used to send government-subsidized rations of similar staples, including American surplus wheat, to the villages. Financial support for the cooperative was raised by selling shares to club members, and profits were divided and distributed annually in proportion to the size of the individual investment. The cooperative also provided a livelihood for a few adult men who preferred to live in Nubia but liked to visit Cairo occasionally for annual business meetings.

In the forties, the clubs built village elementary schools, which the Egyptian government then pledged to maintain and to supply with teachers. The schools were constructed with money sent from the cities and labor provided by men living in the villages. Many men had cash at the time, from compensation for land flooded by raisings of the Aswan dam. Wages were also good, particularly after the Second World War, when the British occupation of Cairo encouraged the opening of a number of new night clubs and restaurants. Here Nubians found employment as waiters, cooks, and, in some cases, managers.

During this period of prosperity, a growing tension between older and younger generations created some problems in the clubs. Many of the young men moved their social life to nearby coffee shops where they could drink tea and play backgammon without worrying about showing continual respect for their elders. In some cases, the loss of young members resulted in partial closing of the clubs. In other instances, compromises were reached whereby the youth were permitted to set up Ping-Pong tables, play backgammon, and enjoy themselves in the early evening, provided they replaced the furniture so the older men could relax more formally later on.

An interest in group sports among the young men also added new life to the clubs for a time. The younger men formed soccer teams to play matches in vacant lots and in city parks; they sold tickets to the matches to their adult relatives, who in turn became interested in the games. The younger and older generations pooled the ticket money to renovate the clubs and buy more recreational equipment.

But another, more serious development threatened the unity of the Nubian migrant communities in the forties and the fifties, when the third generation of Nubians was seeking employment in the city. By this time many Nubian men had profited from their father's ambitions for their education and had moved into white-collar jobs, the teaching and clerking positions to which their secondary education entitled them. A few with some years of college had achieved even higher job status. The new semiprofessional group of achievers was losing interest in the clubs, and this was a source of worry not only to the older men, but also for some of the youngest members. Why were the few educated men deserting the Nubian organizations?

Some members of the third generation, deeply concerned about a possible loss of Nubian culture and cohesion, formed groups to rejuvenate the arts of the Nubian past. A few talented young men, stimulated by Cairo city life but still feeling rooted in Nubian society, met in their spare time to paint, write poetry, and compose and play music. In this way, they hoped eventually to attract the interest and attention of the educated Nubians. They offered their services at weddings and began playing and singing in the evenings at the Nubian clubs. The Abu Simbel club was the first *gamaᶜiyya* to welcome the young Nubian artist-performers, reports Hamza El Din, a member of the original group. (The people of Abu Simbel, he says, have a reputation for being artistic and interested in art, just as the people of Ballana are noted for their hard work.)

"But we never performed at the clubs of our own *nogs*," reports Hamza. "Such behavior would have shamed and humiliated our elders. And of course we could never perform in our own villages."

Yet, when they visited their own villages, the young men did perform, informally, for their mothers and sisters, who were pleased and excited to have their Arabic-speaking city-dwelling offspring come home to sing the old half-remembered Nubian songs of their childhood. The women prayed for the young men and encouraged their efforts in many small practical ways. Gradually, the music of tradition and nostalgia, sung with enthusiasm by a new generation, helped to reestablish the sense of pride in and the consciousness of being Nubian. Partly as a result, two new *gamaᶜiyyas* were formed, uniting all the Kenuz and Fedija in one large assembly; the youth were particularly enthusiastic about this development, which did not replace but merely supplemented the smaller district clubs and served to draw together the men from the two largest regions of Nubia.

Clearly, the institution of the Nubian clubs served important but different purposes for each generation of migrant workers. The first clubs offered a meeting place for lonely, often confused men dealing with the problems of a large, sophisticated city. Unity brought other benefits: the burial plots, the cooperatives, the schools for the villages that aided the new generation. The third generation, of which Hamza was a member, found the association of the clubs a basis for the development of talents that would have remained largely dormant in the villages. The arts have little place in Nubian society, except where they have a traditional purpose—decorating the houses, for example, or providing singing and dancing at weddings or *moulids*. Performing before one's elders in the villages would have been considered disrespectful except on such traditional occasions as weddings. Otherwise, playing instruments and singing was strictly a peergroup activity. But the young artists in the cities found men from other communities who were eager to convert the entertainment regularly enjoyed on Nubian ceremonial occasions to that of a regular pleasure, occupying and enriching one's leisure time. Interested in Nubia, but anxious also to demonstrate their new talents and sophistication, these young men found the performing of traditional Nubian music and the recitation of poetry an acceptable basis upon which they could find common ground with their more conservative, older, or better educated kinsmen.

The artistic and social revival in the Nubian clubs of the fifties and early sixties helped unite the migrants and enabled them more easily to face the crises resettlement. Although the Nubians never became an effective political pressure group, individual clubs submitted many petitions to the various government ministries responsible for resettlement and tried to gain public support for their cause in the press and among the influential artists on the radio and television stations. In return, the ministries used the clubs as a means of communicating with Nubians in Cairo. Perhaps any group of people threatened with loss of land and property becomes politically active, but the Nubians had an organized base from which they could maintain the essential ties between country and city while the society was in the process of traumatic change.

Just before the actual resettlement began in 1963, much traveling took place between village and city, and many adjustments of residence and shares were effected to ensure proper recording of property rights so that adequate compensation would be made by the government to each family and each *nog*. The unique share system of Nubia was not easily transferrable to the government information forms, and the interwoven patterns of interests in *eskalays*, cows, and date palms had to be carefully disentangled and converted into statements of private ownership and specific property, statements that tallied with those of one's neighbors and kinsmen. This process alone was the source of great anxiety, and the fact that the communities survived, without violence, such a potential source of conflict is a further example of the effectiveness of the Nubian polity.

Finally, the young group of performing artists served to unite the Nubian communities in still another way, by presenting benefit concerts. All proceeds from the sale of tickets to these several performances given in Cairo in 1962 and

1963 were donated to a resettlement fund—to aid the old, the sick, the disadvantaged in faraway Nubia as they prepared to move. The young artists' reputation and their appearances in one of Cairo's newest and most attractive theaters attracted not only crowds of Nubians, but also many interested Egyptians and foreigners, which helped draw public attention to the plight of the dislocated peoples and thus aided them in their appeals to government officials.

Nubian migration, as we have described it, emerges as a different phenomenon from much labor migration elsewhere in the world. Instead of separating the Nubian from his society, migration reinforced his ties to his culture. This was partly because migration among the Nubians was frequently a community rather than an individual decision. Men were destined to go to the city, on the basis of whether or not they received enough property to survive as agriculturalists in the home community. The duration of the migratory period varied also; a man might go for a few years before marriage and return to marry, sometimes even settling in the village at that time. He might remain in the city, if his land was insufficient, returning only on holiday every few years. He might eventually retire in Nubia, with a government pension for support, for example.

So long as the pattern remained one in which men left wives and children in the villages, their ties with the community stayed comparatively firm, reinforced by the clubs in the cities. In recent years increasingly large numbers of Nubian women have moved to Cairo or Alexandria or Aswan to live with their husbands, a fact that indicates a greater investment in life in the city than in the past. However, at the same time, the land in Nubia remained in use and the villages were occupied in almost exactly the same proportion of people to arable land as before the larger-scale migrations. All the women and children and older men left behind in the villages, unless they were too old or ill, contributed something to their own support. The movement of Nubian women to the cities was due in part to the fact that for many nothing was left to occupy them in their native villages.

Even for Nubians who had established household *nogs* in the cities, Nubia still remained for many a place of refuge where one went to recover from an illness or an occupational setback, a place where one hoped to retire one day. The "blessed country" remained a place of security and peace—in short, it was home, in the way that many Nubians feel Egypt can never be. Cairo, said the women, had its advantages, particularly if one needed medical care, but basically it was costly, dirty, and full of thieves. With very few exceptions, the women tried to return to Nubia when they were pregnant, "so the child can be born at home." With good Nubian air and family to help, the baby was bound to have a better chance of survival!

If the direction of change before resettlement had involved more and more migrations to the cities by Nubian women, the ability of Nubian culture to maintain itself in more-or-less traditional patterns surely would have gradually diminished. At the time of resettlement, most Nubian women in the city were still uneducated and many did not know Arabic; thus, still speaking the mother tongue, they passed on to their children the traditions and values of the native communities in the language that best expressed them. Whether the village culture would have remained intact as the majority of Nubian women became partially assimilated into Egyptian urban society is questionable; at the time of resettlement this process was definitely underway.

During their time in the city, as we have noted, the Nubians were expected to return to the villages for feasts, such as the *moulids* in the Kenuzi region, or the weddings after the date harvest in the Fedija area; this returning became less possible in recent years, as Nubians became more formally committed to "better" jobs that required their presence for a set number of hours per day, a set number of days per year.

Such was the price Nubians were paying for their success in Cairo, and, had they not been obliged to pay it, the economic condition of their families and homeland would have suffered and their condition now would be far more difficult. As it is, many have jobs with great security and sufficient salaries to have been of key importance to the survival of many Nubian families during the difficult years of adjustment in Kom Ombo just after resettlement. Their history in the cities of Egypt is, then, no less remarkable than their culture in its traditional setting, and their record of urban adjustment compares favorably with that of European immigrants in the United States—though we customarily think of our history as somewhat unique in this respect.

The Nubian experience also demonstrates the narrowness of our belief that rapid change and adaptability is the special province of technological societies. The migrant worker changes his way of life because he is forced to by circumstance; he forgets his traditional culture because it is not applicable in the new community. This was simply not true of the Nubian, who took from the new situation only what he needed and wanted, and rejected the remaining elements in favor of his own values.

The experience did not traumatize but rather seems to have strengthened the Nubians as a group. In the words of the old proverb, "The fire that melts the butter makes the iron hard."

The existing structure of Nubian village communities provided the basis upon which men could organize in the city to cope with new sets of problems, for no social agency existed to take the place of this network of mutual aid. But it is more difficult to account so simply for the intelligence and openness that made the Nubian migrants quick to see and to take advantage of opportunities for bettering their condition, to learn foreign languages—along with foreign cooking and foreign customs—and, finally, to see many of their sons settled as doctors or bureaucrats in Cairo. From the cities and from their contact with foreigners they brought back to Nubia modified tastes in food, ideas for decorating and improving the construction of their houses, radios, and household items of metal and plastic. But, perhaps, because they also saw how little relation exists between contentment and material riches, they did not lose their people-centeredness, their belief that one of the best things in life is conversation and tea with one's friends or close relatives in comfortable, secure surroundings. For this, they have never found a place better than Nubia.

# Footnotes

[1] The survey was conducted by Dr. Peter Geiser, and his bibliography should be consulted for more detailed analyses of the subject ("Some impressions concerning the nature and extent of stabilization and urbanization in Nubia society," in *Contemporary Egyptian Nubia*, ed. Robert A. Fernea, I, 143-169).

# Chapter Sixteen

# The Future

Today the Nubian homeland lies under the waters of Lake Nasser, the shores of which are inhospitable. If the Egyptian government had not undertaken a massive and costly effort to resettle the villagers together and provide them with land to cultivate near the town of Kom Ombo, the more than fifty thousand residents of Nubia would now be dispersed throughout Egypt, in the process of being transformed into an urban minority. For, without fragments of their society still living in villages, still observing traditional patterns of life, it is doubtful they would have survived long as a socially and culturally distinctive part of the urban scene. The villages kept the Nubian language alive, socialized the young children before they went to Cairo, and provided an environment that was a fundamental part of the children's cultural development. Villages remained the dependable check on the process of assimilation, the counterbalance to cities.

The survival of Nubian culture, then, would seem to depend on whether the villages of New Nubia will be able to provide the social functions of Old Nubia. In the new setting a great many circumstances of traditional village life have totally changed. The resettlement area is several miles from the Nile, so the river traffic of the feluccas is irrelevant and the river rituals can no longer be practiced. The isolation of the old communities is gone, for New Nubia is only a few minutes by bus from the towns of Kom Ombo and Aswan, situated on a broad treeless plain that lies in a region of Upper Egypt well suited to the growing of sugar cane. Rather than growing traditional millet and other grains, the Nubians are expected to cultivate sugar cane as their principal cash crop, with the help of canal irrigation and artificial fertilizers. *Eskalays* and cows have no place here. Although palm trees have been planted in Kom Ombo, many years must elapse before their fruit can provide that traditional source of wealth. Thus, several essential elements of both the economic and the ceremonial life of the Nubians are gone.

Of even greater significance is the increased contact between Nubian villagers and Egyptian administrators and institutions. Medical clinics, agricultural extension offices, and a variety of other facilities are a part of the everyday scene. All levels of schooling are available, and most Nubian children will be studying and speaking Arabic from the age of five or six. These factors, combined with the relative ease with which trips can be made to nearby towns, will eventually weaken the use of the Nubian language. Women, who had scarcely any need for Arabic in Nubia, will find themselves at a much greater disadvantage in this new setting. Within two or three generations, it is probable that only the eldest persons in New Nubia will be able to converse in the language of their forefathers.

On the other hand, as the quality of the new land improves, the villages of New Nubia will be far more viable economically than those of Old Nubia, and the pressure for men to migrate to the cities for work will be considerably reduced. According to the terms by which the Nubians were granted land, the beneficiaries are required to live in and cultivate the area themselves. In Old Nubia, pump irrigation projects opened in the 1940s to replace some of the land flooded by the first Aswan Dam, and the men were expected to stay and cultivate the land at that time. But many owners continued working in the cities under sharecropping arrangements whereby resident Nubians, together with a number of hired men from Upper Egypt, undertook the actual farming. This solution is technically illegal now, though reportedly a significant number of neighboring Egyptians are becoming involved in the cultivation of the new lands. More men are still actually present in Kom Ombo than in Old Nubia, and presumably the sex ratios will remain more balanced than in the past.

Perhaps the most positive factor for the future of a distinctive Nubian culture lies in the new range of interaction now possible among rural Nubians. A population once scattered in isolated settlements over two hundred miles along the banks of the Nile today lives in a tenth of that space. Families once separated for years are together again. Relatives who could only with great difficulty visit each other in different villages on special occasions may now do so by walking down the street. The young people, who previously looked forward to a large group of peers only upon moving to Cairo, have found many friends their own age in their own village settlements. In fact, one of the first problems that faced the Nubians after resettlement was that the attendance at ceremonial occasions, such as weddings, deaths, and *moulids* (which were quickly resumed in this new setting), attracted so many people that the food prepared for the feasts was totally inadequate! The ease of communication has had an almost intoxicating effect on younger people, helping to counteract, to some degree, the traumatic shock of resettlement, which, of course, particularly affected the older Nubians.

In the twenties and thirties the growth of the migrant population in Cairo led to formation of the *gamaᶜiyya* clubs, where opportunities arose for the development of artistic and other skills that would not have been possible in the old villages. Perhaps the new villages may experience a similar renaissance. We must remember that the sense of being "Nubian," rather than just a member of a particular tribe or village, has come only recently to this people. Recognition of the Nubians as a group with special rights and interests is also new on the national scene. Already, the Nubians have become aware of the advantage to be gained in remaining together rather than making their way individually. Within a few months of their resettlement, for example, they were able to dominate local elections for the National Assembly and to send Nubian delegates to Cairo.

The aesthetic qualities of Old Nubia—the view of the river, the village situation between mountains and water, surrounded by high green palm groves—were impressive to the outsider and were also much appreciated by the Nubians. But aesthetics are not necessarily the basis of a society. The isolation of the villages carried with the privacy a lack of many of the advantages urban Nubians came to appreciate, particularly medical care and education. Many young men (while seeking as many concessions as possible from the government at the time) regarded the resettlement as a positive step. In spite of all the initial difficulties, the Nubians did not feel altogether pessimistic about the new life they were to develop for themselves.

The Nubians are not, after all, to be compared with the American Indians, whose ways of life were so radically different from the Europeans who came to dominate their land that they were at an almost impossible disadvantage. The Nubians and the Egyptians are in many ways a single people, sharing the all-important fact of a common religious faith. Surely, as the years pass, the Nubian minority will come to share even more with the Egyptian majority. And, while we should be concerned for the future of this small minority, we should remember that in the mosaic of Middle Eastern life, many groups of people have retained their individuality and vitality for generations while living close to other groups distinct from themselves. I believe a Nubian society is likely to persist, for, until the still long distant day arrives when individual achievement and social mobility are the major factors in personal survival and success, bonds of kinship and group allegiance will remain relevant. Rather than indulge in romantic nostalgia for what is indisputably gone, we who care about the fate of this people must take pleasure in the fact that they are so well equipped by experience and circumstance to make the adjustments necessary for their survival. We can only hope that their attachment to what is culturally unique in their own heritage will find new expression among future generations of Nubian Egyptians.

# PART III

# Epilogue

*Robert A. Fernea*
and *Aleya Rouchdy*

# Chapter Seventeen

# Contemporary Egyptian Nubians

". . . ethnic categories provide an organizational vessel that may be given varying amounts and forms of content in different socio-systems. They may be of great relevance to behavior, but they need not be; they may pervade all social life, or they may be relevant only in limited sectors of activity." (Barth 1969, 14.)

"Stable inter-ethnic relations presuppose . . . a set of prescriptions governing situations of contact, and allowing for articulation in some sectors of activity, and a set of proscriptions on social situations preventing inter-ethnic interaction in other sectors, and thus insulating parts of the cultures from confrontation and modification." (Barth 1969, 16.)

The community of Egyptian Nubians, resettled a generation ago when their ancestral lands were covered by the backwaters of the High Dam at Aswan, provide a contemporary example of a people whose sense of their own ethnicity has been redefined and revitalized by this radical change of circumstances. At the same time, there has been a loss of many aspects of their cultural legacy. The relocation of Egyptian Nubians took place in 1963, when the Egyptian government transported the Nubian people from the land along the Nile between Aswan and the Sudanese border at Wadi Halfa to an area at Kom Ombo, 40 kilometers north of Aswan. This event has profoundly affected their personal lives and the nature of their existence as a recognized community among the people of the Egyptian Nile valley. It is almost axiomatic that losing homes and villages

183

and moving to a radically different environment must result in changes of various kinds and degree. Such changes do not simply end after a given period of time however. Twenty-three years, a full generation, has now gone by and the course of Nubian history in Egypt is obviously different from that which it would have taken had these 56,000 people remained in Old Nubia. The question is then not just what has happened to them but in what directions this group of people may be moving: does the contrast between their lives before resettlement and their lives at the present time reveal a course of development which suggests what the future may hold for them?

In the text which follows we shall suggest that though many aspects of Nubian culture and social organization which existed before the building of the High Dam have changed or disappeared, the Nubians in contemporary Egypt, since their resettlement, have become, for the first time, a self-aware ethnic group. As such, we believe the Nubians are likely to play an ever more important role in the political and economic life of Upper Egypt and in the national life of Egypt as a whole.

In using the emergence of ethnicity as the paradigmatic basis for discussing what has happened to the Nubians of Egypt since their resettlement nearly a quarter of a century ago, it is necessary to compare the past with the present. In so doing, we will be concerned with the Nubians primarily, but aware of the context of their transformation: Egypt, still a largely rural, agrarian society in the 1950s, now an urban and industrializing society in the 1980s.

The Nubians in Egypt have moved from isolated communities into a multi-cultural situation in Upper Egypt. But even in the past, many of the men travelled to the cities of Egypt to find work and hence were scarcely isolated. However, the majority of the women rarely if ever left their native communities, which were located along the Nile at some distance from each other and from the Sayiidis, the agricultural people of Upper Egypt. Today the new communities, or "home lands" of the Egyptian Nubians, are not only much closer together and more densely populated but are more nearly contiguous with other peoples within the growing, partially industrialized province of Aswan. The Sayiidi people are now close neighbors. We believe that under these and other related circumstances, to be discussed below, the Nubians of Egypt have become an even stronger *ethnic* group than they were before resettlement, while at the same time losing much of their *cultural* uniqueness. How can this be? What is the nature of Nubian ethnic identity and how stable is it likely to remain? To suggest some answers to these questions we must first examine the nature of "ethnicity" as an analytic paradigm.

The distinction between cultural differences and ethnic identity was most cogently stated in a seminal essay by Fredrik Barth (1969), in which he pointed out that the way a group perceives itself and is perceived by others is a matter of *ascribed* characteristics. These are not restricted to any particular cultural distinctions, neither language, creed, customs nor traditions, though the charac-teristics which are ascribed to a particular group of people may be drawn from any of these (or other) categories—including race, since differences in physical appearance are important ethnically only to the degree that they are *culturally* significant as boundary markers in a particular social setting.

Social anthropologists and archaeologists have traditionally been concerned with the culture of their subjects of study. Whether this has meant the study of material culture or symbolic systems, the focus of attention customarily has been on the unique assemblage of symbolic systems, beliefs, customs, and the like, shared by the members of a group which distinguish them from others.[1] However, as Barth points out, *ethnic* differences cannot be accounted for solely in terms of objective cultural differences. Among groups which are socially distinctive both in their own terms and in the terms of others, "objective" criteria, i.e., cultural content, varies so much in both quality and quantity that an attempt to say how much or what kind of cultural difference is needed to constitute ethnicity would be futile. Placing a persistent, widely shared identity within the context of a larger social system does not depend upon the retention of any particular cultural markers. An ethnic group may select from whatever cultural features as may be present, or can invent such distinctions, as part of a constructed opposition between "us" and "them". Indeed, as we have seen recently in the United States, in the search for "roots" an ethnic identity can be forged out of nothing more than imagination and desire. The problem, as Barth emphasized, is not one of content, but is one of social boundaries made up from ascribed differences which divide "us" from "them."

However, in recognizing the subjective aspect of ethnicity, it is also important to recognize that ethnicity is not merely a state of mind. The pattern of oppositions between one social group and another must relate to a set of life circumstances in which the individual finds significance in his or her ethnic identity, or is so placed in such circumstances by others. Perhaps the issue can be stated thus: 1) In a particular historic setting, 2) social conditions persist which 3) make particular cultural differences assume widespread significance, therefore 4) becoming instrumental in maintaining boundary markers between two social groups. These boundary markers exist at certain points in social practice and in cultural expression.

In the discussion which follows, our intention is to look at the cultural differences and boundary markers between Egyptian Nubians and other Egyptians, attempting in this way to evaluate the importance of the changes in material conditions of social life which have taken place since resettlement. The underlying question we intend to address is whether, under present circumstances, it is likely that such boundaries will be maintained between the Nubians and other Egyptians. To answer this query we will attempt to suggest where social boundaries may be located in everyday life, and how such boundaries relate to the patterns of production and reproduction upon which Nubian subsistence and daily life depends. For while ethnicity may not be directly related to a specific mode of production (it sometimes is, of course), it is indirectly related within the political economy. The members of an ethnic group are always concerned with gaining their livelihood under a specific set of socioeconomic circumstances. We suggest that unless one's ethnic identity is viewed as positively related to one's well-being *or* is imposed upon one's group by others, it will (eventually) disappear.[2]

Ethnicity and its related terms have been used in a number of different ways before and since Barth's article. The definition offered in an article about Mexican Americans refers to both the subjective (ascriptive) and objective (cultural) aspects of ethnicity discussed above:

> "An *ethnic category* or *population* is in the nature of a logical class, objectively defined and embracing individuals according to common *ethnic characteristics*. These common characteristics are real or putative, descent-related cultural features used by members of one population, group, or category to distinguish them from another such population. An *ethnic identity* is the self-ascription to an ethnic category. An *ethnic group* is made up of individuals who have the same ethnic identity and who attempt to use their ethnic identity as a primary principle of social organization." (Melville 1983, 275.)

According to this definition are the Egyptian Nubians an ethnic group? First, let us look at the Nubians before their resettlement in 1963. Until the advent of the High Dam, people from Nubia referred to themselves both by tribal and family origin and according to the name of the district (more than 30) from which they came. Within their districts Nubians were known according to their descent group and their particular village of origin. At that time, the people called "Nubians" did not ordinarily use the term to refer to themselves, nor did they regard as one group all the dark-skinned people speaking a language other than Arabic and living along the banks of the Nile between Aswan and the Sudan. Three distinct linguistic and territorial groups existed in Old Egyptian Nubia: the Kenuz, who lived from Aswan to the south approximately 150 kilometers and spoke the Matoki dialect of Nubian.[3] In the central region of Egyptian Nubia for about 50 kilometers along the river lived related people who spoke Arabic as their native language, though other aspects of their culture were similar to that of their neighbors. South of the Arabic-speaking Nubians lived another Nubian population, speaking a non-Arabic dialect, Fedija (or Fadicca) related to but distinct from the Matoki dialect of the Kenuz. Before resettlement, the Fedija-speaking Nubians had no universally accepted name for themselves or their dialect; a question about a general name would often lead to acrimonious discussion. If pressed, some would say they were called Fedija, though this was in fact a somewhat uncomplimentary term used to refer to them by the Kenuz.[4] In recent years this name seems to have lost much of its pejorative connotation and in this paper is used to refer to this group.

If, before resettlement in 1963, the people of Nubia felt any common identity with each other, it was based on political and economic grievances with the Egyptian government. They had all experienced flooding of palm groves and villages when the first dam at Aswan was built at the turn of the century and again each time the barrage was raised. The last time this happened, in 1933-1934, some families chose to take their compensation money and resettle north of Aswan. The agricultural resource basis of life in most of the region was once and for all destroyed. Many Nubians felt they had never been adequately compensated for their losses. Those who moved above the flood waters in Old Nubia also insisted that the government had neglected them in terms of educational facilities and health clinics — both of which were thinly distributed in the region. However, even in this respect important differences divided the Nubians. The Kenuz, living closer to the dam, suffered greater flooding and could cultivate river shoreland only about two months each year when the reservoir was low: the Fedija to the south had more land left uncovered for longer periods of the year and palm groves still existed in districts near the Sudan border. Furthermore, the government had installed diesel pump irrigation projects in five districts, creating some districts of relative prosperity while the others remained impoverished. Thus, there were real economic differences between the Nubian communities before the High Dam was built.

The number of Nubian labor urban migrants increased after the additional loss of agricultural land in 1935. Often referred to by the pejorative term *"barabra"* in vernacular Egyptian Arabic, many of these migrants worked as servants in private homes and in service jobs in restaurants and hotels. Only a relatively small number of educated Nubians were working as professionals or civil servants at this time. While the Nubians' color and style of dress was a factor identifying them in urban society, their language was even more important. Nubians were said by other Egyptians to speak *"barbari,"* an inferior dialect which resulted in their Arabic being accented and imperfect; thus, the proper recitation of Islamic prayers was impossible. Only in the 1950s, as the High Dam and subsequent flooding of Nubia became imminent, did the stigma attached to this perception of the Nubians begin to shift somewhat.

It was President Gamal Abdul Nasser who first used "Nubian" as a term of reference in the media for the entire population above Aswan. In speaking about the building of the High Dam, he drew attention to the great patriotic sacrifice the Nubians were going to have to make in losing their land and homes for the general benefit of all Egyptians. However, Nasser's comments on the radio and in the newspapers by no means changed the attitudes of all Egyptians, many of whom continued to look down upon the Nubians to some extent. The Egyptian elite and the foreign population which could afford to hire Nubians as servants often praised them for their honesty and faithfulness. It was urban Egyptians in much the same socioeconomic position as the migrant Nubians who continued to express negative attitudes toward them.

Since they were to some degree a stigmatized group in the cities of Egypt, it is not surprising that working class Nubians as far as possible remained within their own social groups. Furthermore, the Kenuz and Fedija had little contact with each other in their leisure time and they rarely worked in the same establishments; indeed, it was usually men from the same communities who helped each other get jobs and worked together.[5] Nubian clubs, established in urban centers to make possible mourning ceremonies for men who died in the city, gradually came to provide recreational facilities, lessons in Arabic, job recruitment, and other services. However, these were individually organized by men from individual districts in Nubia. In short, the Nubians were a long way from thinking of themselves as one group, even in Cairo or Alexandria, away from their native communities.

However, certain opinions about working-class Egyptians were widely shared among all Nubians. The Nubians felt the urban Egyptians to be generally lacking in cleanliness and honesty, behavior which they (and their elite employers) highly valued. They contrasted urban life in lower Egypt with Old Nubia, their "Blessed land", a place where one did not have to worry about thieves or violence, where the peacefulness so lacking in the cities prevailed. Indeed, they shared many of the negative attitudes not infrequently expressed by upper class Egyptians and foreigners about *baladi* Egyptians.[6]

On the other hand, to most *baladi* Egyptians, Nubians were not *baladi* enough, in the positive sense of this term: they lacked the necessary qualities of "Egyptian-ness" connoted by that ambiguous adjective, especially a sharp wit and a gift for ironic repartee, which never leaves a true Egyptian at a loss for words.

Thus, in 1960, before resettlement, Egyptians and Nubians felt superior to each other. For the Nubians this sense rested on two grounds: 1) self-esteem derived from well-deserved reputations among the foreigners and high-status Egyptians for whom they worked and 2) a strong sense of identity with their own communi-ties, a sense of their importance in their own land. For example, the more success-ful men owned homes in Nubia that were truly palaces, with guest rooms, spacious courtyards with shady areas for summer and sunny spaces for winter, storage rooms and rooms for sleeping—in short, a luxury of residence unknown in the cities except to the wealthy class of Egyptians and foreigners for whom many Nubians worked. Even for men who rarely or never visited their natal land, pride in the homes they owned or shared and in the community itself constituted a very important part of their self-respect. It would be difficult to over-estimate the symbolic importance of Old Nubia—and even though it is now under water, much of its symbolic significance remains.[7]

For those Nubians who lived in their own villages, ceremonial life was a tangible demonstration of solidarity among the different local groups, as well as evidence of distinctions between them. For in Old Nubia, the other Egyptians did not exist. Intra-Nubian differences became sharper. Nubians—Kenuz, Arab, and Fedija— spoke their own distinctive dialects and invested their time and energy in their own rites and rituals. Just as the houses reflected the status of individual families, the ceremonies were also of great symbolic importance, reinforcing ties with the community. Among the Fedija, elaborate weddings requiring days of preparation and celebration  drew men home from the cities and attracted relatives from up and down the river. Such weddings were organized by families, but involved patterns of reciprocal assistance within the villages that were of great importance in many aspects of local life.[8] The *aza*, or mourning ceremony following a death, made even more rigorous demands on attendance and on the sending of telegrams of condolence from urban relatives and friends unable to attend because of work in the cities.

Among the Kenuz, the *mulid*-s or saint's day celebrations, were equally im-portant as rites of renewal and reunion. Mulids, to which neighboring groups of similar composition were invited, were organized by tribal descent groups. In the district of Dahmit, there were approximately 150 cenotaphs, or saint shrines, (*qubba*-s) to be found in the 24 villages with a population of about 1,300 people. Shrines were decorated, prayers were recited, food was served, dancing and singing took place. The success of the mulid was judged by the number of outside participants, coming not only from the cities but also from neighboring villages on both sides of the Nile.[9] All of these rituals—weddings, mulids or aza-s— were the Nubians' own, a rich ceremonial life about which much more could be said. The important point is that this symbolic property was part of the way in which Nubians thought of themselves superior to other Egyptians. The same can be said of the traditional Nubian homes (many of which were elaborately rebuilt with compensation money after the 1934 dam heightening). They were a source of pride and satisfaction to their Nubian owners. However, Egyptian neighbors, employers, or fellow workers knew nothing of the special qualities of Nubian life.

It is also important to remember that before their resettlement, the Nubians lived with the illusion of independence in most of their villages; a visible Egyptian presence was rare throughout Nubia. We stopped at communities in 1961 that could not remember a previous non-Nubian visitor. Generally, non-Nubians were only to be found at the Egyptian administrative headquarters for Nubia in Eneba, one of the districts near the center of the region, and there was a border police station in south Ballana. The government's policy of benign neglect was mirrored by the attitudes of non-Nubian Egyptians, for only Nubians wanted to go to Nubia. To other Egyptians, being assigned to a job in Nubia was a form of exile, a sure way to get nowhere in terms of salary and advancement. So Nubia and Nubians were largely left alone. In each district a local Nubian was the chief official (*umda*) who had responsibility for reporting vital statistics and conveying government orders, but there were few Egyptian police in the region and to go to them over local problems was considered disgraceful. For most Nubian districts, a once a week visit from the Sudanese Post Boat was the only contact with the outside world.

A common anthropological view of ethnicity is that it reflects social stratification. Vincent (1974), Benedict (1962), Spiro (1955, 1244), Cohen (1969, 193-194), Hechter and Levi (1979) and Benedict (1962) all argue that ethnicity is primarily an expression of a hierarchical relationship between the social groups involved. This assertion, to be applicable in the Nubian case, would require that a distinction be made between an "objective" political-economic assessment of the situation and the way in which it was understood and experienced by the Nubians themselves. Of course, the Nubians were subordinate within the political economy of the country; they could not prevent the obliteration of their land. But on a day to day basis the illusion of independence and freedom was very strong. No one who ever visited a Nubian village could have overlooked that ambience.

Was the Nubian/Egyptian relationship stratified in Egyptian cities before resettlement? The Nubians' position in the service sector of the pre-industrial labor force was privileged in that they were preferred for the work they did and often had primary responsibility for the day to day aspects of their labor. Also, they greatly influenced the hiring of new employees in many situations. In the still largely agrarian Egypt of colonial times and in the early days of national independence, schooled Nubians were widely employed as servants in private homes and in hotels and restaurants, as mentioned above. A survey in 1962 showed that

66.8 percent of the labor migrants from Egyptian Nubia who were working in Cairo were in some kind of service employment (Kennedy 1966, 361). Others worked in jobs such as boat building or taxi driving in Alexandria. It was characteristic for men from the same community to work together in the same establishment. When a new person was needed, word would be sent back to the village for a relative to be sent to Cairo. It was definitely prestigious to have a Nubian *sufragi* (house boy) or *boab* (doorman). This meant that there was little direct competition between Nubians and other Egyptians for most jobs.

Working as servants, surrounded by non-Nubians, Nubians spoke their own language, a practice which, like the employment itself, was both stigmatizing and at the same time offered a degree of independence. Thus Nubians could discuss their work, criticize their employers and share "inside" jokes, which provided them with a sense of superiority over others, even while their language marked them as *barabra*. Whatever the negative opinions of other Egyptians, the Nubians' ability to control, to a degree, the conditions of their employment made their work more acceptable. Furthermore, many Nubians had jobs requiring high levels of trust and responsibility and intimate contact with people of high status.[10] It seemed to us who lived among Nubians in the 1960s that it was with the elites of Egypt, native and foreign, that many of the Nubian men identified; the elites were the people whose manners they admired and to whose standard of living they aspired.

Considering the above, it is tempting to conclude that before the High Dam, the mystifications of the "Blessed land" (as the Nubians called Nubia), that impoverished shore of the Nile where they felt themselves free in their own beautiful universe, were reinforced by the Nubian experience in urban employment. In the cities, the Nubians, like many white collar office employees, identified with their employers, not with the workers outside. However, the sense of personal worth which seems to have resulted has served the Nubians well, helping them through the radical adjustments of the last twenty years.

What has happened in the last twenty years? Have the Nubians of Egypt been able to maintain their illusions of independence? Can they now reproduce their old symbolic world in a new setting? What has become of their sense of personal identity and their social goals? The answer is complex and to generalize about all Egyptian Nubians today is even more questionable than to generalize about them historically. However, there are some strong tendencies which we can describe, which seem to be part of the direction in which many Nubians are moving. To do so, we must look briefly at the long term effects of the conditions of resettlement as well as their social and economic adjustments within the context of greater Egypt and the Middle East today.

The old Nubian villages were scattered along the banks of the Nile from Aswan to the Sudan border, a distance of 350 kilometers; the new settlements were constructed on a crescent of land about 25 kilometers long. While the districts were lined up as they had been in Nubia, individual villages in the districts have disappeared into the general housing projects. The houses are constructed terrace-fashion, straight rows, wall-to-wall. Houses with the same number of rooms were placed on the same row and assigned according to family size. Thus the new houses have lost their relationship with the organic nature of the community; kinsmen have been scattered far and wide, and old patterns of neighborly reciprocity have been broken.

There is also reason to feel that the new Nubian communities lack the symbolic meaning of the old villages. The houses of Old Nubia also reflected the status of their owners, their success and prosperity. The government-issue houses all looked the same when the Nubians first arrived. In the early years of resettlement, considerable effort and money was expended in remodelling the homes, in plastering the cement walls and painting and decorating the exteriors with Nubian designs like those in Old Nubia. However, such remodelling is no longer going on. People say they do not want to waste money on houses which they do not even own (they still do not have legal title to their homes, as discussed below). Some say that they would rather spend money on furniture and appliances which they can take with them when and if they move one day.

Whether or not they want to be, Nubians are no longer isolated. It is far easier to spend time away from the new communities than it was in the past. Women deliberately make the trip to the several daily markets in New Nubia not only to make purchases but also to visit with their friends. Going and coming to the cities of Kom Ombo, Daraw and even Aswan is easy, a cheap bus ride rather than a long boat trip, as in the past. Cairo is only overnight by train and the trip is relatively inexpensive. Newspapers arrive daily from Cairo, indicative of rising levels of literacy as well as new ease of communication.

The Nubian communities are surrounded by the Sayiidis, the majority population in the region, and many Sayiidis are actually working for the Nubians. Several hundreds of Sayiidis, who had lived in Old Nubia in their own settlements, are now mixed among the Nubians in the new housing projects.[11] Thus interacting with Sayiidis has become a familiar experience for most Nubians, including women. Further, a number of Nubian men have married Egyptian women and brought them to New Nubia.[12] In short, not only are most of the new villages densely populated and residentially arranged without reference to kinship or social networks, but much more movement and contact with non-Nubians is taking place even for the women, children and men who stay at home. Perhaps this is why in 1986 we found the women in New Nubia far less reserved in our presence than in earlier years, taking part in conversations with members of both sexes in a relaxed manner. The *gargar*, a black over-dress traditionally worn by Fedija women, has been shortened and is made of transparent material, revealing colorful and shapely dresses underneath. Our general observation was that both sex and generation gaps had narrowed in the villages.

For younger Nubians, men and women, schooling in an Egyptian setting is a nearly universal experience. Education was always highly regarded in Old Nubia and seen as the avenue to greater personal success. Indeed, even in the 1960s five percent of the Nubian urban migrants held professional and managerial jobs (Kennedy 1966, 361). Today, elementary and secondary schools in New Nubia are overflowing with thousands of children born since resettlement.[13] Nor is it just boys who go to school. There is integrated education at all levels and almost equal attendance between men and women, we were told. This is in part possible because the amount of everyday household work for women (carrying water from the river, gathering fuel and animal fodder, tending gardens) has been greatly reduced from what was necessary in Old Nubia. Although we have no idea how many, some young women now contribute to the family budget by working in shops and offices, a thing unheard of in old Nubia. Thus education is having a tremendous impact on the lives of younger Nubians, all of whom seem to aspire to white collar jobs.

This desire for white collar jobs is consistent with old attitudes about manual labor, especially agricultural work, which we have heard in conversations over many years. The experience of the Egyptian government which in the last twenty years has tried and generally failed to make sugar cane farmers out of the resettled Nubians suggests that distaste for manual labor and associated attitudes have created a serious impediment to the government's original resettlement plans.

Appropriately enough, the resettled Nubians were to be among the first Egyptians to benefit from the land reclamation schemes made possible by the High Dam. In the resettlement area, approximately twenty-seven thousand feddans (one feddan equals 1.038 acres) were set aside for the Nubians. However, at the time of relocation in 1963 only 10 percent of this land was actually ready for use. According to Fahim (1983), only 60 percent of the resettled families had received new land by 1979. The reclaimed land was allotted according to three categories of families: 1) those who had previously owned land in Nubia and cultivated it themselves, 2) those families who had owned land but had not farmed it themselves, and 3) those who had not owned land but had been agricultural laborers. Nubians in the first and second categories received as much land as they had owned, up to five feddans; any land in excess of five feddans was compensated for in cash. The third category of family, the landless Nubians, received two feddans. However, those Nubians who owned less than one feddan were paid cash for their loss, though they protested that they should receive two feddans like their landless neighbors. The government officials explained that the shortage of land made this impossible. This ironic development deprived thousands of families of the means to grow the kitchen crops and animal fodder which were common on even the smallest plots of land in Old Nubia. Nubians who received land allotments were permitted to devote 40 percent of their land to such crops; 60 percent of the allotted land had to be put into sugarcane production.

Clearly, the problems with getting land allotments would have discouraged many Nubians from farming even if they might have wanted to do so. Indeed, some Nubians, especially from the southern Fedija area, are farming their own land under the general supervision of a government-managed agricultural cooperative. However, thousands of Nubians were forced to find other means of subsistence, just as had been the case in Old Nubia, and many who had returned from urban jobs to claim their land and houses and help their families were obliged to resume migratory labor. Among those Nubians who did receive land, the predominant strategy was to sharecrop — the same practice common in Old Nubia. But in New Nubia sharecropping is not being practiced with relatives as much as with local

Sayiidis. The latter, already familiar with the heavy work of sugar cane harvesting, work for wages or a portion of the crop price.

Despite the fact that this practice was contrary to government ideology (landowners should do their own cultivation) the pressure to get the reclaimed land under cultivation and deliver quotas of sugar cane to the local factory made the authorities overlook the question of who was doing the work. It is also important to remember that working for a cooperative and farming a cash crop is very different from traditional Nubian agriculture, which involved subsistence crops and date palm horticulture.[14] As Fahim (1983, 79) observes,

> "The government's plan to incorporate the Nubians into the economic mainstream of the region has proved unsuccessful. These people, with an independent trait characteristic of their culture, have not been able to conform to the agricultural structure that involved almost total intervention on the part of the government."

Nubians do not generally regard the resettlement area as any more self-sufficient than Old Nubia before the High Dam. However, the kind of subsistence agriculture and animal husbandry practiced in the past (goats, sheep and cows constituted the most valuable export from the region in the years after building and heightenings of the first Aswan dam, when date groves were destroyed) much more directly complemented their life-style then than does the present situation. Thus, their enthusiasm for education and for professional or at least white collar jobs for their children is based on a very realistic appraisal of their situation.

In addition to the problems of subsistence, major changes have taken place in the content of Nubian cultural life. The forms of cultural expression brought from Nubia have changed radically, and much of today's cultural experience in the new communities is similar to that of other Egyptians.

Weddings and mulids are now abbreviated in form and content. Rather than not invite new neighbors and friends to weddings, families serve only candies and dates to the guests rather than whole meals as in Old Nubia. The celebrations last only one day rather than three or four. Death ceremonies (aza-s) have been reduced from the fifteen days of mourning necessary to allow absent relatives to return home, to three days, which is seen as time enough, given faster travel connections and tighter work schedules in factories and offices which do not allow much time off. Male circumcision ceremonies seem to be disappearing (Fahim 1983, 66). The number of mulid-s has been greatly reduced. Though in the early days of resettlement, some ishara (dreams telling one to establish a shrine) resulted in the construction of new shrines and while some mulid-s are still celebrated in the Kenuz districts, the number has been greatly reduced, though the number of people participating in those festivals which are held is much greater.

The decline in the number of mulid-s and the changes in wedding ceremonies may not only be a result of the demographic changes but may also signal a growing concern for conformity with what may be considered standard Islamic practice in contemporary Egypt. In the one wedding we attended, the groom and his male kinsmen and other male guests gathered together to pray in the local mosque before a noonday meal. No dancing was held at night and many other traditional Fedija features were missing. This is consistent with a much greater apparent interest in Islam on the part of many Nubians. Many women (who did not do so in Old Nubia) are now performing the five daily prayers, saying them in Arabic, a language which has become far more common even among older women who have not attended school. Male attendance at the Friday mosque prayers is also widespread; in much of Old Nubia Friday prayers in a neighborhood involved a handful of men; hundreds may pray together now. Generally speaking, the growing Islamic consciousness which is so evident elsewhere in Egypt is also part of Nubian life.

The new concern for religious practice goes along with constant exposure to Egyptian television, for this and other aspects of modern Egyptian urban culture is reflected in the programming which the Nubians watch constantly. Every Nubian home seems to have a television set, sometimes more than one, and many video sets are seen as well. Famous Muslim television preachers are a popular entertainment for many, as are films, plays, music programs, documentaries, and news programs. Egyptians soap operas are very important; since for the most part they involve middle class Egyptians and provide a view of the successful life which is just as intimate, even if more romanticized, as the exposure many Nubian men used to get while working among the old elites. In a steady flow of Arabic, the Nubians today are learning how to be both pious Muslims and to aspire to the consumer habits and life-styles of the new middle class. They also are constantly exposed to the "Dallas" and "Dynasty" versions of Western life, which they can both admire and scorn, like many other Egyptians. Thus we heard a successful young Nubian friend worry about the increase in materialism among his people, while he drove us in his new Peugeot sedan, dressed in a jeans suit, listening to Caro Mio on his stereo. (He switched to a Quranic recital after we picked up his uncle, a respected shaykh.)

Almost all the changes mentioned above have in one way or another impacted on what is usually viewed as the core of cultural distinction, the major means of cultural expression—language. The use of Nubian dialects is declining in all sectors of the Nubian population, while there is a general increase in the understanding and use of Arabic. On a recent visit we heard children being addressed by their mothers in the Matoki dialect and responding to them in Arabic. When we asked children of seven or eight whether they knew Matoki they responded shyly in Arabic, "*shwayya*", i.e., "a little". Success in school means an early mastery of Arabic, and many parents are encouraging their children to use that language outside the classroom. But it is not just children who are developing new linguistic competence. We were amazed last January, 1986, to have a woman in her 80s, who had never uttered a word of Arabic to us in Ballana, Old Nubia, make simple conversation with us in Arabic! Some women are using Arabic greetings, we noticed, even if they subsequently converse in Matoki. Our studies reveal that the language is not evidencing new ways of dealing with the changing world through the coining of new Nubian words. While unusually role-conscious speakers of a Nubian language can borrow an Arabic term and supply Nubian morphology, our experiences lead us to believe more and more male conversations now go on in Arabic, even in the Nubian clubs of Cairo which we visited.

We have already alluded to the importance of television as a source of Egyptian influence. Certainly this is a way for non-Arabic speakers (past school age) to learn the language. The greater presence of men in the household, of men working in the region, the more frequent coming and going between the settlement and the cities, including Cairo, all contribute to the use of Arabic among Nubians of all ages and both sexes. In Old Nubia, movement between the villages and cities encouraged bilingualism among the men, who also spoke Nubian dialects among themselves in Cairo. Knowledge of Nubian dialects by the mono-lingual women in the native communities was passed on to their children. This situation is radically changing and once a Nubian dialect ceases to be the language of primary socialization its maintenance is clearly undermined.

But interest in other expressive aspects of Nubian culture is evident, at least as a form of entertainment. Throughout the winter tourist season, the Cultural Center in Aswan, whose director is Nubian, features performances of Nubian (as well as Sayiidi and Bisharyin) dances and songs.[15] All these are choreographed in the ''folkloric'' tradition seen in Cairo theaters. One evening, the auditorium was half full and a number of Nubian couples was present—another departure from the past. Nubian women performed with men. Corridor walls of the Cultural Center were decorated with children's drawings of Old Nubia, though the children had never seen the region. Clearly, many Nubians, young as well as old, feel a sense of pride in their history, and a sense of ethnicity is fostered among the children by the specifically Nubian displays and events sponsored by the Cultural Center. The new Museum of Nubian civilization, scheduled to be built at a cost of 18.6 million dollars, will, when completed, offer another source of cultural identity, though some of our Nubian friends said that putting Nubian history and culture in a museum might well hasten Nubian assimilation.

With regard to assimilation, some commodifying of Nubian culture is taking place, a packaging of expressive forms for the consumption of others, as ''Nubian'' dance acts appear in every hotel and night club of Aswan (and some in Cairo!). On one of the expensive tourist boats anchored in Aswan, we witnessed what was to us an extraordinary performance given at a supper club when the Soviet Ambassador to Egypt happened to be present. The Nubians, wearing bandanna headgear more typical of the American Old South than of Old Nubia, danced to the beat of drums in a well choreographed number, joined in a free-form finale by sturdy, uninhibited young Egyptian men from the audience (medical students on a holiday, a waiter told us). The whole affair, costume, dance and music, seemed much more related to newly prosperous Egyptians' views of ''traditional'' Nubian than anything ever expressed by Nubians in Old Nubia. Nubian tourist guides and tourist shops are now a regular feature in Aswan, added to the Kenuzi fallucas, which for many years have offered boat rides to foreign visitors. Newly middle-class Egyptians are now discovering Aswan, and the Nubians are seeing that their fellow countrymen will not be disappointed.

A serious concern for the preservation of traditions, language and economic interests, also is being expressed by a minority of Nubians, who have attempted to establish new communities along the shores of the lake which covers Old Nubia. There have been several such attempts since 1977, when President Sadat gave limited financial support to the pioneer settlements. In 1980 we visited one such site, a few miles south of Aswan on the west bank of the Nile, near the old Kenuz settlement of Daboud. Wells had been dug by the government, but failed to provide suitable water and thus the settlement had been abandoned.

It is in the old Fedija region that some colonies have actually been established. One, Al-Salam, a satellite of the government settlement at the Abu Simbel temple, is about 25 kilometers south of the temple. Al-Salam has about twenty-five families resident in homes which the government helped build. The community has agricultural equipment, and is using pump irrigation to cultivate virgin desert land. Another colony, Al-Shuhadaa, lies across the river and further south, above the old district of Adendan. When visited in 1981 only men were resident, farming with water pumped from the lake. The Al-Shuhadaa men asserted that it was their intention to preserve Nubian culture in a place free from outside interference and stated they always spoke Fedija among themselves. These 20 or so men seemed to have had considerable formal education and were very articulate in Arabic. President Sadat, who had a Nubian grandparent, it is said, once visited this community and was very supportive. By 1986, however, both of the Fedija colonies were suffering from water problems and we were told that there are only three families in Al-Shuhadaa now. The water level of the lake has dropped to all-time lows since the recent African drought and even the average yearly fluctuation in water levels makes the use of pumps very difficult. Still, the effort has had some success. The cooperative which organized the Al-Shuhadaa settlement has established for Nubians certain long-term rights to settlement and economic development along the shores of the lake and also has secured fishing rights for Nubians. (Fishing has become an industry on the lake, but has been in the hands of non-Nubians.)

Enthusiasm continues to be expressed for the idea of returning to Old Nubia, but many of the older men who once lived in Old Nubia are saying that such a life would be too harsh for them. A group of younger men agreed that they would be interested in going only if the government paid all their expenses. Indeed, between 1981 and 1986 discussion of a return to Old Nubia has noticeably declined. The practical difficulties involving irrigation seem too far from solution and the present government has exhibited much less interest in the pioneering effort than did President Sadat.

As we look at the present situation of the Egyptian Nubians, their strategies for earning a living has turned them away from Old Nubia-and, for many, also away from New Nubia. We cannot provide any quantitative information about the number of Nubians involved but it is clear that today people of Nubian descent are found in almost every part of the Egyptian economy. The Egyptian census does not identify people according to race or ethnicity, this in itself suggesting the absence of any formal boundaries between Nubians and other Egyptians. However, we believe that the Nubians have been fully part of the changes in the

Egyptian economy which have occurred in the last twenty years, the urbanization and industrialization of the country since Sadat's policy of *infatah* opened the country to foreign investment in the mid-70s. The following description, however, must be regarded as impressionistic, based on conversations, not formal surveys of employment statuses.

1) *Work in Upper Egypt*. Public and private offices, hotels and tourist agencies, and probably a wide range of other establishments which we could not visit are filling jobs with Nubian employees in Aswan. We believe they are well on the way toward dominating white collar employment in the area. Many Nubians employed by the Egyptian government prefer to be in Aswan near their families, and this accords well with the preferences of other Egyptians to go to or remain in Cairo. Aswan has become almost like the Wadi Halfa of pre-High Dam days, where Nubians filled jobs at all levels in the local bureaucracies. We strongly suspect that for the majority of Nubians a good white collar job in the Aswan area (including Kom Ombo and Diraw) would be high on their list of job preferences. Certainly this is the pattern well documented by John Kennedy in his study of a Nubian community resettled in 1934. At that time, 46.6 percent of the men were working at professional, managerial, clerical and sales jobs and 3.3 percent were farming, though Aswan was then a far more agricultural region than it is now (Kennedy 1966, 362). The resettled community also had experienced a dramatic rise in educational levels following the move.

2) *Work in Arab oil producing countries*. This has been as much or more of a boon to the Nubian community as to any other sector of the Egyptian population. Older men with service skills have found high paying employment in the homes of the super-wealthy in Saudi Arabia and the Persian Gulf and, until recently, Libya. From such jobs, some Nubians have gone on to acquire managerial positions from their employers. Tape recorded letters and video strips keep families in touch with each other and visits between Arab countries are no more difficult than visits from Cairo before resettlement. Indeed, the Nubians culturally were better prepared than other Egyptians to take advantage of OPEC related opportunities and travel abroad; they were already experienced migrants. The appliances and electronic equipment filling many homes today are explicit evidence of overseas employment. Nor is work limited to Arab countries. In 1978 there were 57 members of the Egyptian Nubian club in London, for instance, men working for wealthy Arab expatriates and in embassies and other Arab offices. This group has a well-appointed and active social club. Some Nubian women have joined their husbands in London, but one study suggests that this is not an entirely successful social arrangement (Helmer 1983, 133-157). It is also difficult to bring families to the Arab oil countries, but again this is no new hardship for the Nubians.

3) *Employment in Cairo and other lower Egyptian cities*. This has certainly increased since resettlement; the economic limitations of the resettlement economy necessitated what may in any case have remained a preferred choice. Visits to Nubian clubs in Cairo and talks with the men who crowd them indicate a wide variety of employment in private and governmental offices. Nubians are found working at all levels in banks, news agencies and in many private concerns. In

other words, Nubian employment in Egypt even now appears to be primarily in the service sector, as before resettlement but now more in white collar occupations; this is also the nature of their employment abroad. In Egypt, Nubian men, and numbers of women, have entered the modern, urbanized, Western sector employment market with considerable success, we believe.[16]

4) *The cultivation of sugar cane on the reclaimed land.* This occupies a considerable number of Nubians, whether they actually do the work or manage their own and others' holdings. Male absence from New Nubia was reported as high as 50 percent by an under-secretary of the Ministry of Land Reclamation in 1973; the 1976 census revealed sex ratios of from 38 to 50 percent of men among the Kenuz, 62:100 among the Arab-Nubians and 80:100 among the Fedija (Fahim 1983). The rates of migration have certainly increased by this time and many of the locally resident Nubians are working in the nearby urban centers. However, some men have become involved with agriculture. As 52 percent of the land claims were in the names of women, the management of some of this land may fall to either a returned spouse or another male relative. While there is clearly a strong preference for city work, it is interesting to speculate that working on the sugar cane may be a kind of safety net for unemployed Nubians, who can still find work in the fields when the urban employment opportunities decline. The current contractions in the Egyptian economy might conceivably make it necessary for Nubians to replace Sayiidi sharecroppers, though the Nubians insist that they cannot make as much money working their five feddans as they can by sharecropping it and working in the city (Fahim 1983,82). A recent study shows that compared with cotton, sugar cane is a very profitable cash crop (Adams 1986, 71). Once irrigation and drainage problems in presently blighted areas of reclaimed land are solved, more Nubians may turn to cash farming. However unsatisfactory the present situation may be, the Nubians will never abandon the reclaimed land, but as the population grows the percentage of descendants who can actually be fully supported by this resource will continue to decrease.

*Conclusion.* What then of Nubian culture and ethnicity? Much of our discussion has centered around the loss of language, traditional customs and ceremonies, even the commercialization of dance and music. Yet the Nubians are far from disappearing as a distinctive part of Egyptian society. First, they share economic interests in the new settlement and residual claims to the land of Old Nubia. The government has still not granted them full title to their homes or lands and until this is done, the Nubians cannot sell their property or homes.[17] While some of the houses are presently empty, their owners settled in lower Egypt use them as vacation homes, sending their children and elderly parents there part of year and maintaining their claims. Perhaps, when title is granted, houses may be sold and the heterogeneity of the communities will increase as non-Nubians, such as the Sayiidis, move in, but this is still not possible. In fact, some Nubians are actually building new homes of their own in New Nubia with the petro-dollars they have earned abroad. These homes, unlike the government issued houses, are registered as their own private property. While spending more money on the government houses has stopped, the new homes represent a significant investment and indicate a positive attitude toward the new settlements.

In addition to their common economic interests in New Nubia, the Nubians are becoming an increasingly important economic and political force in Upper Egypt. Educated Nubians are taking administrative jobs in every branch of the local government. They were able to fill most of the key posts in the local hierarchy of the Arab Socialist Party when it was the only permitted political organization. While the gap between local Nubians and the educated administrators still exists, as the levels of education rise in the new settlement this will gradually lessen and the ability of the local population to influence administrative decisions presumably increase. In short, the Nubians are becoming—may already have become—the dominant political and administrative group in the Aswan region. On the other hand, it would be a mistake to ignore the potential for factional disputes within the Nubian population, based on old social and linguistic divisions combined with new interests. There have been quarrels of various kinds, but information is lacking to assess how serious these differences may be or may become.

Nationally, the Nubians are taken far more seriously than was the case twenty years ago. They have excellent contacts with both the government and the media in Cairo. In January, 1986, three articles about the Nubians appeared in *al-Ahram*, Cairo's most influential newspaper. The first article critically discussed the fact that the Nubians still do not have proper title to their lands and asked why this is so. The second article described plans for the new Museum in Aswan, and the third discussed the problems of the pioneer settlements in Old Nubia and Nubian land and water rights in the region above the High Dam.

It is also important to remember that access to employment in Cairo still involves the use of personal contacts, networks of common interests, even in the Western sectors of the economy. The Nubian urban clubs in Cairo date from as early as the 1920s and 1930s; they now occupy quarters which have in many cases become prime locations in the city, on some of the most fashionable streets. It is comparatively easy for them to evolve into middle class establishments as the occupational status of the membership improves. Indeed, this is exactly what is happening in the one we visited on Kasr el Nil street, where men in Western style business suits drank coffee and visited while young men in jeans played pool. The clubs offer many advantages as a facility for weddings and funerals, but probably the most important may be in the way in which jobs are passed out and news of common interest disseminated. As in the past, they are a means of adjustment in the city and both a source and an expression of modern ethnicity. The Nubian clubs remain a valuable asset to the Nubians for this reason, but they are also of political importance. They have organized conferences and workshops to discuss their common problems with government officials. In 1975 they began to publish a monthly newsletter called *Akhbar el-Nuba*, and they provided financial assistance for the pioneer settlements in Old Nubia, among other functions. In short, Nubian clubs have become political as well as economic and social organizations, working for the well-being of their membership in the city and in Upper Egypt.

In this regard, Nubian women university graduates in Cairo also formed a club of their own in 1978, received a grant of land from the government to build a headquarters, and began the publication of *Ganoub el- Wadi*, "Southern Valley," which includes information about the entire region. They also were active in supporting the efforts to establish communities above the High Dam. This parallels the civic interests of the women living in New Nubia, whose votes were a major factor in the 1976 election: out of twenty thousand votes cast, fourteen thousand were women. In this respect, they are far more politically active than the Sayiidi women in the region (Fahim 1983, 99).

Finally, interest in the future of the lands above the High Dam still remains strong, even if the current condition of the new communities there is not encouraging. In this respect, the possibilities of a common claim to whatever economic development may take place in Old Nubia is a unifying, common cause among all Nubians. Even if the hopes and dreams about future possibilities are still a long way from realization, they remain a subject of common concern among all the descendants of the Nubians who were born there.

Returning to the definition of ethnicity which began this discussion, we see that the contemporary setting still provides a persistent set of conditions, involving shared political and economic interests which make being a Nubian important in defining this group's interests in opposition to those of others. Nubians both share common interests among themselves and compete with other Egyptians in an ever wider variety of jobs. The alienating forces of modern urban employment have still not overcome group identity; being a Nubian will remain a significant difference to a great many people who have inherited this social status as long as real and potential economic interests remain viable, reinforced by the history they have shared and the self-ascribed characteristics of being Nubian.

At the same time, so far as other Egyptians are concerned, individual Nubians are free to pursue paths of individual mobility and become part of the population at large, as many Nubians have done in past generations. The urban, capitalist society of contemporary Egypt, with its growing middle class, makes individual social mobility far easier than in the more static agrarian past. Moreover, Egypt is not a racist society and being a Muslim is a serious claim to equality, superseding all other social characteristics. While color may be judged on aesthetic grounds to be more attractive if lighter and less so if dark, personal achievement is of far greater importance in establishing one's social status. Thus, with greater access to educational opportunities and new job possibilities, the Nubians of Egypt are free to disappear as an ethnic group. But the great majority of Nubians have no desire to do so at the present time. It seems doubtful that this attitude will soon change.

## Footnotes

[1] If anthropological practice and theory have shifted away from such concerns in recent years this is surely as much because culturally unique societies are rapidly disappearing as it is because of changes in theoretical interests.

2 Unfortunately circumstances have not permitted us to make a study of contemporary Egyptian Nubian society such as would constitute a solid empirical basis for our discussion. However, one of us (Rouchdy) has spent nine months investigating changes in Nubian language performance with particular interest in changes in their knowledge of their native languages. The other of us (Fernea) has made five extended visits to New Nubia since resettlement and to the pioneering villages which the Nubians have established along the shores of the High Dam reservoir; the most recent visit was in January, 1986, when we visited New Nubia together. However, both of us have been restricted to a relatively small number of contacts. We have depended on what our Nubian friends have told us and what we could see from visiting the communities and Nubian clubs in Cairo, and are thus also indebted to the work of other scholars. Our personal knowledge of Egyptian Nubia does, however, go back to years of research in Old Nubia before resettlement (1960-1964).

3 Linguists have debated over correct use of the terms "language" and "dialect". Though they are closely related as members of the Nile Nubian language group, Matoki and Fadija are not mutually intelligible, which some linguists would argue makes them both "languages". However, Arabic speaking Nubians and other Egyptians call these languages *lahja*, which is usually translated as "dialect" in English. Egyptians also refer to the Nubian dialects as *rutana* because they are not written.

4 *Fadicca* is the way this term is pronounced in the urban centers of Lower Egypt; in Upper Egypt the pronunciation is *Fedija*, consistent with the regional sound shifts in Egyptian Arabic. Some of the people referred to in this paper as Fedija sometimes also call themselves and their language *Nubiyiin*, which avoids the pejorative connotations of Fedija.

5 During the early research in Old Nubia, the Fedija hinted at days in which the Kenuz were slave traders and sometimes raided the Fedija communities. The Kenuz, on the other hand, sometimes made derogatory remarks about Fedija intelligence and work habits. There was a definite residue of bad feeling between the two groups in the 1960s, though personal contacts sometimes bridged the difference. For instance, Mekki, a Kenuz boat merchant, regularly traveled south to trade in the Fedija communities while we were there, but the Fedija said that it was only in the 1950s that he had begun to sail into their districts.

6 *Baladi* generally means someone belonging to a lower class, a native Egyptian, but it can also mean stupid, tasteless, with no savoir-faire, depending on the context of its use.

7 The concept of symbolic inversion of social status seems useful in understanding the self-identity of the Nubians before the inundation of their homelands. In their nearly rainless, isolated homeland, the Nubians could create from mud brick and mud plaster spacious homes with elaborate decoration, fantastic dwellings far grander than those of the working class Egyptians, equaled only by palaces and country homes of the Pashas and Beys of the ancient regime (see Fernea and Gerster 1973). The symbolic significance of this homeland encouraged a sense of superiority among the Nubians, which perhaps was reinforced through their employment by members of the Egyptian elite and wealthy foreigners (see Babcock, ed. *The Reversible World: Symbolic Inversion in Art and Society*, Ithaca, London 1978).

8 See Fernea 1966.

9 See Messiri Nadim 1966.

10 Perhaps it is worth thinking about the Mamluks, the Muslim slaves who became rulers in Egypt, however anomalous their rise to power may seem to western observers.

11 Sayiidis were in Old Nubia after 1934, working on pump irrigated project land for absentee Nubian landowners. However, in Ballana, at least, their settlements were apart from the local Nubians and, of course, they were very much in the minority.

12 Intermarriage is still not favorably looked upon, especially among the Nubian women, for when it happens it always involves a Nubian man marrying a non-Nubian woman. However, marriage between Fedija and Kenuz is said to be occurring now; this was very rare in pre-resettlement days. Also, there is a lot more freedom in the choice of marriage partners. Young people, often meeting in the integrated secondary and training schools, or colleges, take the initiative, though their mothers and others make the arrangements.

13 Census data showed the Kenuz population increased 24.8 percent from 1960 to 1966, to a total of almost 21,000. But by 1976 their number had dropped to only 15,856. The Arab group almost doubled by 1966 — from 4,418 in 1960 to 8,846 in 1966 — but dropped to 6,284 in 1976. "Similarly the Fedija, who showed a slight increase during the period 1960-66, witnessed a considerable rate of population decrease (5.6 percent) over the period 1966-76." The Fedija were 64 percent of the total population of some 56,000 persons at the time of resettlement. The total Nubian population in both the cities and villages was estimated to be 120,000 at that time (Fahim 1983, 98). The recent Egyptian census cannot be used to determine the number of Nubians in Egypt, since the population is identified in terms of religious affiliation only, and all Nubians are Muslims.

[14] Judging from a recent study, the Nubians seem justified in their dislike of the agricultural cooperative. Adams reports the irritation of the farmers in Lower Egypt, who complain that the cooperatives are just another form of government control by officials who refuse to come to the fields and know little about their problems. Many farmers also hate growing the cotton cash crop they are obliged to cultivate and would far rather grow food crops for their own consumption and for sale. (So would the Nubians who farm.) The cooperatives were introduced to promote modernization of small-sized plots. "Despite such well-founded intentions, the agricultural cooperatives have failed miserably as a mechanism for promoting the mechanization of Egyptian agriculture" (Adams, 1986, 61). Adams is generally very critical of Egyptian farm policy and of cooperative cash crop farming in particular.

[15] The Bisharyin are nomadic herdsmen living in the desert of Southern Egypt.

[16] An urban survey conducted by Dr. Peter Geiser as part of the Nubian Research Project in 1962-63 showed 11.2 percent of Nubian labor urban migrants from the old communities were at work in professional, managerial, clerical and sales jobs at that time. However, 46.6 percent of the men from the 1934 resettled community of Dar el Salam were in these kinds of jobs in the same year! Upward mobility has long been well-established among Nubians.

[17] It is not fully clear why the government has not proceeded to grant full title to the houses, but there are Nubians who fear that their neighbors would sell their homes to non-Nubians if they legally could, thus diluting the Nubian character of the settlement. Some say that government officials are afraid of land speculation, for there is no question but that this real estate is becoming more valuable as the population of Upper Egypt steadily increases.

## Bibliography

Adams, R.H.J. 1986: *Development and Social Change in Rural Egypt*, Syracuse.

Barth, F. 1969: Introduction to *Ethnic Groups and Boundaries: The Social Organization of Cultural Difference* (ed. F. Barth), Boston.

Benedict, B. 1962: "Stratification in Plural Societies," *American Anthropologist* 64, 1235-1246.

Cohen, A. 1969: *Custom and Politics in Urban Africa*, Berkeley.

Cohen, R. 1978: "Ethnicity: Problem and Focus in Anthropology," *Annual Review of Anthropology* 7, 379-403.

Fahim, H.M. 1983: *Egyptian Nubians: Resettlement and Years of Coping*, Salt Lake City.

Fernea, R.A. 1966: "Integrating Factors in a Non-Corporate Community," *Contemporary Egyptian Nubia* II (ed. R.A. Fernea), New Haven.

Fernea, R.A.,and G. Gerster 1973: *Nubians in Egypt; Peaceful People*, Austin, Texas.

Geiser, P. 1986: *The Egyptian Nubian: A Study in Social Symbiosis*, Cairo.

Hechter, M., and M. Levi 1979: "The Comparative Analysis of Ethnoregional Movements," *Ethnic and Racial Studies* 2, 260-274.

Helmer, K. 1983: "The Egyptian Benevolent Society of London," *Egyptian Nubians: Resettlement and Years of Coping* (ed. H.M. Fahim), Salt Lake City.

Kennedy, G.J. 1966: "Occupational Adjustment in a Previously Resettled Nubian Village," *Contemporary Egyptian Nubia* II (ed. R.A. Fernea), New Haven.

Melville, M.B. 1983: "Ethnicity: An Analysis of Its Dynamism and Variability Focusing on the Mexican/Anglo/Mexican American Interface," *American Ethnologist* 10, 272-289.

Nadim, N. El Messiri 1966: "The Sheikh Cult in Dahmit Life," *Contemporary Egyptian Nubia* (ed. R.A. Fernea), New Haven.

Rouchdy, A. 1980: "Languages in Contact: Arabic-Nubian," *Anthropological Linguistics*, 334-344.

Spiro, M. 1955: "The Acculturation of American Ethnic Groups," *American Anthropologist* 57, 1240-1251.

Vincent, I. 1974: "The Structuring of Ethnicity," *Human Organization* 33, 375-379.

# Additional Bibliography

Adams, William Y., 1977. *Nubia, Corridor to Africa*. Princeton, NJ: Princeton University Press.

Fahim, Hussein M., 1981. *Dams, People and Development: The Nubian Case*. New York: Pergamon Press.

Geiser, Peter, 1980. *Cairo's Nubian Families*. Cairo: American University Press.

Kennedy, J. G. and H. Fahim, 1974. "Nubian Ohiker Rituals and Cultural Change." *Muslim World* 64(3): 205-219.

_____, 1977. *Struggle for Change in a Nubian Community: An Individual in Society and History*. Palo Alto, CA: Mayfield Publishing.

_____, 1979. *Nubian Ceremonial Life: Studies in Islamic Syncretism and Cultural Change*. Berkeley, CA: University of California Press.

Salem-Murdock, Muneera, 1989. *Arabs and Nubians in New Halfa*. Salt Lake City: University of Utah Press.